G000122747

WAYGOOK

LAOWAI

Five Years in the Far East

By Paul Bacon

As this book has taken so long to write, there are plenty of people to whom it needs to be dedicated. Firstly, my good buddy Ossie who features heavily in these pages. Secondly, my long-suffering mother who I am sure missed me in the many years I worked overseas. Finally, my wonderful wife and beautiful baby boy with whom I hope to visit many of the places detailed in this book for a second time.

PROLOGUE

This book has been many years in the writing. I lived in the Far East between 2004 and 2010 and ever since I boarded my Air China flight home to depart from Norman Foster's beautifully designed airport in Beijing, I was keen to get my experiences down on paper. However, a combination of undeniable procrastination and life getting in the way - in the intervening years I lived in Turkey, Oman, France, Dubai and Germany before finally moving back to the UK - meant that it was pushing a decade before things actually got moving. It was the onset of the COVID pandemic that gave me a nudge by providing me the time and the need for a project that things actually got moving.

One of the major factors behind my continued procrastination was that I really wasn't sure what kind of format the book should take. This was because living in a country is very different to travelling through one. A standard travelogue is a linear and chronological experience. The narrative has a very clear beginning, middle and end. But, I didn't feel what I had to say fit into that format. There was, of course, a starting point (Arriving in Seoul in September 2004) and an end (Leaving Beijing in January 2010) but in between things didn't really happen in a straight line. As a consequence, this book takes a slightly disorganised form.

I have, where at all possible, tried to follow as logical and chronological an approach as I could. The three sections of the book are very much linear as: I lived in Korea from September 2004 to September 2005, then visited China in September and October 2005 in order to see if I would like to live there before moving there in 2006 and staying until 2010. However, within each section there are areas tha3t are focused more on particular themes and, in those parts, the narrative does flip backwards and forwards at times.

Because of the approach I have taken, the book may seem illogical and lacking an overarching narrative. I agonized about this for quite some time whilst writing but, ultimately, decided that I am unapologetic. I feel the structure I have chosen reflects the experience of living overseas as accurately as possible because, in all honesty, it was an unpredictable experience that took in many adventures and defied a clear direction.

So, if this book is not a travelogue and doesn't have a clear and simple narrative, then what is it? To be frank, I am not sure. It is, of course, part travel book as it is about my experiences in foreign lands. It is also part memoir as it deals with my personal experiences. I would also argue that it is also partially a history book as it details a fascinating period for both Korea and China, one which has already given way to a new era. The China of 2006 was a very different place to the one we see today.

PART 1: Korea

MOVING EAST

It has been many years since I made the life-changing decision to move from the UK to Korea in order to teach English. However, despite the intervening decade and a half, I still vividly remember the slightly bizarre logic I applied to the decision-making process. For many educators, teaching is a deep-rooted calling or lifelong vocation that is part of their very identity. In the years since I first picked up a whiteboard pen and textbook, this has also become the case for me as I have worked as a teacher of English for over fifteen years in several countries across the world. However, at the time, I saw entering the whiteboard jungle as merely a means to an end. I just wanted to use it as an opportunity to see a distant part of the world and to get paid for the privilege.

My decision to throw myself into teaching was a relatively simple one and came from what I would term as an 'excitement hangover'. A few months before I went to Korea, I had been living in the frozen reaches of Mongolia. It had been a truly amazing experience, one which still gives me goosebumps and fuels my desire to travel to unusual places. I worked as a volunteer journalist at the country's only independent English-language newspaper writing stories about such varied subjects as government corruption, impoverished street children and the rise of Mongolian sumo wrestlers in Japan. I also got the opportunity to travel across one of the most unique and unexplored countries on the planet. I hiked through the Gobi Desert, I climbed mountains and I rode horses around a frozen lake on the Russian border. It was thrilling. It was slightly dangerous. It was glorious. I do not wish to drift into the area of hyperbole, but it really was an experience that undeniably altered the way I saw the world. Then, I went home … to the north of England.

As you might expect, it did not go so well. When I arrived back in Sheffield, I looked for an exciting and challenging job that would keep me motivated and full of energy and that wouldn't leave me pining for the adventures I had just enjoyed. Sadly, that was not to be and I fell into that vicious circle which many young university graduates (I was 24 at the time) face: I had very little practical working experience and no-one wanted to hire me and provide me with the opportunity to gain that experience. My work in Mongolia made a funky little talking point in an interview and stood out on my CV, but it was not really enough to seal the deal with any decent employers. As a consequence, I found myself temping and working in call-centres for minimum wage. It was no kind of life. No amount of football or cricket at the weekend or beers with the boys - and I drank plenty of beers - could satisfy my sense of adventure and make it feel like the life I was living was worthwhile. I knew that I needed more.

That desire for more didn't immediately push me towards teaching. At first, I was hoping to follow on from my working experiences in Mongolia and find a job at a newspaper or a magazine somewhere exotic. I had, in a quite magnificently naive way, heady visions of living a Hemingway type existence in a remote corner of the world. I had just read Hunter Thompson's *The Rum Diary* - since butchered on celluloid by Johnny Depp - and had visions of sitting by a beach somewhere rattling away at a vintage typewriter. Sadly, and not at all surprisingly, this did not come to pass. Apparently, my experience at the UB Post - published just once a week with a circulation of just 350 - was not quite as impressive as I thought it was. Consequently, job offers from overseas publications were not forthcoming. So, I went to plan B.

From a bit of rudimentary internet research, I knew there were plenty of jobs available around the world teaching English, even for people with no experience and no teaching qualifications. That was fortunate for me as I had neither of those. Most of those jobs were located in the Far East rather than in Europe, which also worked out pretty well as it was a part of the world that held a lot of appeal for me and that I desperately wanted to visit. It was - and I realise that looking at a huge area that is home to well over two billion people as one homogenous lump is a pretty massive generalisation - an area that felt genuinely exciting compared to the more mundane confines of Europe or North America.

This brings us to the question of why I chose Korea and not China, Taiwan or Japan. It is at this point that my reasoning begins to, quite spectacularly, lose its clarity and logic. To find jobs, I used the teaching recruitment website teachermania - now sadly defunct - and found a plentiful supply of openings in China, Japan, Taiwan and Korea. The site had separate pages for each country, all of which were extremely well-stocked with English teaching vacancies. This gave me great encouragement and assuaged some of the worries I had about my rather spartan CV. If there were so many schools looking for teachers, I figured that one of them was bound to want me even if I had no experience or qualifications.

The problem I faced, though, was that all of the places on the site captured my imagination and I wanted to travel to each of them with a fairly equal desire. Viewed from the context of demeaning service sector work, all of them looked fabulous. Whilst I lacked solid and substantial knowledge about any of them, they all had a sense of the exotic about them and they were all very different to England. As I sat calling people who didn't want to change their energy supplier and wanted very firmly to hang up on me, I weighed up the pros and cons of each place over and over in my head. Ultimately, though, I made my final decision to go to Korea based on the whimsiest of whims.

When I was young, sometime around 1986 or 1987, my mum bought me a large black poster from the Rotherham branch of Woolworths - also now sadly defunct - with a map of the world at its centre and flags of all the countries of the world filling the rest of the area along with minor information about each such as capital city and population. I loved that poster! To this day, I am still able to recognise some of the most obscure flags and identify some of the tiniest capital cities from around the world - I am not being immodest to say that I am an absolute star in the geography round of pub quizzes. As the map was a product of the 1980s, I can also even identify flags and capitals that no longer exist or have been since renamed or redesigned such as the old Afghan flag from the era of the Soviet invasion or South Africa's apartheid version.

One of the flags that always stuck in my head was that of South Korea (The Republic of Korea to use the correct name). The blue and red circle and dashed lines surrounding it always looked rather pretty and fostered a degree of curiosity about the country. It was far more interesting than the boring red spot of Japan or the imposing solid block of Chinese red. This curiosity, I suppose, stayed with me and was enough to sway me in favour of choosing Korea as my teaching destination. That was it: I loved the flag! I am under no illusions as to just how crazy this sounds and how ridiculous it is to make a major career and life decision that way, but that was where my gut led me.

My actual knowledge of Korea was extremely minimal. This was, it is important to remember, before globalisation had exerted a major influence on the world and was also a good while before social media had brought people from around the world so much closer than ever possible before. It was also before a lot of things that we now consider quintessentially Korean were particularly well known. For example, Samsung had not become quite the global powerhouse it is today - although it was still a relatively large and well-known company - and it was many years before the world was able to 'enjoy' the dubious wonders of GangNam Style or some of the more cultured delights of Korean cinema such as OldBoy or the Oscar-winning Parasite. If I am honest, I knew nothing of Korean culture, fashion or cuisine. I would have struggled to name a famous Korean and the only thing I could tell you about Korean food was that it was famous for dog being a national dish.

On a political or governmental level, I also knew very little aside from the rather obvious fact that the country had been divided for the previous fifty years between North and South. Ironically, the regime of Kim Jung Il in North Korea garnered far more media attention. This meant that I had significantly more knowledge of the despotic and secretive North than I did of the democratic and transparent South. I would easily have recognised Kim Jong-Il and his movie star sunglasses as he was in the UK media relatively often, but I couldn't have picked Roh Moo-Hyun out of a lineup. I guess my only real concrete knowledge of Korea came in the form of sport. If I strained my mind back to my childhood, I was able to recall the 1988 Summer Olympics in Seoul and some of the accompanying footage that featured the sprawling mass of the city. And, on a more recent level, I had also followed the 2002 World Cup - hosted jointly by Korea and Japan - in which Korea reached the semifinals.

GETTING A JOB

Having made the decision to move to Korea, you might have imagined that there could have been something of an obstacle in my path: I was completely unqualified to teach and had absolutely no experience whatsoever in education. However, my utter lack of prerequisites for a teaching position was genuinely - and in all honesty, as I would be shaping young minds, quite alarmingly - not an issue. Getting a job was frighteningly easy. To give a better insight into this bizarre situation, it is probably best for me to provide a brief overview of the Korean education system. By British or American standards, it is incredibly harsh on the kids and genuinely feeds into the stereotype of Asian kids excelling at maths and in standardized tests through insane hard work and a robotic approach to learning.

When I think back to my own school days, I remember going to primary school from 9am to 4pm and then going home without the pressure of any homework. I could play football, see my friends or chill out with my mum and dad. Then, at comprehensive school, it was 8:45 to 3:20 with a couple of hours of homework per night. Korean kids would consider that nirvana and would probably have no idea what to do with all the free time it afforded them. Most begin their classes at 8am or before. They then work well into the afternoon: primary school kids are there until around 2pm and the older kids are there until 4 or 5pm. All of them, regardless of age, leave with a hefty pile of homework for the next day. On the surface, this might not sound too horrendous. However, the system I have described thus far is only what the government provides as part of the state syllabus. Most parents do not see this as anywhere near enough and want to push their kids harder and further. So, the state provision is only the start.

Not only is the parents' desire to have their kids learning almost without a break based on a genuine love of education - one which is much stronger than you might see in the UK - and a burning desire to get them into the best universities in the country, but it is also built on a need for child care. This stems from another far-eastern cliche that is based very firmly on reality. As most Korean adults also work extremely long hours - it is not uncommon for employees of big corporations to be at work from 7am and stay well into the evening - they need someone to look after their kids until quitting time. To deal with these two issues, a separate education industry has sprung-up that centers on private schools known as *hogwans*. These schools provide a combination of supplementary education and babysitting services. Typically, they offer education in many different subjects, but they usually make the majority of their money through English.

The *hogwan* industry is fiercely competitive. There are *hogwans* almost everywhere in big cities like Seoul or Busan. It might be a bit of an exaggeration to say that they are as prevalent as fast food joints, but it would not be a large one. Even small towns will have three or four of them competing over students from the local state school. The basic prerequisite they must all meet in order to be competitive is to have a native English speaking teacher. In many cases, this is more of a marketing tool than a legitimate educational resource. No *hogwan* wants to be the only one in town without a foreigner - it simply would not attract customers. This is where I found my opportunity. As the *hogwans* have such massive need for teachers, I guessed that despite my glaring professional deficiencies I had the chance to find a decent opportunity.

Even with the knowledge that the job market in Korea was tilted massively in the applicant's favour, I could never have possibly imagined how the hiring process would pan out. It really was astounding. I kicked things off on a balmy Monday evening. I sat in the spare room of my mother's house, where we kept the computer, and sent out a bunch of CVs on which I had tried desperately to make eighteen months in an entry level marketing job and six months in Mongolia look more heavyweight and desirable than they actually were. After firing out five or six emails to recruitment companies, I went to bed and awaited responses. I was not at all prepared for what happened next.

By the time I awoke the next morning - just before noon as I was in between demeaning service sector jobs - I had six recruiters vying for my, as yet unproven, services with a surprising degree of ferocity. Pleasantly surprised at my rapidly improving employment prospects, I responded to all of them, but the most professional and enthusiastic was a guy called John Lee who had a wide selection of jobs available and was by far the most transparent and honest about the hiring process.

John explained that he worked purely with hogwans in Seoul and the northwest of Korea and added that, because I was a native-speaker with a university degree, he could easily find me a job with a decent salary and free accommodation. That was amazing news, but it certainly surprised me a little. When I questioned whether or not the schools might prefer someone with experience and teaching qualifications, he made it clear that while they most certainly would prefer experienced teachers, there were nowhere near enough of these to satisfy demand. Therefore, they would be happy with any native-speaker with a degree as being a university graduate was a requirement for a visa application.

After we finished our little Q/A session via email, John asked me where I would prefer to work: Seoul or outside. As I felt a little nervous about living in such a sprawling metropolis and was worried about making friends in such an intimidating environment, I opted for outside. Just a few minutes after I had sent that email, he responded and asked me if I was free for an interview with a school in the almost unpronounceable province of Chungchonnam-Do. He informed me that the school's last teacher had returned home because her grandfather had died and, consequently, they were keen to hire quickly. I confirmed that I was indeed available and was told that I would speak to a lady named Christine the next morning.

It was by far and away the easiest and simultaneously the strangest interview I have ever experienced, either in general or in the ESL field. She began by, quite routinely, asking me to introduce myself and then slipped into some rather bewildering questions:

"Do you like kids?"

"Well, yes, of course".

"Do you want to come to Korea?"

"Errrrr .... Yes".

"Great. Do you think you will be a good teacher?"

"Yes, I do".

"Great, OK, thank you. That was a good interview. John will call you soon".

Within ten minutes John had emailed to offer me the job. It came with a surprisingly good salary, much better than I was earning in Sheffield, and free accommodation - a relatively normal perk for most teaching jobs in Korea. As the prospect of more temping loomed on my short-term horizon, I thought that there was nothing else for it but to jump in and to begin a new adventure.

The recruitment and subsequent administration process was frighteningly easy and breathtakingly fast. John explained that because the school did not have a native English speaker in situ, it was running the risk of losing students to competing schools that had a foreigner in place. Because of this, the school would happily have put me on a plane the same day as my interview - this also explained the less than probing questions. The only thing stopping them was the process of arranging a visa. So, the next day, I sent my degree certificate to Korea via DHL and waited for them to process the application.

The brief period between receiving the job offer and departing for Seoul was extremely hectic. The speed of things completely astounded me. I had been expecting it to take weeks and maybe even a month, but they got my visa and arranged my flight in a matter of days. I was also a little shocked at the ease of the process as I thought it might, and perhaps should, have been a little more stringent. As I were to be working with kids, I thought the school might have checked out my references - obviously I had no teaching experience to check but I thought they might look for a character reference at least - or ask for a police-check to prove I wasn't a sex offender or something similar. Apparently, though, the need for a foreigner to arrive quickly superseded such trifling concerns.

Because I had made my decision based on a rather basic desire to find adventure somewhere exotic and on the silly notion of how pretty the Korean flag was,, I was in a position of ignorance. I really didn't know very much about Korea. To combat this knowledge shortfall, I purchased a copy of Lonely Planet - this was in the days before Tripadvisor - and began reading up. There was plenty to learn about the bright lights of Seoul and Busan and some good information about the country as a whole, but I would be heading to a small coastal town called Taean about which there was far less information.

The book really didn't offer me much. In fact, it gave less than 200 words, of which 100 talked about an arboretum by the beach. Admittedly, that sounded nice but there was scant detail on either the town of Taean or the wider area in general. The adjective 'sleepy' was used a disproportionate number of times and there were rather a lot of references to fishing... and, that was it. I followed this reading up with a

Google search, but it yielded little more. That was frustrating, but I won't pretend it bothered me too much. I was young and looking for adventure, so the air of mystery was probably a positive thing for me.

INTO THE 'LAND OF THE MORNING CALM'

I landed at Seoul-Incheon airport excited about doing something new and fun, but also feeling just a bit nervous about the whole undertaking. The plan was for John Lee to meet me there and then drive me to Taean, which was about two hours away. It was late in the afternoon when, after clearing customs and having my visa stamped, he lifted my backpack into his Hyundai sedan and pointed us towards the freeway heading southwest. On first viewing, I was surprised by just how green everything was. I had been expecting to find a huge degree of urban sprawl as Seoul is one the biggest and most built-up cities in the world, but the tower blocks very quickly gave way to countryside that looked lush and humid.

I am not sure if I appeared visibly nervous - I would like to think not - but John did his best to make me feel comfortable. He had a collection of Franz Ferdinand, Muse and Oasis CDs - very popular at the time in the UK - in his glove compartment that he proudly offered to put on. He seemed mildly disappointed when I declined and explained that none of them were really my cup of tea. To break the ensuing silence, I asked whether those bands were particularly popular with Koreans in their mid-40s. He laughed and confirmed he was no big fan and confessed that he had a teenage daughter who liked them. He explained that he had the CDs to make new teachers feel comfortable on arrival. It was a nice touch and left me feeling encouraged about my new adventure.

It was a pleasant and surprisingly rural drive. Around halfway, we stopped for coffee and John offered me sea-weed and dried squid for a snack - my first exposure to some of the 'delights' of Korean food - which I politely refused. Consequently, it was dark as we got off the highway which meant that my first glimpse of Taean was both ghostly and slightly surreal. The first things to loom into view as we took the local roads towards the centre of town were a series of neon red crucifixes that stood above the churches in the town. I had - again, rather ignorantly - assumed Korea was predominantly Buddhist, so I was surprised to see such overt Christian symbolism but John explained that the American presence from WWII onwards had created a large Christian presence.

As we drew nearer to town, the crucifixes grew larger and a plethora of other neon lights began to pop up. John navigated us through these and drove us towards the rear entrance of the *hogwan* to find parking. He then, despite my protestations, lugged my backpack to the second floor and I had arrived.

My *hogwan* was part of a national chain of franchises called Jung Chul that could be easily identified across the country by its bright yellow signs and its bizarre mascot that looked like a strange combination of cat and bear. The Taean branch was owned by Mr Kim who, alongside his father, had been very successful in running a small chain of shoe shops in a nearby town and decided that the next logical step was to move into the *hogwan* business. It seemed a bizarre progression to me. However, over the following few weeks, I would learn first-hand that the *hogwan* industry really was very big business in Korea and the potential gains of running a successful school were very much worth such a bizarre dog-leg in strategy. There was also another reason behind Mr Kim's change in business strategy: Mrs Kim. Before she married Mr Kim and had their daughter Cathy, Christine - who had conducted my 'interview' - had worked as an English teacher and wanted to continue this career. Therefore, where the school was concerned, she wore the trousers.

John and Mr Kim quickly introduced me to the rest of the team, who had all stayed late to welcome me to Taean. There were four members. Mr Kim was the boss. He ran the show and taught some maths classes. His own English was patchy at best, so he didn't really do any language classes. Then, there was Christine. Aside from being the driving force and the only truly experienced teacher in the team, she taught English and ruled her classroom with an iron fist. The third member of the team was Mr Jang who spoke excellent English and was engaged to Christine's sister. He was not actually a trained teacher, but as his English was very good and he would soon become Mr Kim's brother-in-law, he took a lot of classes. The final member of the gang was Ms Ahn who was in her mid-twenties, was very sweet and rarely missed an opportunity to tell people that she was only working as a teacher until she found a man and got married - it was literally the second or third thing she said to me and she repeated it on an almost daily basis.

On my first evening in Taean, John and Mr Kim took us all out for dinner. We had kalbi, a delicious barbeque dish made from pork ribs and the surrounding belly meat, which is cut into small pieces, cooked on a grill and eaten in a lettuce leaf with spicy pepper paste and garlic. It kinda felt like a Far-Eastern burrito and was fantastic. We washed this down with some Korean beer and soju (Korean rice wine). It was a very pleasant start to my time in Korea. However, even as I savoured the rich kalbi and winced at the harsh rice wine, I had some doubts nagging at the back of my mind. They revolved around whether I was actually going to be able to teach Korean children at all well. Christine assured me that the next day she and Mr Kim would ensure that I was 100% ready.

Unfortunately, the training session I got really did not offer too much in the way of help. As it was a Sunday, the school was closed. This meant I did not get the chance to sit and watch the preexisting teachers give any classes. In almost every other job I have since done in the EFL industry, shadowing and observing an experienced teacher was one of the key elements of training - in any job in any industry, a bit of shadowing is usually seen as a good way to learn. Sadly, it was not to be as Mr Kim explained that they needed me in the classroom as soon as possible. So come Monday, he wanted me teaching rather than observing. It was going to be very much a case of being dropped in at the deep-end.

The actual training that I did receive was sparse to say the least. Christine showed me the classroom and equipped me with attendance lists and marker pens before handing me over to Ms Ahn and going back to playing with her daughter in the apartment they had above the school. It seemed rather odd that the school would invest so much in hiring me and flying me out yet they palmed my training off onto the youngest teacher in the school, but I figured that I would take whatever help I could get.

Alas, from the get go, I could tell that Ms Ahn was not so invested. She seemed happy to be getting the overtime for the day, but was not so keen on actually training me. Instead, we quickly flicked through the textbooks before she decided we should stop for lunch. She ordered Ja Jang noodles - thick noodles cooked in black bean sauce. They were absolutely delicious, but I was getting frustrated that while my knowledge of Korean cuisine was improving, my classroom readiness was not. So, I pushed Ms Ann to help me more.

"Isn't there more we could be covering? I really am quite nervous and I have never taught before".

Ms Ahn smiled a little and then dropped something of a truth bomb on me.

"I wouldn't worry about it too much. Look, you are the *wae gook* (foreigner). All the kids will be excited to have your class. It won't matter if you are not so great at first, nobody will notice. As long as you are friendly and polite, Mr Kim and the parents will be happy".

It was a pretty direct and cynical summary of the situation and did not fill me with joy. Basically, because I was the foreigner, nobody cared if I was actually any good. I must admit that I felt a tad objectified and disheartened, but Ms Ahn seemed to have Mr Kim's mindset perfectly defined. When he dropped by later in the day, he echoed her words with unerring similarity, albeit in slightly less well-polished language. As we chatted about the school, he showed exactly where he was coming from.

"Now you here. Parents send children for foreigner".

When I asked if he had any advice for me, he responded with the following gem:

"Just be nice. They will love you. They are very excited to see foreigner"

INTO THE CLASSROOM

As the previous chapter shows, Mr Kim dropped me straight in at the deep-end. My teaching schedule was a full 30 hours of classes per week from my second day on the job. A typical day was broken up into two major parts. In the morning, I had kindergarten classes and in the afternoon/evening I had elementary and middle school students. I was a little disappointed that we had no high school students because I presumed that it would be easier to deal with older students as they would probably speak slightly better English. At that point of my life, not only did I have no meaningful teaching experience, but I had absolutely no experience of working with young children in any capacity whatsoever. This meant it was going to be a major leap into the unknown for me. Despite my inexperience, it would prove to be unbelievable fun as I hope the following pages will attest.

Going into my early classes, I was extremely nervous. My lack of experience in both teaching and dealing with kids in general was weighing on my mind and my school's abject lack of preparation had also left me mildly concerned. Thankfully, as Ms Ahn's advice suggested, I needn't have worried as the expectations of me in terms of actually teaching the kids anything were pretty low. Mr Kim was no great education professional and did not buy into the majority of modern academic conventions. To him, learning objectives and lesson plans were needless frivolities. He absolutely did not care one jot how I went about my class. He had no concern as to whether or not I wanted to use a communicative approach or whether I wanted to focus on the audio-linguistic method. He did not even know what those words meant - to be fair, at the time, neither did I. He just wanted me and my foreignness in the room. I could actually perhaps go as far as saying he had his own educational methodology when it came to his school: Magic Foreigner Syndrome.

MFS - which is a term I have coined here rather than something you will see written in any teaching textbooks - is a technique that was, and in many regions still is, a hugely prevalent approach to teaching. It is most common in East Asia where schools and parents alike seem to be under the almost religious belief that children will improve their language exponentially by simply being in the same room as a foreigner. It doesn't matter whether the foreigner is at all skilled in education - and in many areas where schools are desperate for a British or American teacher, they really are not - his or her mere presence is enough. I quickly learned to think of the mind-set as a type of 'education by osmosis'. The belief was that the kids would pick up language skills simply by listening to someone who spoke that language as their mother tongue. Whilst there is a degree of logic to that in one regard as hearing language from an authentic source is certainly important, I didn't really buy into it too much myself, but it paid my wages so who was I to complain?

My kindergarten classes were based around basic vocabulary and a little bit of pronunciation. To teach these, I was given two major resources. A large pack of flashcards with various pieces of basic vocabulary illustrated in cartoon form and some phonics books that practiced basic vowel sounds such as cat/hat/bat and sit/hit/mit. We did lots of classes with me sitting on a frighteningly small chair at the front of the classroom - trying desperately not to slip off - while ten tiny Korean children sat in front of me and stared. I would say a word in English and they would repeat it. Or, I would show them a picture and they would shout the word out at me. It really wasn't rocket science and, at times over my year in Taean, I genuinely questioned whether it was a sensible way of utilising an honours degree from a respectable red-brick university in the UK.

Despite my misgivings, the first week of classes seemed to go pretty well, albeit a little quietly. The students were extremely curious about their *waegook* teacher. I could sense they all wanted to play and have fun with the new novelty that had just walked into their lives, but they all also seemed rather wary of the large figure with a big nose and grey eyes that sat in front of them. There were quite a few of them who looked decidedly shy and would hide behind chairs or avert their eyes and giggle whenever I tried to talk to them.

Things all seemed rather cagey and I felt that I wasn't really getting through to them. So, I asked some of my colleagues for their opinion on how I could break the ice. I asked them what I thought were some sensible questions: Were there any ice-breaking activities they could recommend? Were there any cultural issues I was maybe overlooking that made the children shy? Were there any resources I could think about bringing into the classroom? Could I use multimedia? These inquiries generated little more than a derisive grunt. Apparently, my questions were naive to the point of stupidity and I had another truth bomb coming my way from Ms Ahn: "Just give them candy!" was the rather direct answer I received.

So, the following Monday, the prize for getting a correct answer in the flashcard game was a piece of sweet candy. Suddenly, the strange looking foreigner was not so scary anymore! This was shameless and completely unadulterated bribery. It was unethical, it was completely unhealthy and it certainly wouldn't have been acceptable in the UK. But, it worked. Paul *Sungsangnim* - The Korean word for Teacher, which is used in a similar style to how we might say Doctor in the UK - quickly became everyone's favorite. From there on in, the kindergarten boys and girls were all over me. The boys wanted to run around and play-fight and the girls wanted to be lifted up in the air. The world was suddenly a great place. Not only did the kids start to have fun, but to my own surprise, I began to love it too. I had never really contemplated the possibility of finding working with kids, particularly younger kids, so rewarding. Until that point, I had just been in Korea to see a different part of the world and experience another culture. However, barely a month into my new career, I found myself smiling like a crazy man at the end of every day.

There was also another factor that really seemed to make a difference to my relationship with the students: I learned their names. I realise how ridiculous this comment may sound, but there is actually quite a lot of significance in it. The majority of Korean kids have their own Korean names but also adopt a western nickname. So, Lee Ji Son might become Ellie Lee and Park Ji Won becomes Sabrina Park. This was something I also encountered later when I lived in China and, in both countries, I was a little perplexed as to why the students and teachers felt the need to add these names to the children's identities. I could understand that part of it was the idea of getting students to fully embrace the language they were learning, but Koreans also argued that it was to make it easier for westerners as their names were so complicated. This I found ridiculous. What was difficult about names like Ji Sun or In Young?

I found that one of the negative up-shots of the western nickname policy was that, particularly with kindergarten students, it was really difficult to get their attention. Kindergarten kids are often quite difficult to control regardless of the situation. They are young, full of beans and easily distracted. They are fun to work with but it is, without doubt, a tough job. If you add in the fact that if you address them but don't actually use the name their parents use with them and they are accustomed to hearing every day, it makes things very difficult indeed. I found that it was possible to shout "Ellie", Ellie", "Ellie" until I was blue in the face and I would have a relatively minimal chance of getting Ellie to sit down and be quiet for a few minutes. But, if I shouted "Lee Ji Sun", she might just recognise I was talking to her and give me her attention.

With the candy working as an effective bribery technique and the children's Korean names giving me an element of control, I was beginning to feel confident in my kindergarten classroom. This feeling of confidence got something of a simultaneous boost and jolt when I met one of my students' parents. Jimmy or Eun Joh was in my second year kindergarten class. This meant he was about four-years old. He was a big chunky fella for his age and was great fun in class. He was always friendly, was very energetic and generally behaved well. One morning after class his mother brought coffee and cakes for all the teachers from the bakery down the street. It was a nice gesture and, as she spoke pretty good English, we quickly fell into conversation.

"Thank you for the coffee and cakes".

"No problem. Jimmy really likes to have his classes with you, you are his favourite teacher".

This was music to my ears. The comment certainly massaged my ego a little bit, but it also helped assuage my fears about whether or not the students were enjoying my classes and benefitting from them. However, as she continued and gave me some slightly more detailed information, my heart sank just a little bit.

"Yes, he really likes the *waegook* teacher". "He likes your bald head and big eyes. He thinks you look really funny".

I struggled to hide my disappointment that Jimmy was quite clearly objectifying me. He liked me just for the novelty value; it wasn't really anything to do with my classes. I was also a tad pissed at young Jimmy in regards to his comment on my hair. At the time, I was going through the onset of the male pattern baldness that has ravaged my father's side of the family and now leaves the top of my head smooth and shiny. Therefore, I was a tad sensitive about my hair-loss. Jimmy describing it as 'funny' didn't do much for my fragile ego. The whole scenario was also a clear example of MFS in its bluntest form. Jimmy liked me because I was foreign and a bit unusual - also because I gave him candy I imagine - and his mother was happy because her son liked the foreigner. All through this conversation, Christine stood there beaming because one of her customers was happy with her new teacher. Everybody seemed to be delighted with my performance ... yet no-one seemed bothered if I was actually teaching the kids anything!

GETTING OUT OF THE CLASSROOM

As fun as things were in the classroom, I was in Korea for more than just a teaching job. Thankfully, my life in Taean was not limited to the confines of the Jung Chul classroom and I succeeded in getting out and about quite a bit. At first, this was primarily with my colleagues as Mr Kim was keen to help me to settle into life in Taean. This started with quite a few team dinners - lots more kalbi - but after a couple of weeks he decided that I was becoming one of the guys and it was time to do something different. This meant that Christine and Ms Ahn were left by the wayside and he, Mr Jang and I had boys' nights. These would generally prove to be fun but also a tad weird and, usually, extremely inappropriate.

The first of these was a trip to the neighbouring town of Seosan, where there was a bigger branch of Jung Chul run by a friend of Mr Kim's, also named Mr Kim. After work on a Tuesday evening, my Mr Kim declared that the three of us were going out for dinner and ushered me towards Mr Jang's Hyundai sedan. We met Mr Kim v2.0, a couple of his Korean staff and his foreign teacher, a Canadian guy whose name is now lost to the ether. We enjoyed a large dinner - kalbi again - and a lot of beer and soju. As the average Korean has a lower tolerance to alcohol than most westerners, whilst I was feeling a little tipsy, Mr Kim - both versions - and Mr Jang were resplendent in their drunkenness. As the clock reached 23h00 both of my colleagues were in something of a state. Consequently, I was concerned as to how we would get home. When I asked them what the plan was, Mr Kim just shouted out "Sauna" and laughed. Whilst he seemed very excited, the statement left me no closer to knowing what on earth was happening. However, when we left the restaurant Mr Jang led us through the streets of Seosan to a four-storey building with the word 'Sauna', in both Korean and English in neon, written boldly across the front.

As we walked towards the entrance, Mr Jang explained, in slightly slurred speech, that the sauna had places to sleep and that we would spend the night there. Even in a mildly drunken state, I was not super excited at the concept of spending the night in a sauna with two male colleagues I had only known for three or four weeks. However, I was surprised to learn that it was not at all unusual in Korea to go out drinking and then spend the night in the sauna as a way to avoid drinking and driving and also to save money on a hotel - or perhaps also to avoid going home to your wife drunk.

I am not sure exactly what I had in mind when I stepped into the sauna. I guess I was expecting something seedy. I was, though, hugely surprised. The whole place was really nice. It was clean, well-decorated and pretty luxurious. The first two floors of the building had different baths and saunas, segregated by gender. The third floor was a sleeping area for women and the fourth floor was the same for men. The whole experience was very organised.

When we arrived, Mr Kim paid for the three of us and we were each given a slightly strange pair of baggy shorts to sleep in, an oddly small towel and a locker key. We then headed upstairs and deposited everything in the lockers. After this, we headed to the bathing area. I cannot say I felt 100% comfortable walking naked with my two colleagues into a bathing area that was full of other naked Koreans. I had suggested just going to the sleeping room and skipping the communal bathing, but apparently that was not how things were done.

The bathing area contained three or four large marble-lined pools of warm water that were occupied by a bizarrely large number of Korean men - I am by no means exaggerating here as it was well and truly rammed. It was almost midnight on a Tuesday in a relatively small town in rural Korea yet there were dozens of guys sitting naked in the water. It was odd, and I cannot deny that I felt very uncomfortable. As the only foreigner there, I attracted plenty of attention. Everyone was staring at me and - much to my embarrassment, but weirdly not theirs - not usually at my face. Whilst all the Koreans had something on which to focus, I genuinely didn't know where to look. There were large bushes of pubic hair in whichever direction I looked and lots of, invariably quite tiny, penises. It really was not how I had thought my evening would pan out. Things were made worse by Mr Kim who was really getting into the spirit of boys night and wanted to sit with his arm around me in the pool. I was less keen.

After the rather uncomfortable bathing session, we went back to our lockers to don our sleeping shorts and then take the lift to the fourth floor where we would sleep. Whilst this was not the strangest part of our evening, it was still a little odd. There were no beds or mattresses, just a bunch of small square pillows that you picked up when you entered the floor. Basically, you just then plonked your pillow down on the hard wooden floor and went to sleep. It was definitely not the best night's sleep I had ever had and I woke stiff and cranky at 6am the next morning, just in time to use the same bath again and then jump in Mr Jang's car to go back to Taean in time for classes at 8am.

Korean karaoke

Whilst the drinks and dinner portion of our trip to Seosan was quite good fun, I made it clear to Mr Kim that I was not particularly keen on getting naked together again any time soon. Thankfully, he took my feedback to heart and there were no more sauna escapades. However, he still had plenty of unusual plans up his sleeve. The first of these was team karaoke. Hiring a room for a small group of friends or colleagues to sing together is hugely popular in Asia. So, on a Friday evening during my third or fourth week in Korea, we all trooped down the street to the local *Noh Rae Bang* - this roughly translates as singing room.

Things started off rather sedately. Ms Ahn monopolized the early part of the session by singing three or four K-pop ballads. Whilst she did, Mr Kim ordered us some fruit and seaweed - not served together - and a bottle of beer each. After a while, Mr Jang jumped in with another K-pop ballad that sounded oddly feminine. Then, they decided it was time for me to sing. To offer full and frank disclosure here, I am utterly tone death and have a horrific singing voice. So, my attempts at doing Living on a Prayer were of very low quality. Thankfully, everybody was very nice and I got an over-generous round of applause.

A couple more K-pop numbers later and Christine and Ms Ahn declared they were done for the evening. In all honesty, I wouldn't have minded following them out, but Mr Kim was keen to enjoy the freedom of not having Christine around. So, he insisted we stay. As the girls left, he ordered several more beers and a bottle of soju. I was more than a little concerned that three men sitting in a semi-darkened room serenading each other might be just as weird as the same three men going for a bath together. However, Mr Kim had a cunning plan.

He clearly realised that three guys singing to each other did not lay the foundations for a fabulous night out. So, he decided to address the gender imbalance by getting on the phone to call for coffee girls. This was a particularly Korean thing to do - I haven't seen anything exactly like it anywhere else I have travelled. Coffee girls are, generally, attractive young women who you can call and who will come to your office, to a bar or in our case to a singing room. They are usually delivered on the back of a scooter, although I suspect ours may have already been in situ at the Noh Rae Bang. Their job is to serve coffee and make conversation. I guess you could define them as very low budget geisha girls. They are a highly prevalent phenomenon in Korea. It was really common to see them all over Taean either on the back of a scooter zipping through the town centre or popping up in the local billiard hall. I presume that, in reality, the majority of Korean men who ordered these girls didn't actually want coffee on the go. Rather, they wanted the girls to come, sit there looking pretty and giggle at their jokes.

I am sure there are also situations in which things go beyond a little giggle, but even in the more 'platonic' form I found the idea of coffee girls very seedy and a little too misogynistic for my liking. Mr Kim did not share my misgivings. Therefore, 15 minutes after Christine and Ms Ahn had departed, we were joined by three young women in high heels and short skirts. They each sat down next to one of us, fluttered their eyelashes and poured our beers for us. 'My' girl tried to strike up a conversation but, as I spoke no Korean, things foundered very quickly. With the rather imposing language barrier, Mr Kim decided to skip the uncomfortable conversation and asked the girls to serenade us with yet more K-pop ballads. As you might expect, the whole thing was pretty cringeworthy. However, as you might also have expected, Mr Kim loved it and quickly had his girl sitting on his lap. Mr Jang and I, in contrast, were clearly both very uncomfortable. I don't think either of us really knew where to look. Mercifully, Mr Kim had only booked the girls for an hour, so our awkwardness didn't last too long.

Expat Endeavours

Getting out with the Jung Chul team was always fun, but it was also quite predictable as it generally involved drinking lots of soju in and around Taean before watching Mr Kim do something foolish. Being in a new country so far away from home, I didn't want to limit my social life to a small fishing town and my everyday colleagues. Thankfully, because there are so many *hogwans* in Korea, there were loads of other foreigners to socialise with. In Taean alone, there were four *hogwans*, which meant four foreign teachers. Two of those were quite odd - this was not entirely unusual as the ESL industry attracts a wide variety of people, many of who are not necessarily superstars in their native countries - and not at all sociable. However, in Taean and Seosan there were five or six *wae gook* with whom I got on pretty well.

For the first few weeks I lived in Korea, if I spent time with westerners we would generally do one of two things: i) go out to bars in Seosan before finishing the evening with some terrible karaoke, albeit without the accompaniment of ladies whose presence we had paid for, or ii) spend the weekend in the bright lights of Seoul. Whilst the first of these options could certainly be a lot of fun, experiencing one of the world's biggest and fastest-growing cities had significantly more allure to it. To get there, we would generally jump on the express bus - Korea doesn't have much of a rail network, but it has amazing bus services all over the country - on a Saturday morning and arrive in Seoul just before lunchtime. We would then usually grab something western for lunch, as neither Taean nor Seosan had much to offer in that regard, before going out into the city to explore.

We spent a lot of time in areas of Seoul like *Don Dae Mun* and *Gan Nam*. Both of these areas were great for shopping. *Don Dae Mun* had loads of small shops selling all kinds of tech as well as a giant flea market that was located under the bleachers of a disused baseball stadium. *Gan Nam* - later made famous in the song GanNam Style - was a little different. The area was just a giant subterranean marvel with a huge shopping centre attached to the metro station. It was so big that it was easy to get lost and completely miss your train.

Those areas were cool as they were vibrant and bustling, but, in truth, they seemed to lack a bit of colour and character. They were very modern and shiny but felt just a tad soulless. The fact that I have described them both in one single paragraph as I had nothing more to say about them is probably testament to this. In contrast, one part of the city that certainly didn't lack 'character', although I don't necessarily mean that as a compliment, was Itaewon.

As Seoul sits barely 100km from the military might of North Korea, the US maintains a significant military presence in the city in the form of the Yongsan garrison. The base has been in continuous operation for pushing 60 years, so it is no surprise that a whole localised economy has grown up around it. The epicentre of this is in the Itaewon district of the city. In many western cities, you can find Chinatowns; in Seoul,

Itaewon was Americatown.

As it had so many western goodies, we went to Itaewon quite a bit. It was a great place to buy western clothes or pirate DVDs and it had some amazing places to eat. To this day, the Philly Cheese Steak I had in a bar there and the burrito I got at a food truck on one of the sidestreets remain two of the best versions of those particular dishes I have ever eaten. However, despite some of the plus points to the area, Itaewon had a horrifically seedy underbelly that made it a slightly dicey place to visit at times.

The first element of this was prostitution, which was quite clearly aimed at the large G.I. population. Parts of Itaewon are located on a small hill with a few streets running parallel to each other up the incline. Some of those streets played host to some small bars, kalbi restaurants and karaoke rooms. One other street though, was dedicated to bars filled with ladies whose 'services' you could purchase for an hour .. or longer if you felt the need. There were also a series of windows that were reminiscent of Amsterdam with women standing there in their underwear attempting to beckon the *wae gook* males into their rooms.

When we took trips to Seoul, we generally stayed over for the night as we wanted to get on the beers and soju. However, Seoul is not a cheap city and major hotel chains were very expensive. So, we generally tried to find budget options. Eventually, I managed to find a couple of traditional guest houses that were both cheap and lovely but, at first, we generally just went for the cheapest options in central Seoul. Often this meant 'love' hotels. These are a particularly Asian creation (They are popular in Japan as well I believe). You can rent rooms in a moderately priced but often bizarrely decorated hotel - there was one in Seosan that looked like the fairytale Disney palace - for either a night or a shorter period of time. A large proportion of the clientele are generally young couples who live with their respective parents and want a little privacy. As we just wanted a cheap place to crash, in most areas of Seoul they usually did the trick … even if there was a vending machine for condoms, lube and sex toys on each floor. In Itaewon, though, things were different.

On one particular Saturday, a few of us had left Seosan at around 10am with the plan of grabbing a burger in one Itaewon's many bars before getting some shirts made at a tailors - I am not sure why, but there was a multitude of places to get a sharp suit made on Itaewon's main street and these offered tailored shirts at a crazy low price. After I had been measured up, we went in search of a place to stay. It was the first time we had stayed in Itaewon as we normally stayed in the university areas around Sinchon and Hongdae, so we didn't know where was a good place to crash and which places we ought to have avoided like the plague. We didn't want to stay too close to the main intersection as it was surrounded by some pretty rowdy bars. So, we climbed the hill and found a very plain looking hotel that we presumed would be safe and relatively quiet. It didn't look anything special but seemed pretty clean, so we presumed it would be safe and sedate. However, we had no idea of the horrors that would unfold in the early hours of the morning.

We stayed out until after 2am and had been putting away plenty of beers. Consequently, ordinarily, I would have been comatose until the early parts of the following afternoon. However, at some point just after 5am, I was awoken by an almost indescribable cacophony. It was deafening and I was genuinely worried that someone or something was going to burst through the walls. Not best pleased at being so rudely roused from my slumber and also worrying slightly for my safety, I decided to drag my half-drunk and half-hungover body into the corridor to investigate and to tell the perpetrators to put a sock in it. However, as soon as my eyes adjusted to the light in the corridor, I realised that I wasn't going to be telling anyone to keep it down. It was full of muscled young Americans, clearly GIs, and three Korean girls in short skirts and skimpy tops. Aside from the occasional giggle, the girls were pretty quiet. The guys on the other hand were loud, evidently drunk and obnoxious.

Not wanting to get involved in a fracas I couldn't possibly emerge from unscathed, I decided that it was best not to blunderbuss my way in there. So, I slinked off back to bed and covered my head with a pillow to drown out the sound of noisy sex that quickly followed from a room across the corridor. The repetitive banging and the squeals of pleasure from the girls - although as they were being paid for their time it is dubious how genuine their enjoyment actually was - continued for longer than I had hoped. Sadly, this was exacerbated by the demographics of the group. There were about ten guys and three girls. This meant that we had to deal with three separate waves of noise as the guys took turns.

As you might expect, that was the last time we ever picked Itaewon for a place to stay. Sadly, it was a relatively typical example of a Saturday night in that particular part of Seoul. The G.I. population was always a slightly unpredictable element to any evening out. On most Saturdays, in the majority of the district's bars, which could get crazily busy, there would be two distinct populations: i) regular expats, many of whom would be teachers, and who were generally relatively well-behaved, and ii) the military element. who were almost never quiet or well-behaved.

It was really not uncommon to see Military Police pile into bars at around 2am and start dragging off-duty soldiers out by the scruff of the neck. On one particular evening, I got a very close-up taste of this. It was somewhere in the small hours of Sunday morning and I was standing at the bar of a large Irish pub in the centre of Itaewon drinking my final pint of overpriced Guinness of the night when my shaved head caused an over-zealous MP to grab the arm of my shirt and try to drag me away. Only when I cursed drunkenly at him in my British accent did he let go and, rather grudgingly, apologise.

I don't want to over-intellectualise Itaewon. I was there because it was a lively place to go on a night out. However, the more I look back on it, the more I realise that it was perhaps one of the last vestiges of a world that everywhere else on the planet had long since disappeared. Nowhere else in the world have I ever seen bars dedicated to soldiers on R&R as though it were the 1940s, 50s or 60s. In a way, it really felt like something from decades past. It was a remnant of the Cold War still playing itself out every Friday and Saturday night. I am sure it was certainly not 100% the same, but at times I wondered if Itaewon was not a million miles away from Saigon in the late 1960s - it wouldn't be like Seoul or Busan in the early 1950s as nothing was left standing back in those days.

I did have plenty of good times with my expat friends. However, it was not always smooth sailing. As I noted earlier in this chapter, some of the expats living in Korea were a tad on the odd side. This was a reflection of the overall teaching environment in Asia. There were some pretty fun and exciting people to meet, but there were also some - let's be blunt - weirdos and losers. This stemmed from the ridiculously flimsy standards of recruitment that a lot of *hogwans*, including mine, employed. It didn't matter who the *wae gook* was; they just wanted a warm English-speaking body in the classroom. This meant that whilst you saw a lot of adventurous people who were keen to experience another culture, you also got people who were there for less palatable reasons.

Sadly, there were plenty of teachers across the Far East who weren't the type of people you would want to see teaching young children. Many of them really did not have the right motivation for being there. There were plenty of 'teachers' who were there because they saw teaching in Korea as a way to make a quick buck and there was also a disappointingly large number of male teachers who were simply there to try to hook up with Korean girls. As I have already detailed, my initial motivations for moving to Korea were not hugely academic and I did feel quite self-conscious about this at times. However, when I saw some of the other teachers living and working in Korea, I began to feel a whole lot better about myself.

For example, one of the other hogwans in Taean had a teacher from Ireland called David. Not only was he a teacher of dubious quality, like me he had no teaching certificates or classroom experience, but he was also in Korea primarily for sexual and financial reasons. Back in Cork, he had been unemployed and very single. He had moved to Korea for easy work and to find a girlfriend. I don't know if this is still the same today, but at the time there were plenty of Korean girls who were interested in the novelty value of foreign men and it often didn't really matter which foreign man. After finding such a girl online, he left his job in Taean early - in the dead of night so the school didn't see him go - in order to move in with her in Seoul.

I was not at all sad to see David go as I found him very creepy. However, little did I know that when he scurried off my life would change dramatically! In truth, I had not spent much time at all with him, we met for a beer a couple of times after I first arrived, but I soon decided to give him a wide berth. To my delight, the hogwan replaced him with a teacher from Northern Ireland who was far more likeable and far less seedy. Ossie was well-educated and liked a beer. His arrival made life in Taean a lot more fun. Many of the adventures detailed in the coming chapters - in both Korea and China - took place with him at my side.

THE LEGEND OF THE DONG CHIP ... AND THE HORRORS OF KOREAN PUNISHMENT

As I explained in an earlier chapter, my teaching career began with quite the jolt. 30 hours a week in front of a bunch of walking talking little guys was certainly a daunting scenario. My lack of experience and Mr Kim's abject disregard for training and preparation meant that it took me a while to feel comfortable in my own teaching skin. Consequently, I was always on the lookout for a bit of reassurance. The conversation with Jimmy's mum had provided me with a modicum of that assurance, even though it was lacking in any great detail and objectified me a little. Nevertheless, as things progressed over the first couple of months, I began to feel just a bit better as the kids seemed happy and a couple of other parents also dropped by to say good things. As great as all that was though, it paled in comparison to some 'feedback' I received from one of my kindergarten kids.

Kim Sang Min was not one of my superstar students. He never said very much in class and was genuinely terrible at the flashcards game, but he was absolutely lovely. He always had the cutest of smiles and was the only student who ever helped me tidy my classroom at the end of the day. Over a decade and a half after my time in Korea, I still remember him vividly. I would like to believe that I would have remembered him anyway, but his bizarre form of praise is still wedged firmly in my memory.

It was a Wednesday lunchtime at Jung Chul and I was finishing up a few things after a tough morning of kindergarten classes before stepping into the lunchroom for a spot of rice. I tidied up the pens and discarded candy wrappers on my classroom floor before popping over into the reception area to hand my attendance lists to our receptionist, Eun Kyu. As I chatted with her, our conversation was interrupted by one of the most shocking things to ever happen to me. I know that sounds quite dramatic, but it really was quite alarming.

Sang Min was a very quiet boy, so he was always able to approach you very secretively. You would often not know that he was around until you actually laid eyes on him. This stealth ability allowed him to sneak up on me with anonymity. On this particular day, he managed to do this perfectly and moved directly behind me as I stood there unawares. As he approached my rear area, he put his index fingers together to make a rather thick point. He then got as close to me as possible and ... pushed his fingers into my ass. It was a painful and shocking moment that caused me to leap off my feet and scream, both in surprise and discomfort. To clarify, it was not a gentle little prod. He really jabbed them in there and were it not for the fabric of my trousers he might well have done me a little bit of damage.

In the seconds immediately following the incident, I felt as though I were in a state of shock. I had just been - to my mind at least - violated in a chillingly intimate way. I looked down at Sang Min who was sporting a grin that seemed to blend in equal measure innocence and mischief. In any other situation, it would have been wonderfully cute. But, not then. As the initial shock wore off and the sharp pain in my ass began to subside a little, I started to feel mad, very mad. I lifted Sang Min clean off his feet, stuck him under my arm - he was only tiny and easy to lift - and set off towards Mr Kim's office with the little boy starting to kick and scream as we went.

When I arrived at the office, I dropped Sang Min down on Mr Kim's couch and began screaming:

"Mr Kim, do you know what he did? Do you know what he just did to me?"

As I burst into my speech and my indignation flared, my self-consciousness also started to assert itself and I felt a little embarrassed as I divulged the rather personal details.

"What he did?" Asked Mr Kim.

"He … er … well … he … . Ok, he stuck his fingers into my ass".

Mr Kim's reaction shocked me to my core and left me genuinely speechless.

"Wow! Paul, that is great! I so happy!"

"Excuse me? What?"

"Yes, this very good."

"Why? Why? … Why on earth is this very good news Mr Kim? He shouldn't do that!"

By this point, my rage had begun to boil over and get the better of me. Not only had a student pushed his fingers into my ass, but my boss was happy - nae delighted - about the fact. So, I stormed outside in order to find Mr Jang. Whenever there was a language or cultural boundary that needed crossing, I would search out Mr Jang who was usually able to translate for me and explain the situation. In the most part, he had a far more logical and level-headed approach than Mr Kim.

"Mr Jang, Sang Min just pushed his fingers into my ass. I am, as you might imagine, quite upset about this, but Mr Kim seems quite happy. I don't understand what is happening".

"Oh wow! That is good news!"

"What? Whyyyyyyyy?????

"This is called Dong Chip and it is a way for Korean children to show their affection to their teacher. They only do it to teachers they like. He must like you. That is great!"

Mr Jang then began to explain the crazy phenomenon that was the Dong Chip. Apparently, it was a common and well-known way of showing affection for your teacher. I asked him if it was something he had needed to deal with in his career. He informed me that it was but that it had taken his students a bit longer to feel comfortable with him. He then sighed rather wistfully with an air of genuine disappointment. It almost made me feel sympathetic for him, before I remembered that we were discussing kids sticking their fingers into our respective asses.

I cannot pretend that getting perilously close to being anally violated didn't get me a little bit agitated. I also cannot pretend that, as I lifted Sang Min into the air, I didn't want to see him receive some form of punishment. I was genuinely mad. However, after Mr. Jang explained the situation, I calmed down a little and changed my mind in regards to seeing Sang Min punished. This was partially because I kind of understood why he did it, but also because I knew that the punishment he would receive would be difficult for me to stomach.

Korean attitudes to discipline were very different to those we have in England. Ideas like the 'naughty step' or 'taking a time out' were seen as wishy-washy and ineffectual in Korea. Mr Kim and the rest of the team preferred a more physical approach. The following passages may sound almost unbelievable, but I attest that for those where I was present they are entirely truthful. I wish they were not.

I will begin with an anecdote cum rumour that I cannot verify as true, but which all of my friends and colleagues were talking about for weeks. The story went that a Korean teacher in Busan was so enraged by the disobedience of a middle school student in his class that he struck him repeatedly on the hands with a cane. He did so with such force that he drew blood. He then forced the errant child to write an apology on the classroom whiteboard … in his own blood! I cannot be sure of the veracity of this story. It could be false or dramatically embellished. However, the point I am coming to by including this potentially apocryphal tale is that the attitude to discipline in Korea that I encountered on a day to day level was such that nobody I knew was fully convinced that it wasn't true.

Jung Chul did not quite reach the levels of the Busan story, but there was plenty or treatment that I would describe as nothing other than brutal. I will start by describing what happened with Joen, one of my junior school kids. Ordinarily, she was a very nice and very well-behaved kid. However, on one particular Wednesday afternoon, she just seemed to have spiralled out of control. No matter what I did, she would just not quiet down or pay attention. I tried asking nicely. I tried a sterner tone. I tried raising my voice. I tried threatening to send her to Mr. Kim. Nothing worked, so I made good on my threat and sent her to see the boss

Mr. Kim did not bother to ask nicely or raise his voice. Instead, he took out a long wooden ruler and cracked it across Joen's palm. When she returned to class her face was red and flushed from crying and she had a large red stripe across her quivering hand. It was a sobering experience for me, for Joen and for the rest of the class. Nobody wanted a repeat of that situation, so a tacit agreement developed within that particular class: the kids would behave and I would not involve Mr. Kim. If the kids acted up, all I needed to do was glance in the direction of Mr. Kim's office and everyone would quieten down.

The episode with Joen was not at all pleasant and certainly offended my British sensibilities. However, it was nowhere close to being the worst thing I saw at Jung Chul. There were a couple of examples that went way beyond. The first occurred when Ms Ahn was sick and Mr Kim drafted in a female supply teacher. Whilst Ms Ahn was not averse to giving the kids a gentle little slap, her methods were positively angelic compared to her stand-in. Rather than starting with smaller reprimands or sending the kids to Mr Kim, the supply teacher went big from the outset and banished the kids to the hallway where they were forced to bend double and balance with their fists on the floor forming a triangle with their body with their asses pointing into the air. They were not allowed to bend their knees, which meant there was huge pressure on their knuckles. It didn't take long for the skin on the outside of their fingers to be worn away and for the floor to be left bloodstained.

However, even an incident as brutal as that came a comfortable second place in terms of the cruelty I witnessed at Jung Chul. The dubious honour of being the worst thing I saw went to an incident with Mr Jang and a six-year old called Ka-Eun. It was genuinely harrowing. Apparently, Ka Eun had been behaving very badly in class, although I am not entirely sure exactly what she had done. She was only six years old and generally pretty nice albeit occasionally a bit loud, so I really couldn't imagine anything too heinous. However, Mr. Jang was clearly furious with her and inflicted punishment that seemed to be in no way proportionate to anything a six-year old could do.

Things began when Mr. Jang dragged Ka-Eun out of his classroom and into the corridor and started screaming at her. He then told her to say sorry for what she had done. She refused. He told her again. She refused again. So, he went back into his classroom and returned with a stick. He gave her one final chance to apologise. She refused again. So, he cracked the stick across the back of her legs. She let out a small yelp but didn't cry. This didn't impress Mr. Jang, so he demanded once more that she apologise. She refused yet again. With an exasperated sigh, he cracked the stick across her legs for a second time. This time she fell to her knees and began to cry. However, she was still adamant in her refusal to apologise. So, with an even bigger sigh of exasperation, the stick went across her calves again. This vicious back and forth went on at least three more times with no change in the result.

As things progressed, it clearly began to pose Mr. Jang a problem. Whilst I may not have agreed with his approach to discipline both in general and in this particular situation, he was a genuinely nice guy and was certainly no great sadist. However, Ka-Eun's obstinance was turning common a garden corporal punishment into bona fide torture. I am sure that a couple of cracks on the legs would ordinarily have satisfied him and I am certain that he didn't want to viciously beat Ka-Eun. Yet, he needed her to apologise. If not, he would have felt he had looked weak in front of the other kids. So, after one final crack across the back of the legs, he took the only course of action open to him. He sent Ka-Eun to Mr. Kim. I don't know what happened in the office, but

Ka-Eun was back in class the next day and nobody in Jung Chul - except me - seemed to think anything untoward had gone on.

The incidents with Joen, the supply teacher and Ka-Eun surprised me in the brutality that my colleagues believed to be acceptable. However, I was perhaps even more shocked that the parents seemed to think it was ok too. Demanding dads and pushy mums would change their kids' *hogwans* for all kinds of reasons: if their son or daughter didn't do well in an English test, if the school didn't have a foreign teacher, if the kid didn't like the foreign teacher, if the school wasn't doing the right kind of activities. However, I never heard of Jung Chul losing any students over corporal punishment. It seemed like an odd set of standards.

This type of attitude was not confined to Jung Chul or to Taean. A friend I met in Seoul used to tell a fantastic story - he insisted it was true but I felt it may have been accurate in its general message but perhaps exaggerated in places - in which he shared a father's reaction to disciplining his son. Apparently, the boy - an unruly teenager - was causing havoc in class. My friend went through the same kind of process as I had with Joen. However, just as with Joen, the boy was unresponsive and continued to cause problems. So, he clipped him around the ear. The boy burst out crying and fled the classroom. At the time, my friend chuckled to himself at the sight of a fifteen year old boy running out of the classroom crying, but things would get much more interesting as the day went on.

Later that evening, the boy's father arrived at the school with the child in tow. My friend was asked to go to the *hogwan* manager's office where they all sat around a coffee table. The *hogwan* manager explained that the father was angry that my friend had struck the child without a good reason. Affronted by the allegation, my friend explained that the boy had been misbehaving and proceeded to detail what had happened in the classroom. The father turned to look at the boy and asked if the list of allegations were true. When the boy sheepishly admitted that it was, the father got up and stormed out of the office.

My friend, the manager and the tearful boy sat in the office in a bizarrely uncomfortable silence. None of them were sure when or if the father would return. His son's behaviour had clearly been a source of major embarrassment. Ten minutes later he barged back in and was carrying a long wooden stick that he had apparently retrieved from the boot of his car. He handed it to my friend and informed him that if the

boy were to misbehave again, he should use it to beat him across the
legs and not bother with effeminate clips to the ear.

ONTO THE FOOTBALL PITCH

Regardless of where I am in the world, I love to get involved with some football. I like both to get to local matches and to try to find a team to play for myself. In Mongolia, I actually managed to combine the two by playing for a team in the national league. That may sound quite boastful, but in truth, the level was not world-class. In fact, it was nothing more than an average amateur level in the UK. However, it was an amazing experience and I was keen to enjoy something similar in Korea. So, one Sunday morning, I dragged myself out of bed at a frighteningly early hour - as apparently most matches started at 8am - and walked to one of Taean's football pitches to see if I could find a game with one of the local teams.

I was a tad nervous when I arrived at the pitch. Taean was a small town, so I was concerned that i) They would not speak any English, and ii) They wouldn't be welcoming to a foreigner just pitching up with his boots. I would later learn that I was right to be concerned about the second of those issues. However, on that Sunday morning, things went very smoothly. They spoke enough English for us to get by and they invited me to join their team, Lee-Wah FC. I was even able to play in a friendly match they were having that very day.

Over the subsequent few weeks, things seemed to go really well and I genuinely enjoyed myself. Dragging myself out of bed at 7am on Sunday was always hard work, but it felt worthwhile. The football was great fun and I succeeded in doing pretty well in the matches we played as the standard of play was, in all honesty, not at all great. In fact, it made the Mongolians look like the Brazilian national team!

A big reason for the less than stellar standard was that Taean was a small town, so there was not a huge talent pool to draw from. Additionally, because it was so small and there were not so many good jobs going with big corporations, the majority of younger fitter guys generally moved to Seoul, Busan or Daejon. This meant that I usually played against guys in their mid-thirties or older. Also, as your average Korean is significantly shorter and slighter than your average *wae gook*, at 182cm and 75kg I was bigger and stronger than almost all of my opponents.

For two or three months, the above factors combined to make things go very well and I scored plenty of goals, which helped Lee Wah win quite a few matches. The guys on the team seemed to like their new foreign friend and were keen to replicate Mr Kim in creating some slightly odd socializing opportunities. This began at half-time in my third or fourth game and came in the form of a bottle of soju and a tupperware container full of meat cut from a pig's face. In England, at half-time, we might have water, an orange or maybe a cup of tea. So, pig's face and booze was a bit of a departure for me.

Despite really not finding rice wine and the pig's face hugely appealing, I tried to be one of the boys by chewing away on a piece of the pig's ear and following it up with a soju chaser. It was genuinely disgusting. However, my teammates were delighted at my reaction and it seemed to spur them on. Consequently, the following week the soju and assorted pork products were served not out of one of our defender's tupperware containers from home, but on a nice plate … by coffee girls!

Despite our game being deadlocked at 0-0, the young ladies appeared to be genuinely impressed by Lee-Wah's first half performance and giggled approvingly at the jokes my teammates made. My fellow striker and the team's best English speaker, Yop, slapped me on the back and joked "Good for half-time"! Apparently, pig's face and bitter rice wine tastes better when served by a girl wearing heavy make-up with a very short mini-skirt and who had absolutely no idea whatsoever what was happening on the pitch!

After January and Ossie's arrival, there were suddenly two foreigners in the Lee-Wah starting lineup. We continued to do well on the pitch and the guys loved coming for beers with me and Ossie on a Friday night. It became the highlight of Yop's week to meet us in one of Taean's bars and knock back a pitcher of beer. Everything seemed to be going swimmingly. However, sadly, things would take a pretty massive turn for the worst in a couple of ways. One of these would cause me quite a bit of physical pain and the other would shock me to my core and cause a good deal of emotional distress.

The first problem struck when I was involved in a crunching tackle whilst playing against a team from a naval base 20km from Taean. A lot of their guys were members of the Korean version of the marines, so they were a lot fitter and faster than the collection of overweight 35 and 40 year olds I usually played against. This probably explains why some of the challenges going in were a little more robust than usual. I am not exactly sure what happened, but after one such challenge my knee quickly swelled up like a balloon and I was done for the game and for the subsequent few weeks.

The following morning, as I was in quite a bit of discomfort, Christine took me to the local physiotherapist. This proved to be a strange experience as the majority of the treatment he gave me was based on traditional Asian medicine, which was something I had never experienced before. His office was located in a very rickety old building that looked like it dated back to the Korean War and was decorated in a manner more akin to a Buddhist shrine than a medical practice. However, I'd had trouble getting my trousers over my swollen knee when I got dressed that morning and was unable to bend my leg. So, I suspended my scepticism and decided to buy into whatever he suggested.

After a bit of poking and prodding, he diagnosed strained ligaments and then began to place a series of strange suction cups around the knee. He attached these to some form of machine and then set them off pulling on the skin around my knee. It didn't really seem to have any impact and only served to feed into the apprehension I was trying to quell. However, after that, he used physio tape to strap the knee up and wrote me a prescription for some anti-inflammatories, which reassured me a little. He also wrote out a recipe for some herbal tea, which didn't reassure me at all.

After the initial visit, I underwent a couple more physio sessions. These involved some similarly strange approaches and plenty of herbal tea as well as slightly more incense than I thought necessary. Despite my efforts to be open to the new approach, I eventually decided that even though the sessions were really cheap - they were less than £5 a go - I was probably wasting my time and money. So, I resolved to stay at home, to rest the leg, to do the yoga-style stretching exercises he had recommended and to keep taking the anti-inflammatories.

During my first appointment, when I had asked how long it might take for the swelling to go down and for me to be able to run again, he told me that it usually took about six weeks to recover from that type of injury. This was terrible news for me as there was a big tournament coming in around two months and I desperately wanted to play. The recovery date didn't give me much wiggle room in getting fit on time. So, I continued to do my stretches religiously, took all my pills and crossed my fingers. Alas, as it turned out, I really shouldn't have wasted either the time or the effort.

On the day of the tournament, I was delighted to be fit and was raring to go. Ossie and I arrived an hour before the game was due to start and warmed up with the rest of the guys. Everything seemed normal. Except it wasn't. Because it was a fully blown competition rather than a friendly game, there would be a photographer from the local newspaper present to take a picture of the respective starting elevens. This meant that, unfortunately, neither Ossie nor I would be in Lee-Wah's line-up as some members of the Lee-Wah team didn't want said picture to be 'tainted' by the presence of a white face.

In pure footballing terms, this was a ridiculous decision. We were two of the youngest and fittest members of the team and, with us playing together, we invariably won the majority of our games. But, it very quickly became clear that there were no sporting considerations involved. We were, essentially, witnessing segregation. It was a horrific thing to experience, which felt worse because of how blunt and unapologetic they were about it.

They clearly didn't feel the need to dress their prejudice up in any way. Had they wanted to be diplomatic, they had an easy opportunity to be much more conciliatory about things. As I was only just back from my injury, they could simply have told me that I would be on the bench for fitness reasons. That would not have been illogical. But, instead, they decided not to bother with such niceties and went with the blunt racism approach. The exact wording they used when they told us we weren't playing was, "For the photo, no white faces. Only Koreans" .

It was a horrific thing to hear. Initially, I presumed something had been lost in translation. I just assumed that they couldn't actually really have said what I thought they had said, after all these were guys I had eaten pig's face with and gone for beers with. I thought we were friends. So, as I tried to keep a lid on the toxic anger that was bubbling up inside me, I asked Yop to explain what was going on. His response didn't help.

"Yop, why aren't we playing today? I don't understand".

"Sorry Paul but maybe this photo will go in the local newspaper and some of the team think it won't be good to have *wae gook* in the picture. They want only Koreans. They want it to be pure".

The dialog ended there as I really had nothing more to say to that. I simply took off my Lee-Wah kit, dropped it - hurled it might be a more accurate description - on the ground and left Unfortunately, there followed a very awkward moment when I realised my street clothes were in Yop's car, which meant I had to stand there in my underpants cursing to myself and anyone else who would listen whilst he went for my jeans.

In the years that have followed, I have often tried to rationalise what happened at the side of that football pitch. Yet, no matter how much I go over it, I cannot conclude that it was anything other than unadulterated racism and was something I had never expected to encounter - maybe my shock says something about my being a heterosexual white male and never having experienced such terrible treatment, but nonetheless it still stung. The only real insight or depth I can offer, aside from the fact that Koreans can in general be frighteningly nationalistic, was that I was dealing with older generations and maybe their old-school 'values' came out that way. Had I been dealing with younger people, maybe things would have been different. I didn't really think that was any kind of excuse, though. So, I decided I needed to find myself a new team.

That proved to be much easier than I thought it might have been. A couple of days after the incident, I was walking down the street in Taean when a taxi pulled up alongside me and the driver jumped out and walked towards me with a mildly alarming degree of purpose. At first I was a little alarmed as I worried I was perhaps about to get robbed. However, it soon dawned on me that I recognised him. He was a tallish guy with a spectacular pot-belly whose team I had played against a couple of weeks before my injury. From what I could recall, they were a terrible side and we had thumped them 6-0 or 7-0. He had clearly learned what had happened with Lee Wah - as I had already discovered, news travels fast in a small town - and he wanted me to bolster their ranks. It was all super easy and I would be playing the following Sunday.

My new team was just awful. We lost almost every game we played, and we often lost them spectacularly heavily. However, they were generally a nice group of guys and were happy to have their picture taken with me should the need arise. Some of the older members of the team were clearly a little reticent around me. Fir example the captain had no idea what to make of me and really didn't like it if I put in a hard tackle or argued with the referee, but they were happy for me to play whenever a competition came around.

It was after one of these tournaments that one of the most memorable things that happened to me in Korea - and, in truth, in all my years of travelling - took place. We had played our first game at around 9am and had lost on penalties after drawing 2-2, which put us out of the competition. That may sound disappointing, but to actually draw a game was quite the success for us. As I trudged dejectedly away from the pitch, one of the older guys, who spoke almost no English, approached me and put his hand to his mouth in an eating motion. I was not really in the mood for a team lunch - I am a terribly sore loser - so I said "No, thanks" in my best Korean. However, he was insistent and began to make some funny noises, "Mong, mong". At first this seemed just plain weird, but after a few seconds I remembered that instead of "woof", Koreans say "mong".

Obviously, Korea is well known for dog being one of its traditional dishes. Until that point though, as it was not something I was particularly keen on, I had been able to avoid eating it. Mr Kim had invited me once but I had politely declined and he had not forced the issue. That was my plan again. However, my teammate then began making hand gestures that looked remarkably like a gun and then added some "bang bang" sound effects for good measure. "You shot a dog?", I asked with unconcealed apprehension. He clapped his hands triumphantly and responded, "Yes, I shoot dog … for you".

I was not so keen on a Sunday brunch involving a four-legged friend. It was not really my cup of tea. However, it didn't look as though I had the option to refuse as the dog's life had been ended with my eating pleasure in mind. That was quite a bit of pressure! Despite my misgivings and clear reluctance, the whole team began ushering me towards the guy's car. Before I could get in though, they opened the boot to reveal the body of a dog that was missing it's head and fur - although, curiously, not its tail. It was not the most appetising of sights, but the rest of the guys seemed super excited and I was quickly bundled into the back seat and we headed out into the local countryside.

We drove at breakneck speed along a series of narrow lanes until we arrived at a very pleasant little picnic spot. We all piled out of the car, laid a straw mat on the floor and opened the soju. Whilst we did this, our driver pulled the dog out of his boot and one of the others dragged an oil drum out of the pick up truck he had driven there. What followed was truly harrowing. They dragged the headless dog carcass onto the straw and set about hacking it into eight pieces before throwing them into the oil drum with some cooking oil and some greens that I guess were either spinach or cabbage.

Having watched the cleaver go in between the dogs ribs and wrench the animal into pieces, I cannot say my appetite was getting any stronger. However, as the animal cooked in the oil drum and as I drank more soju, the aroma started to really grip me. It genuinely smelled delicious and I began to feel very torn. I was not keen on eating dog - in England they are pets for goodness sake and I was conditioned not to think of them as food - but, after my exertions on the football field and several glasses of booze, I was beginning to feel ravenous and when the animal came out of the drum it looked very inviting.

Even today, years after the actual event, I still feel very self-conscious about finding the dog delicious. But, it really was! We started with the ribs. We ate them in the same way you would eat pork bbq pork ribs in an American bar. They were amazing. The flesh fell delicately off the bone and I quickly went back for more. Then, after the ribs, we tucked into the legs and something that would best be described as fillet. It was all bizarrely good. The closest comparison I could make with other meat would be a slightly tougher but leaner version of lamb. Make no mistake, I have eaten several worse dishes in England!

At the time, as I ate and drank with my team, the canine cuisine went down very well. However, the following morning I woke up in something of a state. Having drunk soju for the majority of the afternoon, I arrived home in the evening and passed out on my bed. I awoke around 5am with the sun drenching my apartment - I had not succeeded in closing my curtains when I got back - and a pounding headache. It was only as I began to brush my teeth and the small chunks of dog meat dropped into the sink that I started to recall the events of the previous day and groaned to myself. A raging soju hangover and the residual taste of dog was no way to start a day teaching kindergarten.

When I told my mother, my father and my friends about my culinary escapades, their reactions varied from surprise to outright revulsion. However, all of their comments had one factor in common: they all compared the Korean cuisine to eating a beloved family pet. But, that is not really an accurate reflection of reality. In Korea, dog meat is raised and reared in a similar way to pork or beef in the UK. There are farms where a specific breed of dog is raised to be eaten - Koreans only eat larger dogs as they believe they are not as intelligent as smaller ones, which means smaller dogs are pets and certain bigger ones go in the pot. Therefore, Koreans view these dogs in the same way English people look at pigs or cows. There is a certain logic to it. At no point is anyone popping around to their neighbours to steal their Jack Russel and stick it on the bbq.

Playing football in Taean was a big part of my time in Korea, but it was not my only experience of football there. Ossie and I also decided to get out and about and head to see some K-League and national team matches. Exploring Korean football was a fun and interesting experience, during which I learned quite a lot about the sport and Korea as a nation. Our first exposure to professional football in Korea came when my friend Matt came to visit and he, Ossie and I went to the national stadium in Seoul to watch Korea play a World Cup Qualifying match against Kuwait.

It was February and bitterly cold. The game started around 19h00 in the evening, so we grabbed an early dinner and a few beers before heading to the stadium. We were looking forward to the match as at the World Cup two years before Korea had surprised everyone by reaching the semi-final and upsetting some major players along the way. Quite famously they defeated both Spain and Italy before losing in the semi-final to Germany. It ranked as one of the World Cup's biggest surprises and genuinely captured the world's imagination. Prior to that, they were something of an international football whipping-boy. In the 1998, 1994, 1990 and 1986 World Cups, they had failed to win a single match and had only four draws to show for all their efforts. So, becoming the first team from outside Europe or South America to reach a semi-final was a major achievement.

During the tournament, the whole country worked itself into a footballing frenzy. Two years later and there was still plenty of residual euphoria bubbling about. On my first day in the country, the second or third question John Lee had asked me was whether or not I liked football. When I answered in the affirmative, he was really keen to ask me if I had seen Korea in the World Cup and waxed lyrical about how fabulous it was. He was not the only one. During the World Cup, almost everyone in Korea was wearing a red t.shirt with the slogan "Be The Reds" emblazoned across the front. These were still hugely prevalent around the country - so much so in fact that I would often teach classes where four or five of the kids would be wearing them. I found that a touch weird as Korea's shirts were closer to pink than to red!. On a slightly more bizarre level, I also had kids wearing t.shirts featuring a black and white photo of a rather schoolmasterly looking Dutch man in his mid-fifties.

South Korea's World Cup success was masterminded by Gus Hiddink, the renowned coach from the Netherlands who had coached PSV Eindhoven (where he won a European Cup) the Netherlands (who he took to the semi-finals of the 1998 World Cup) and Real Madrid. It is with him that Korea's World Cup story gets very interesting. Hiddink is almost deified in Korea - something that remains true to this day. He is the only foreigner to be granted honorary Korean citizenship and has a stadium named after him. Paradoxically, this adoration came despite Hiddink making a concerted effort to do things in a very unKorean way.

My time with Lee-Wah showed how nationalistic - and, let's be blunt, even xenophobic - Koreans can be. However, Hiddink blew past this and changed the way the country approached the game on a professional level. The first example came with the national team's preparation for the World Cup. Qualifying had generally been a relatively simple process for Korea as Asia was not a particularly competitive part of the footballing world. However, thumping the likes of Vietnam, Thailand and Cambodia didn't provide much in the way of preparation for a major international tournament. Prior to Hiddink, Korea's coaches exacerbated this problem by arranging pre-tournament friendlies against teams they could easily defeat as they didn't want to look bad in the national media by losing. The end result was, of course, terrible performances at major tournaments where the underprepared Koreans simply couldn't cope with stronger nations from Europe or South America.

Rather than booking games against other Asian nations, Hiddink decided to put his side up against those major European and South American sides. The theory was that playing against better teams would prepare Korea for the tough games they would have in the World Cup. At first, it didn't go at all well and Korea took some beatings. In fact, at one point, some of the Korean newspapers nicknamed Hiddink '0-5' because his team were always on the wrong end of some unflattering scorelines. It would seem unthinkable now in Korea, but the Dutchman was under quite a bit of pressure to improve results quickly and also received lots of criticism for openly spending time with his girlfriend when the papers felt he would be better served working with the players on the training pitch.

The second big change was a more fundamental one. Korean culture places a huge amount of emphasis on the importance of age and seniority. I saw this a lot in my everyday life. For example, I got a few glimpses of it at work. Ordinarily, the hierarchy at Jung Chul was pretty clear and pretty simple. Mr Kim was the boss and was also the oldest member of the team. Therefore, in most meetings, he ruled the roost and almost always had the last word. However, this wasn't always the case. Occasionally, at busier times we had a substitute teacher called William who was older than Mr Kim. When William was there, we had to listen to his ideas and opinions … regardless of whether they were worthwhile and also regardless of the fact that he was only a temporary employee. We had the rather odd situation of meetings being held up for 10 or 15 minutes just so the oldest person could have his say. Weirdly, everyone would nod along and give great reverence to his words before Mr. Kim would either decide to follow his own path or to adopt what Christine or Mr. Jang had suggested.

Similar values were also visible on the football pitch for both the teams I played for. Admittedly, we didn't have a huge amount of younger players that were actively available, but nevertheless both sides preferred to play older players rather than younger ones. For example, my new team had a defensive line with an average age of well over 45, which often showed as we regularly shipped 6 or 7 goals in a game. Also, whenever we got a penalty kick, we didn't pick the taker based on the likelihood of him scoring. But, rather, we gave the oldest member of the team the chance to take the kick. Invariably, we would not score.

Whilst things were not quite so clear-cut or ridiculous in the Korean national team, prior to Hiddink's arrival age played a huge factor. Previous coaches all picked older players and rarely gambled on playing youngsters. There were also similar issues amongst the players themselves. Younger players often went to great lengths to show deference to older members of the team. In fact, there were stories of younger players passing to their elders in situations where they would have been better placed themselves simply because it was seen as the correct thing to do. It was no way to operate an international sports team. Hiddink changed things by dispensing with the Korean way. He managed to oust several older players that he had inherited and instead picked a squad of younger players.

On a side note, Korea's success was also extremely interesting because there are plenty of rumours suggesting it was an example of horrific corruption. Whilst the Koreans see the World Cup as a national triumph, others have asked whether it was all one big fix. The main voices behind the corruption allegations came from the Italian press - who, admittedly, were not necessarily balanced and impartial as Italy were the supposed victims. They alleged that the Ecuadorian referee, who took charge of the game between Italy and Korea was a 'questionable' character. During the game he made a plethora of controversial decisions, including sending off Italy's star striker Francesco Totti for diving when he really should have given Italy a penalty and also disallowing a seemingly legal goal for the Italians. After the World Cup, he was banned by the Ecuadorian F.A. for 20 matches and also arrested, and subsequently imprisoned, for smuggling 6kg of heroin into JFK airport in New York.

With such an interesting, complex and dramatic recent history to Korean football, I was expecting big things from our trip to Seoul's World Cup Stadium. Sadly, it did not quite meet expectations. As the opponents were Kuwait rather than Italy, Spain or Germany, the quality of the football was not so great and Korea won very comfortably. Kuwait were not a very good team and they really didn't seem to be loving the frigid temperatures, as you would imagine with a team from the Gulf. In all honesty, nobody in the whole stadium seemed to be liking the cold. We certainly didn't. My feet felt like they had frozen solid. The majority of the Korean fans seemed to feel the same as the stadium was oddly quiet and there was very little of the excitement seen at the World Cup. It left us feeling as though we had somehow missed out.

The trip to the World Cup Stadium might not have been the most exciting, but we enjoyed the spectacle of seeing the stadium and watching Korea's national team. We saw it as a decent start to our footballing adventure and decided to also try and watch some national league games. Korea's K.League was formed in the late 1990s. This came a few years after the launch of the J.League in Japan, which had been wildly successful and had attracted some high profile international players such as Zico from Brazil and England's Gary Lineker. A new league in Korea was part of the infrastructure created for the World Cup - just as the MLS had been in the USA in 1994 - and would see the creation of several new teams and the construction of new stadiums that would be used both for the tournament and the league.

The league was pretty successful and, whilst it was no Serie A or English Premier League, some sides quickly became hugely popular and developed strong fan bases. For example, we often saw Suwon Bluewings or Pohang Steelers on TV playing in front of very sizable crowds. Each of the teams in the K.League generally followed a similar pattern: they were usually made up of young Korean players - boosted by their World Cup success, the majority of the senior team played in either Japan or Europe, such as Park Ji Sung who had moved to Manchester United - and three or four mid-level players from South America or Eastern Europe.

Ossie and I started our K.League journey with a trip to the city of Bucheon, which is located between Seoul and Incheon in the northwest of Korea about two hours from Taean on the express bus.. We made the trip on a very wet Saturday afternoon for what we thought would be a big game as Bucheon were playing Incheon United. We presumed that, because the two cities were so close to each other, there might have been some sort of fierce local rivalry and that we might experience the type of atmosphere that had been missing when we watched the national team. Alas, this was not the case as the stadium was all but empty.

Ossie and I arrived about an hour before kick-off and went in search of tickets. It took us a while to find these as half of the stadium - which held almost 35,000 people - was not open. Eventually, we found a ticket office and saw that we could buy tickets for either end of the stadium: the home fans were behind one goal and the visitors were behind the other goal. The only other tickets available were in the VIP section on the halfway line. Admission was not at all expensive. Seats behind the goal were just five or six pounds and the VIP seats were only about fifteen pounds. As we were both used to paying a lot more to watch matches in England, we thought we would push the boat out and decided to go for VIP tickets.

As it transpired, we really would feel like VIPs. Our seats were excellent and we got complimentary tea to sip whilst we watched the game. This was lovely, but it was secondary compared to the people we were sitting close to. After the 2002 World Cup, Hiddink left his role as coach to move back to Europe where he would coach PSV Eindhoven again as well as Chelsea and the Dutch National team for a second time. He was replaced by a Portuguese coach who was significantly less successful and was fired within a year. Therefore, in an effort to improve results, the Korean F.A. decided to go Dutch again and hired the far less well-known Jo Bonfrere. To our surprise, Hiddink 2.0 was seated in the row in front of us and, in a humorous echo of my adventures with Mr. Kim and the Lee Wah boys, he and his staff were laughing and joking with a selection of coffee girls who were doing a pretty decent job of batting their eyelids and distracting everyone from the rather dull game before them.

For the record, Incheon won the game 1-0. Perhaps Bonfrere should have paid a bit more attention to events on the pitch and a bit less to the coffee girls because he failed to get the Korean team playing at all well and was out of a job before I had left Korea. Ossie and I had enjoyed the trip out, but we were feeling a bit disappointed in our choices of footballing events in Korea as neither game had been too exciting. Therefore, to get over the massive letdown in Bucheon, we decided to go to a second game. We picked one at the Incheon Munhak Stadium, home of Incheon United - the same side who had defeated Bucheon - and one of the venues for the 2002 World Cup: it hosted three group games, including Korea's win over Portugal.

Thankfully, things would get a lot better. We managed to pick a weekend when the weather was better and there were plenty of fans in the stadium. It was a balmy 28 degrees and there were about 13,000 people watching the match and making a lot of noise. We were able to sit and watch Incheon lose 3-1 to Ulsan with a beer in our hand - it was finally a great taste of Korean football for us!

HITTING THE ROAD

The first few weeks of my teaching career were quite dramatic and a little stressful at times. I had to learn a lot about my new vocation whilst simultaneously fending off offers to spend time in the sauna with my boss and worrying about being intimately violated by my students. Thankfully, after a while things began to settle down and the remainder of my time teaching the kindergarten students was a little more sedate. To my great delight, I did not need to discuss my ass - and the violation thereof - in any further detail, which was a blessed relief. However, despite things calming down in my classroom, Mr Kim still wanted to emphasize the benefits of the Magic Foreigner approach to language learning. This manifested itself in a host of different events and field-trips where I was wheeled out in-front of curious parents and where I was captured in countless photos posing with the students. These trips were, generally, pretty tiring and I soon got rather sick of the constant photo-calls. However, they did give me a chance to see quite a bit of Korea - they were also quite fun at times.

Mr Kim's program of tours started locally at Baek-Wah mountain, which was situated about 3 or 4km outside Taean. In truth, it was more of a small hill than a mountain, but it was home to a small Buddhist shrine and was quite pretty. It also afforded some great views across the rice fields and out to sea. So, it was deemed worthy of a trip. To my dismay, though, I was informed that the mountain was best viewed at sunrise, which meant I would be up much too early for my liking. I was sceptical about this but, nevertheless, I squeezed myself onto the school bus at just before 6am.

I had assumed that everyone else on the trip would feel the same as I did about starting off in the pitch black of the very early morning. I was wrong. Korea is known as the 'Land of the Morning Calm' because everybody gets up so early. It is typical for office workers to be up before 5.30 and to be at their desks before 7.00. Because of this, everyone else on the trip was in fine fettle as we set-out at stupid o'clock. Ms Ahn - who had taken the English name Anne, to make her full name Anne Ahn - decided that it would be a great idea to start the day with a bit of a sing-song. It was only a short journey to the mountain but we managed to get through "Wheels on the Bus" and several green bottles falling from the wall before we arrived. As the kids had barely mastered vowel sounds and basic vocabulary, the din the songs created was horrific and did absolutely nothing for my early morning grumpiness.

When we arrived at Baek-Wah, it was a genuinely serene and peaceful sight. After getting off the bus into the darkness, the kids quieted down a bit and things felt nice and calm. The sight of the sun cracking the horizon and gently raising itself above the rice fields that surrounded Taean was very nice. As I flicked open my third coke of the morning, I began to feel a little less resentful at being woken so early. A small part of me - with a heavy emphasis on the word small - was beginning to see why the Koreans enjoyed their early mornings and I began to feel very calm and centered. Then, as the sun began to climb and the daylight fully asserted itself, the silence was shattered.

As it got lighter, the kids started to fully wake up. With this awakening came a great deal of shouting, screaming, crying and arguing over toys and candy. There were a few parents on the trip who tried to help Ms Ahn and Mr Jang keep control, but they failed miserably. The whole escapade quickly began to descend into a mist of candy-fuelled chaos. As the kids shrieked and hurled themselves around the shrine area, I began to worry that Buddha would not be best impressed at getting his serenity shattered and my thoughts turned to the karmic consequences that might await us. Clearly, Ms Ahn and Mr Jang were of the same opinion and we decided that it was time to draw the trip to a close.

At the start of the excursion, the bus had driven up the mountain and deposited us close to the shrine. The driver had then returned to the bottom, where he was waiting for us - and, most probably, enjoying a sly sleep. The plan, therefore, was for everyone to walk down the hill to meet him. It was a plan that sounded fantastic in theory. It would have been great to take the kids for a gentle stroll down the mountain. We could have pointed out different trees and plants and the kids would have got some nice exercise. In reality, though, nothing of the sort was ever on the cards.

As soon as Ms Ahn shouted "Let's Go!", utter unbridled chaos gripped the mountainside. Fuelled by candy and fizzy drinks, the kids set off at full pace. At first, they charged down in conventional style. However, many of them soon discovered that it was far more fun to lie down and roll down the slope. All this was happening on a public road, albeit a very quiet one, so there was the worrying and very real prospect of a small child rolling under the front wheels of an approaching Hyundai. Obviously, I was quite perturbed. We had 30 out of control kids loose on the mountain. Mr Jang and I quickly began sprinting down the slope to try and restore some order, but Ms Ahn and some of the mums who had accompanied us on the trip were next to useless. They all looked resplendent in full make-up and high-heels, but were able to do little more than totter precariously down towards the car park and shout ineffectual instructions as the children disappeared into the distance.

Thankfully, Mr Jang and I managed to avert any major injuries or fatalities. There was the odd bruised shin and scraped knee but, miraculously, nothing worse. After we had corralled all of the kids back onto the bus we set off back to the hogwon. I was expecting some of the parents to be concerned at the total lack of health and safety precautions and to file complaints with Mr. Kim. However, by early evening, Eun Kyu was fielding a stream of calls from delighted parents who wanted to inform Mr Kim of how much their kids had learned and how much fun they had had running down the mountain with Paul *sungsannim*. MFS was clearly proving its worth and the success of the Baek-Wah trip had Mr Kim searching for other ideas.

His next brainchild was one that actually got me a little excited. It was a trip to a theme-park on the outskirts of Daejon, the closest major city to Taean. As much as I love Buddha and early morning sprinting, this idea was much more my cup of tea. To my great relief, we set off at a very reasonable 8am. This time I was fully prepared for Ms Ahn's love of orchestrated vocal butchery and I had my discman turned up to full volume. This allowed the two hour drive to fly by and helped me arrive at the park feeling genuinely enthusiastic. There were plenty of small rides and animals to distract the children and there were also a few bigger attractions that I had my eye on.

Sadly, I began my day by making something of a rookie mistake. The car park was quite a distance from the main entrance to the theme park, so we had a bit of a walk. As we made our way towards the gates, a student named Choi Ji Yun ran up behind me and tried to jump on my back. Relieved that he wasn't trying to Dong Chip me, I gave him a quick piggy-back. He loved it and started shouting at his classmates to watch him. This was not a good turn of events for my shoulders or lower back. One lesson I had quickly learned teaching Korean kids is that no-one wants to be left out. If you give one kid candy, you have to give every kid candy. Therefore, one piggy-back actually equates to thirty piggy-backs. Suddenly, the theme park was a secondary concern for everyone on the trip. The kids seemed more content to ride their foreign teacher around the parking lot like a horse and Mr Kim enjoyed the photo-op tremendously.

By the time we actually got inside the park, I was exhausted. Thankfully, some of the animals in the zoo section of the park did a really good job of distracting the kids, which meant all I really needed to do was occasionally jump in with the English name for each different animal. The kids seemed happy enough staring at the animals and Mr Kim was engrossed in taking pictures of the kids (with me somehow captured in the background).

The animal area of the park and a few of the smaller rides managed to take up the majority of the afternoon. This meant that whilst I had a relaxed afternoon, I did not get too much time to enjoy any of the park's more grown-up attractions. This was a massive shame as some of them looked genuinely terrifying. However, I managed to console myself with the knowledge that there had been precious little chaos and I was getting paid overtime for the day. However, the day would end with an unexpected twist.

As we began to make our way back to the bus, Mr Jang slid in stealthily beside me and informed me that we were about to pass the park's main attraction, an extremely high vertical-drop ride. These were hugely popular in Korea at the time. There was one at Lotte World in Seoul that was positively huge and gave an amazing, albeit very brief, view of the city. The ride near Daejon towered over 150m in the air and plummeted to earth at frightening speed. It sounded like just my cup of tea, and Mr Jang looked keen too. Ms Ahn, as expected, was petrified at the idea and didn't want to mess up her hair or make-up. Mr Jang, though, was also feeling mischievous and had his eyes on getting us and, for maximum entertainment value, Mr Kim onto the attraction. To do this, he delivered a Machiavellian masterclass.

Even though he was a pretty friendly and approachable guy, Mr Kim still bought heavily into the Korean idea of respect and reverence for seniority. Therefore, he was no great fan of anything that could make him look foolish in front of the children. Accordingly, we knew he might be reluctant to go on the ride voluntarily for fear of looking scared in front of the kids. Mr Jang was aware of this, but had a cunning plan up his sleeve to harness Mr.Kim's pride and fear of looking foolish. As we passed the ride he shouted:

"Shall Teacher Paul and I go on the ride?"

He was met by a chorus of screams in the affirmative from the kids. He then said to Mr Kim:

"I presume you don't want to join us".

"No, I think I will be ok" came Mr Kim's cagey response.

Then, just loud enough for the kids and Ms Ahn to hear, he delivered the knock-out blow:

"Yes, it could be quite scary".

This put Mr Kim in a difficult position. If he had a go on the ride and looked scared, he wouldn't look good in front of the kids. But, not going on it at all might look even worse. What was he to do? After a moment's consideration, he passed his giant camera to Ms Ahn and, with impressive bravado, walked towards the ride.

As we strapped ourselves in, the kids began to chant "Wong Jan Nim" over and over again. (This is Korean for headmaster). A wry smile broke out at the edge of Mr Kim's mouth, but it could not mask the fear he was clearly feeling. As the ride began and we steadily started to rise above the park, the tiny voices became scarcely audible and the figures below looked smaller and smaller. As we moved above the treetops I turned to Mr Kim. His teeth were clenched and he looked genuinely petrified. Mr Jang, who was in the next seat, was grinning from ear to ear at having quite spectacularly stitched up his boss/future brother-in-law.

When we reached the top, there was a short and sharp clicking sound. There was then just the briefest of pauses before we fell to earth at speed. The air above the trees had felt oddly silent. However, as we began to drop I could hear the air whistling past my ears and Mr Kim screaming uncontrollably beside me. Then, as we neared the bottom of our descent, Mr Kim's girlish squeelings were drowned out by the eager cheers of the kids who were clearly very excited by the whole escapade … much more so than Mr Kim. We disembarked the ride amidst quite the fanfare, which was just as well for Mr Kim was still whimpering rather audibly.

The vertical drop was great fun. I enjoyed it tremendously both for its own intrinsic value and for the opportunity it afforded to see my boss in genuine discomfort. As much fun as it was, though, the ride actually managed to cause me some pain as I made yet another rookie mistake. After getting off and meeting the kids again, a few of them ran up to me demanding hugs and high-fives. Without thinking, I lifted one of them up in the air and then pretended to drop him in the same way as the ride before catching him before his feet landed on the ground. He loved it. Just as with the piggy-backs earlier in the day, it was a big mistake. You vertical drop one kindergarten student, you vertical drop 30 kindergarten students. By the time I slumped into my seat on the bus, I was exhausted and my back, shoulders and forearms ached beyond comprehension.

Christmas in Korea

The first few trips out had been a great success with kids and parents alike, so Mr Kim decided that we should branch out and organize a Christmas event with our very own Santa Claus going to visit students in their homes.. Consequently, it was planned that on the 23rd of December the whole team would go and visit the kids at home with Santa dropping off gifts. Mr Kim had organized things so that the parents could give us gifts they had bought ahead of time for Santa to deliver. It seemed like a sound enough plan. The only remaining question was who would play the role of Santa. The logical decision would have been for me to do it - Santa, clearly, does not look particularly Korean. However, Mr Kim was worried that the kids would recognize me and this would mean they might figure out that Santa was not actually real. This caused a bit of head-scratching before Mr Kim came up with the slightly insane solution of asking Mr Jang's fiancee to don the Santa suit: Nothing says Christmas like a thin Korean woman wearing heavy eye-shadow putting on an ill-fitting Santa suit!

On the evening of the 23rd we finished classes early before Mr Jang, the future Mrs Jang, Mr Kim, Ms Ahn and I set off in the school bus to visit a selection of the students' homes. We started at the home of Eun Jae, one of our smallest and cutest little guys. We arrived at around 4pm to find him waiting patiently by the front door with his mum. We piled out of the van to greet him and give him the gift. As Mrs Jang handed him the neatly wrapped package he stared at her with a look of complete and utter confusion - he was probably under the impression that Santa was i) Male, ii) Quite portly, and iii) Not Korean. He hesitantly took the gift and then hid behind his mother's leg. Mr Kim tried to coax him out for a picture. Unfortunately, the sight of Mrs Jang and her fake white beard proved just a little too much and he burst into tears before running into the house. His mother shrugged apologetically before following him inside.

Despite the initial setback, Mr Kim stuck to his guns and we proceeded to the next house. Sadly, the rest of the evening followed a similar pattern. We would arrive at a house and within a couple of minutes the child would have quite spectacularly freaked out at the sight of a thin, female, Korean Santa. To minimize the damage, after the fourth or fifth house, Mr Kim started to call ahead to explain to the parents that we were coming and that Santa might not be exactly what they were expecting. On at least one occasion, the parents thought that it would simply confuse the children too much and Santa had to sit disconsolately in the van whilst Mr Kim took pictures of me holding a child with a gift.

Winter Wonders and Woes

The trip to the theme park had been great fun and whilst the Christmas excursion had been farcical at times, I had enjoyed seeing the kids in their home environments and meeting some of their parents. Therefore, when Mr Kim suggested another trip I was happy to go along again. As it was the middle of winter, the trip would have a particularly snowy theme as we would be going to the mountains to enjoy some winter sports.

One of the things that had surprised me most about Korea was the severity of the winter. Having spent the previous February in Mongolia, I knew a thing or two about frigid temperatures. However, when November rolled around I was genuinely shocked as the snow fell and Taean began to freeze. Things weren't as cold as Mongolia had been, but the mercury dropped a long way below zero.

In Mongolia, I had seen temperatures as low as -45. Thankfully, though, my apartment there came with central heating that was permanently on and cranked up to maximum. In Korea, this was not the case. The apartment Mr. Kim had provided for me, whilst well-furnished and generally comfortable, was metallic and perched on the top of the five storey building in which the school was located. There was precious little insulation against the bitter winds outside. It was heated by a system of underfloor pipes that used oil for fuel. This kept me warm, but the exorbitant cost of the oil - the purchase of which Mr. Kim, rather suspiciously, insisted on arranging - ensured that I spent over 20% of my salary on heating.

When the first winter showers hit Taean and I had to start paying for heating fuel my mood soured on Korea a little bit. However, this proved to be just the start of my winter woes.

My first major mishap came on December 30th and stuck a spanner in the works in regards to my new year plans. Whilst trying to retrieve my clothes from the washing line out on the roof, I slipped on a patch of black ice and fell awkwardly. In doing so, I managed to strain my neck to such an extent that I was only able to turn my head to the right. It was so bad that I was unable to see a person standing next to me on my left. It also hurt like hell. As it was so uncomfortable, it scuppered my plans of spending New Year's Eve partying in Seoul. Instead, I rang in the new year watching movies - lying in a very awkward position - on my couch..

Not being able to enjoy New Year in Seoul was a bit of a bummer, but things would get a lot worse! In February, the winter decided to kick me in the ass once more. With the football pitches in Taean frozen, Ossie and I decided there was nothing keeping us there for the weekend and so made our way to Seoul for a large quantity of beers in Itaewon. We were away for two full days and, when I returned, the water-pipes running to my house had frozen solid as the water in them had been standing and the insulation covering them was not up to scratch. This meant it was impossible to have a shower, do my laundry or flush the toilet for almost a week. I found myself showering in the school - which, thankfully, had a very cramped toilet/shower room - and flushing the toilet with bottles of water I filled in the school bathroom.

Because of those problems, I was keen to get away and enjoy the benefits of a Korean winter rather than experience the drawbacks. As I boarded the bus on a chilly Saturday morning, I was feeling good about the trip. I wasn't quite sure what "winter theme park" meant, but it sounded fun. Things got even better when after about forty minutes, the bus stopped and the kids began to get off. Confused at what was happening - there was little snow to be seen and Mr Kim had told me that the journey was two hours long - I asked Ms Ahn what was going on. In response, I got a quick lesson in Korean infrastructure. As the country is very rocky and mountainous, particularly in the centre, there isn't much of a rail network. Instead, just as I usually did when travelling to Seoul, people took the bus to get where they were going. Because of this, none of the kids had ever been on a train before. Therefore, as part of our excursion, the kids got the opportunity to ride a train - on one of the country's few lines - for the first time and Ms Ahn and I got the chance to spend the journey in peace.

As cool as all the animals were on the previous trip, they paled in comparison to the fun in the snow that was on offer. The winter sports park wasn't quite like the French Alps, but it had a few nice ski-slopes and a cool looking snowboarding park. I am no great alpinist but, having spent a year of my university life in northern New York close to the Adirondack Mountains, I am not totally inept on skis and was eyeing the slopes excitedly. Sadly, Mr Kim felt that my time would be better spent with the kids and never too far from his roving camera lens. I did try adopting Mr Jang's technique of suggesting he should come with me, but the kids were too excited about getting into the snow themselves to care about the idea of watching me and Mr Kim try to ski.

Rather than swishing my way down the slopes, I spent the majority of the afternoon working as little more than a pack mule. As the majority of our group was below ten years old, they went onto the baby slopes where Mr Kim had rented a bunch of plastic sledges. The kids all loved gliding down the 'piste', but they were significantly less excited about the prospect of dragging the sledges back up the slope. So, it was left to me. It was really hard work! Thankfully, though, a lot of them also wanted to go down the slope with Paul teacher on the sledge, so at least I got to experience a very small taste of adventure in the snow. This really pleased Mr Kim who, of course, was waiting at the bottom to snap a picture of the happy kids with their foreign buddy.

A Korean Wedding

Perhaps the most interesting trip I took during my time in Korea came in early Spring and gave me a fascinating glimpse into Korean culture. We - just the staff from the school; thankfully there were no kids involved this time - went to the JungChul event of the year: Mr Jang's wedding … to the lady who was also known as Santa Claus. As Mr Jang was from Daejon, in the centre of Korea, we would not only get to see a traditional ceremony but we would also have an interesting journey across the country.

When I looked at a map of Korea, Taean didn't look to be too far from Daejon. It seemed to be the same kind of distance as Seoul, which usually took just under two hours to reach on the express bus. However, I was surprised to learn that it would take a minimum of three hours to reach the wedding hall on the outskirts of the city. This longer journey time was a result of the rather dramatic terrain between Taean and Daejon: Whereas the journey to Seoul was almost all undertaken on flat highways, the trip southeast would involve a slog through an imposing mountain range.

Just as with a regular journey to Seoul, the first part of our trip was relatively smooth and serene as we took a highway that led south from the Taean peninsula. It felt very much like every other journey I had been on in Korea, so I slipped my headphones in and dosed off. I only drifted out of my slumber when we pulled off the highway just over an hour later. This proved to be a good piece of timing as it was at that point in the journey that things got significantly more picturesque and like nothing else I had seen in Korea.

After leaving the highway and then stopping briefly for gas, we started climbing into the mountains along a winding single-carriageway road. To get to Daejon, we had to pass a few kilometres north of the Gyeyoson National Park. The scenery in this part of the journey was spectacular as the mountains were steep, tall and covered in lush greenery. As it was Spring, the weather was pretty cloudy. This made for a fabulous effect as the bus regularly poked up through low clouds so that we were staring down at the veiled valleys below.

The journey in itself was fantastic. I have been to few places with such amazing scenery. However, I also loved it for the magnificent juxtaposition it provided. Until that point, I had only really seen two faces of Korea: the massive urban sprawl of Seoul and the slightly more rural climes of Taean. The route to Daejon was nothing like either of these and represented a huge contrast to the modern urbanisation that I had come to associate with Korea. It was a genuinely refreshing change not to be surrounded by glass and concrete. The mountain roads gave a glimpse into a different and more natural side of Korea, one that doesn't instantly spring to mind and one I regret I didn't see more of.

We arrived at the wedding venue about thirty minutes before the ceremony was scheduled to start. It was all very exciting, but I certainly found a lot of what I encountered to be a little bizarre and very different to an English wedding - there was plenty of stuff I am sure my wife would have baulked at had I suggested it for our nuptials! This started at the entrance to the hall where there were a series of life-sized pictures of the happy couple.

Some of these, whilst being a little bit extravagant, were actually pretty nice and did not seem too odd. The more sensible pictures included shots where they were captured in a dinner jacket and an elegant ball gown; in a western style white wedding dress and a morning suit; and, in summer clothes at the beach. However, there were some that would have raised a few eyebrows in England. For instance, we saw them dressed in matching Burberry travel suits and as European aristocracy from the seventeenth century with powdered wigs and all the associated trappings.

In one way, I was rather surprised to see such indulgent and rather strange photos. Mr Jang was generally a pretty straight forward kind of guy. There was absolutely nothing about him that suggested he was secretly into dressing up in ridiculous outfits in his free time. However, that impression failed to take into account Korea's love for a staged photo - this was a country that loved a selfie before selfies were even really a thing. This was a phenomenon that was prevalent on many levels.

On a simple level, most younger Koreans loved to snap pictures either with their Samsung digital cameras or mobile phones, which were just starting to come with decent sized cameras. During my first few weeks at Jung Chul, all of my middle school kids wanted to have their picture taken with me. On another level, there was also a huge trend where kids - and many adults for that matter too - used a type of novelty photo booth in which they could have photos taken with different backgrounds or with cute graphics like bunny ears superimposed onto the top of their head. It was kind of like a fixed and slightly more analog version of Instagram or Snapchat.

Just like their modern successors, the photo booths were immensely popular. In the stationery store down the street from Jung Chul there was a row of them and they almost always seemed to be packed.. On more than one occasion I stopped in there to buy candy to bribe my kindergarteners with and found Ms Ahn getting pictures of herself that would be pinned onto the noticeboard in her classroom..

As the above context might suggest, I was in the minority when it came to thinking that the pictures were a little on the silly side. My chief critic when I aired my bewilderment at the pictures was Ms Ahn who thought they were fantastic. I may be in danger of painting Ms Ahn as something of a caricature as I have already focused on her predilection for high heels and make-up, her overwhelming desire to find a husband and her love of indulgent photos. This is absolutely not my intention as she was one of the nicest people I met in Korea. However, the image is not inaccurate as she really did make it clear Jung Chul was only a temporary gig for her until she met Mr Right and, whilst she did have a pair of Converse sneakers, she clearly loved wearing heels whenever possible. Hers was, by western standards at least, a rather dated way of looking at gender roles.

Ms Ahn was not alone in the way she viewed the photos and the way she viewed gender roles in Korea. As there were only two female staff members at Jung Chul, my workplace didn't give me a definitive picture of Korean women and the role they play in society. However, there were plenty of other examples in Taean that showed how Korea had, on a rather wide level, what we might consider in the UK to be a slightly outmoded view on the role women play in society. For example, Yop with whom I played football for Lee Wah was married to a woman he met at university where they both studied finance. He worked in a bank and she had given up work to be a housewife and look after their two kids. It was the same with almost all the guys I played with. They went to work whilst their wives stayed at home with the kids. Similarly, whenever we did job vocab in class, the majority of the kids described their mums as housewives. I had been hoping that Mr Jang's wedding would give me a different and slightly more modern taste of things ... I would be disappointed.

Once we actually got inside the hall, I was pretty surprised by what I encountered. More specifically, the wedding party and the way everyone was dressed certainly seemed unusual.. All of the guys - Mr Jang's buddies and a couple of his relatives - were dressed in very sober black and grey suits with white shirts and rather bland ties, the type of thing they would have worn to their day jobs at the office. Lots of the women, on the other hand, were dressed in traditional Korean hanbok. These were long and baggy robes that came in striking bright colours. It seemed a very strange dichotomy to see between the genders. In all honesty, I cannot say why I found it a slightly uncomfortable sight. Perhaps it was the emphasising of antiquated gender roles in a modern society. But, the whole thing had me feeling a little odd.

Sadly, I cannot pretend that I found the ceremony beautiful or romantic. Primarily, this was because everything was - as you would expect - in Korean and, whilst I could follow the general gist of what was going on, I didn't understand any of the more intimate details.. However, Ms Ahn also took a bit of the lustre off things by leaning across and explaining that we should pay strict attention to the bride's face. She explained that Korean's believed that the bride absolutely positively had to cry during the ceremony. If she didn't, both her family and the groom's family would view her as not being appropriately emotional or romantic. It seemed to be undue pressure on a day when she would be feeling pretty nervous anyway. I was petrified for the poor girl. On the few occasions I had met her, she had seemed lovely and it felt desperately unfair that she was having such antiquated rules forced upon her when she should have been enjoying the happiest day of her life.

Thankfully, she was appropriately emotional. At one point during the ceremony, she stopped and dabbled her face - quite pointedly in my opinion - and everyone seemed to relax a little. The rest of the proceedings went off without a hitch and were relatively uneventful. Vows were exchanged in Korean and the couple walked back down the aisle together just as in a western wedding.

Also in the same vein as western nuptials, everyone then retired outside for the photographs. As I only knew Mr Jang from work, I was certainly not expecting to be involved. However, after the photographer snapped some pics with close family and friends, he called me and Ms Ahn over for a large wide-angle shot with the groom's friends on the left and the bride's on the right. Having Ms Ahn on the girls' side was no great issue as she blended in perfectly with all the other petite dark haired Korean ladies. I, on the other hand, could not have been more conspicuous.

Mr Jang had thirty or so friends to his left. All were shorter than me, all had dark hair and all were wearing very sensible suits and white shirts. Prior to the wedding, I had asked what to wear and Mr Jang had simply said to look smart and suggested a work shirt would be fine. He didn't specify any style or colour. Therefore, wanting to look bright and create a celebratory mood, I picked a white and violet striped shirt and a blue tie. As the weather was good and I didn't have a suit in Korea, I went with just the shirt and tie. This put me in marked contrast with the rest of the male guests. However, as silly as that made me look, it was nothing compared to the hair disparities.

I was 24 when I moved to Korea. By that point in life, I had reconciled myself with the fact that I was following firmly in the footsteps of my father and paternal grandfather in losing my hair. Therefore, I had taken to using clippers to take my hair down to a grade zero. Even though it wasn't my first hair styling choice, the closely cropped look worked for me and mitigated the appearance of hair loss. Unfortunately, Mr Kim was not so keen. He worried that my hair might scare some of the children as it made me look like a soldier. So, one proviso in my recruitment was that I should grow my hair. It was an experiment that did not work for anyone. In all honesty, it made no difference to the kids and it made me look genuinely ridiculous. Therefore, a few weeks after the wedding - perhaps because of how bad I looked at the wedding - Mr Kim agreed to allow me to shave it again. At the ceremony, though, it looked plain awful.

My hair growth in Korea went through a few different, but all horrific, stages. The first was when I arrived and the hair that was growing had failed to really kick in: There was nothing on the temples and I managed to cultivate a sparse covering on top with a small fringe in the centre. Think of a less robust version of Bruce Willis's hair in Die Hard. Then, as it grew, it succeeded only in covering the top of my head partially and thinly. To be fair to Mr Kim, this did soften my appearance a little but made me look ten years older than I actually was.

To combat my thinning hair and ageing appearance, I had a bit of a brainwave. I figured that one of the problems was that my darkish hair showed my pale scalp off because of the contrast between the two. The logical conclusion I drew was that if I lightened my hair colour I could reduce the contrast and look less bald. Solid logic, surely?

With a plan firmly hatched, I asked Sarah - and English woman who worked at one of the other hogwan in Taean - to go with me to a local supermarket to help me pick out the correct shade of blonde. From there, we returned to my apartment where she helped me dye it over the tub in my bathroom. It did not go well. One of the factors we had not considered was the difference between European and Asian hair. As hair in the Far East tends to be thicker and darker, the dyes used are different to those in the UK. Consequently, my hair didn't go a bright and crisp shade of blonde. Rather, it turned a slightly metallic peach colour.

I did this around three weeks before Mr Jang's wedding, which meant that by the time I stepped into the photo, my hair still had that peachy look but was also beginning to grow out, so my darker roots were showing and again exposing my scalp. It looked genuinely terrible. Because of this, one of Mr and Mrs Jang's wedding photos has a truly ridiculous blip in it. It includes roughly thirty Korean men who may as well have been dressed in uniform and then one westerner stuck on the end of the bottom row glowing like a peach and purple beacon. If I were them, I would have put that one to the back of the album!

After the photos, we all headed inside for food, and some celebratory soju. This was the area of the wedding that surprised me the most! The first element of this was the type of food and the way it was served. Essentially, it was like eating at a school canteen. We all sat down at rather bland looking tables where we were given some soup with dumplings and some kimchi and rice. It was all pretty basic compared to weddings I have attended in other countries where food tends to be more lavish. After we had eaten, there were then a few toasts given with soju - which, as we all expected, Mr Kim reveled in - and then Ms Ahn announced we should all get on the bus to go home.

I was really shocked. We had a long journey back to Taean, but we had been there less than two hours and as the toasts had just been sunk and Mr Kim was getting into a good rhythm, I presumed the party was only just getting started. I must clearly have looked confused because Ms Ahn came over to explain that the wedding hall was only booked for two hours and another couple would be coming in for their canteen style lunch in a few minutes, so we needed to leave. It all seemed rather brief and disappointing.

INTO THE COUNTRY

As I have explained in previous pages, Seoul was a huge modern city that grabbed me by the shoulders and demanded my undivided attention. It was full of so many modern wonders and many ways to have a great time. However, for history lovers, Korea doesn't have that much to offer as almost everything of note was flattened during the Korean war in the 1950s. There are scarcely any of the temples you might find in China or southeast Asia and you don't really find 'old towns' in any of the major cities. In Seoul, people often like to describe the In Sa Dong district as 'Old Seoul', but there was one single street of older buildings and they seemed to have been heavily rebuilt and restored. In Taean or Seosan, there was nothing that wasn't built from the 1960s onwards.

This all meant that genuinely interesting or unusual travel options were pretty thin on the ground. It was easy to get buses across the country but when we did, we found the same thing: Huge modern cities bedecked in neon. Not to put things too simplistically, but it was all very samey. This didn't mean we didn't have fun. We had lots of nights out in Seoul and enjoyed the nightlife, the theme parks and other modern attractions. But, truth be told, I wanted more. Having spent four months in the natural wonders of Mongolia, skyscrapers and karaoke rooms just seemed a bit shallow and materialistic.

To get a wider view of the country, Ossie and I travelled to Busan, which took about four hours on the bus. In all honesty, it wasn't worth such a long journey. To be fair to Korea's second city, it was fun and it was cool. There was a super cable car that took us up a mountain to Yongdusan Park, which overlooked the city. We were also able to stand on the shores of the Sea of Japan, which remains the furthest east I have ever travelled. However, we were there for the weekend and by Saturday afternoon we felt we had exhausted the non-alcohol fuelled entertainment options the city had to offer. So, we hit the beers early.

In fairness, it really was a fun city at night. We found lots of cool places to drink and also chanced upon thousands of young Koreans partying on Haeundae beach well into the early hours. We were even able to get fake tattoos done in gravelly printers' ink at 3am from a stall on the promenade. It was all cool, but we spent Sunday in a hungover fog looking for something more interesting to do and didn't really find anything.

What we found in Busan was typical of Korea as a whole. However, what Korea lacks in ancient history, it makes up for in slightly more contemporary matters. By far and away Korea's most famous tourist attraction is the DMZ, the border area that separates North and South Korea. The 4km wide area of no-man's land stretches 250km across the entire Korean peninsular. It intersects but does not completely follow the 38th parallel. It was created at the end of the Korean War and follows the front line as it stood in 1953 when the two sides signed an armistice agreement. As they didn't go further and sign a fully-blown peace treaty, the two sides are still technically at war. Therefore, the DMZ remains one of the most heavily fortified frontiers in the world.

To get to the DMZ, we first had to travel to Seoul and take a train. The DMZ is actually located frighteningly close to the huge population density of Seoul. Just 50km separate the capital of the South from the heavily-militarised border with the North. It is a permanent and daunting concern for the government in the South that North Korea's huge standing army - apparently upwards of one million men - could conceivably reach Seoul in a matter of hours.

I didn't really grasp the significance of the railway at first, but the train to the last station in South Korea - Imjingang - actually operated on the line that once linked Seoul and Pyongyang. From the station at Imjingang, we had to take buses that ran to the edge of the DMZ and were controlled and monitored by Korean Military Police. After we bought our tickets but before the bus moved an inch, one of the MPs boarded the bus and gave a very strict briefing on security and how we were to behave in the areas close to the DMZ. As one might expect, we were not allowed to stray anywhere beyond the designated paths and roads and it was heavily emphasized that we couldn't take pictures of any military installations or personnel on the southern side of the fence. The North, on the other hand, was fair game. We could take as many pictures as we wanted.

The first stop on our DMZ tour was the Dorasan viewing point from which we could look over the whole area and into North Korea. It provided a fantastic view of the area. However, the first thing that struck me was the instructions on i) from where you can view the DMZ, and ii) from where you can take photos. These were not the same thing. There are a series of tourist binoculars along the edge of the viewing point from which you could look into the DMZ and beyond to North

Korea, but look is all you could do. You were not permitted to take any photos. Instead, if you wanted to take any photographs, you had to stand behind a yellow line several metres from the edge. The angle that position offers prevented people from taking pictures of the South Korean military positions below the mountain.

The view north from Dorasan was fascinating. There was the open expanse of the DMZ below and then within that area was the North Korean propaganda village of Kijong-dong, which is also known in the North as the Peace Village. The North Koreans claim it is home to a collective farm of over 200 people. However, the South claims that it is largely uninhabited and that telescopic photos show that the apartment buildings are actually just empty shells.

Even though there are no people in the village, it is home to a powerful transmitter that plays propaganda radio, which we could hear faintly drifting across the barbed wire. It is also home to one of the world's largest, and pettiest, flagpoles. The structure measures 160m in height and is topped only by poles in Tajikistan and Saudi Arabia. It was built in the 1980s in response to South Korea building a pole that was 98m high and remains as a piece of classic and rather futile one-upmanship.

From Dorasan we took the bus to another really interesting sight, the Third Tunnel of Aggression - the less than catchy name was coined by South Korea. It was dug by the North Koreans in 1978 and extends almost half a kilometre into South Korean territory. It was discovered by the South Koreans when they heard explosions beneath their territory. Initially, the North denied responsibility but later claimed - rather ridiculously - that it was a coal mining tunnel rather than anything with a military purpose. Our tour guide explained that the North had painted some of the rock black to try to make it look as though it were coal. It was a claustrophobic but exciting experience. When you placed your hands on the wall, you could feel the blast marks from where the North Korean soldiers had placed their dynamite. These all pointed north and painted a series of abstract lines along the tunnel wall.

The most famous part of the DMZ is Panmunjeon, where the armistice treaty was signed in 1953. It is located on the military demarcation line and is the only place where the two Koreas physically meet. It is where, in recent years, leaders of the two Koreas have met for talks. It is also, apparently, the most chilling sight in Korea as soldiers from both sides stand metres apart and are essentially eyeball to eyeball. As Panmunjeon is so militarily and diplomatically sensitive, it is not like other tourist attractions as its opening hours are determined not just by one country but by both sides of the divide and, consequently, the international political climate. Sadly, when we visited, it was not open as relations were at a frosty moment.

The tour culminated at Dorasan train station. Unlike Imjingang a few hundred metres further South, Dorasan was not really a functioning train station. Rather, it was more a symbol of division and potential reunification in Korea. It has been built to modern South Korean standards as though it were part of a line operating between Seoul and Pyongyang, as it was before World War II. On one side of the tracks is a platform for trains running in the direction of Imjingang and beyond that, Seoul. On the other side, is a platform for trains running to Pyongyang - it even had signs showing the stations that were on the line that went to the North Korean capital. It was an interesting sight, but despite the best intentions behind its construction, it was merely a ghostly shell of future possibilities.

Unlike most fully operational stations, from Dorasan it was possible to walk along the tracks. These lead to a metal fence that spans the tracks and stops trains - or pedestrians - moving onto a rather forlorn looking bridge that leads into the DMZ. There have been a few tourist trains over the past couple of decades and there was briefly a rail freight service running to a joint industrial zone in the North Korean city of Kaesong - between 2002 and 2016, the two countries worked together to operate factories to produce goods for South Korean companies using North Korean labour - but, in general, the fence acts as a very permanent barrier.

The fence itself was very interesting to see. The first reason for this was that it represented a stunning and exceptionally poignant visual of the type that is not so prevalent in the twentieth century: there was barbed wire separating freedom and tyranny. It was one of the final vestiges of the Cold War staring us right in the face. As we will see quite a bit as the book progresses, I have always been a fan of Cold War history and have always felt a bit sad that I was born a little bit late to experience things first-hand. However, I was still able to get a small taste of the conflict in Korea. With the Berlin Wall gone and barbed wire fences across Eastern Europe and the former Soviet Union torn down, the fence was one of the few sights that remained of a fascinating but frightening period of world history.

The second reason that the fence hit home was the emotional element it provided. The metal wire was covered in flowers and notes left by people living in the South for friends and relatives stranded in the North. It was a sad sight as firstly the notes and flowers signified a separation of - at the time - just over fifty years. Secondly, the fence and the whole DMZ area highlighted that things were in no great danger of changing anytime soon - as the subsequent fifteen years have shown. Thirdly, as things in the North have grown increasingly bleak with political executions combined with mass famine in the mid-1990s and a life expectancy ten years lower than the South, in all likelihood the people for whom the flowers and notes were placed were quite probably dead already.

Whereas the Dorasan viewing point gave a very militarised view of the Korean divide, the railway fence made things far more personal. This continued inside the station where there were several displays that talked about the DMZ and relations on the Korean peninsula. The most interesting of these focused on a speech by George W. Bush in which he spoke about satellite images of the peninsula at night where you can see the South is lit up like a Christmas tree. The North, in complete contrast, is almost completely blacked out. There are lots of ways to see the difference between the two Koreas in terms of development. However, talk of GDP and poverty rates doesn't really put things in such clear terms. The satellite images really were a case of seeing things in black and white.

The displays in the visitor centre - along with a bit of follow-up research - also gave some really interesting information about the differences between North and South. The first of these was a very physical metric: average height. The people from the two Koreas are, obviously, from the same genetic background as there were countless families divided at the end of the war. Therefore, you would imagine they would be physically similar. However, that is not the case. The majority of North Korean refugees who have reached South Korea are smaller than their brethren in Seoul. This is thought to be caused by malnutrition and the horrific living conditions - in the 1990s the country was ravaged by a famine that killed between 200,000, if you believe the North Koreans themselves, and over 3million people if you believe more reputable sources - in the North.

Another aspect of the DMZ that was genuinely fascinating was biodiversity. Korea is not a country that is renowned for the beauty of its nature. Parts of Taean and the surrounding area - and of course the areas en route to Daejon - were relatively rural, but the majority of Korea was covered with urban sprawl that has grown almost unchecked since the 1960s. The narrow sliver of land between the two heavily guarded barbed wire fences, on the other hand, has been unaffected by South Korea's development and remains pristine and untouched. Apparently, it is home to a fabulous array of wildlife including 100 species of fish, 45 species of amphibians and even Asiatic black bears. Of course, there is no chance of seeing any of it up close.

The DMZ was by far and away the most interesting tourist spot in Korea. However, a close second was my visit to the small coastal town of Boryeong in southern Chungcheongnam Do, which provided one of my most unusual experiences in Korea. For the majority of the year, Boryeong is a relatively sleepy seaside town, much like Taean. However, each July it is transformed into one of Korea's most visited towns as it hosts the Mud Festival.

Just off the coast near Boryeong are a series of mud flats that contain a rich array of minerals that are, supposedly, great for the skin - just like the Dead Sea. In the early 1990s, companies began to sell products containing the mud as cosmetics. Then, in 1998, initially as a marketing tool for said cosmetics, the mud festival was launched. It is a celebration of all things mud. There are so many cool things to do ... all involving getting covered in vast quantities of mud.

We started our day by taking a dip in one of the giant mud pits, which were like huge mud swimming pools that could accommodate hundreds of people. It was fabulous. We all came out caked in mud, which dried very quickly in the summer heat. In all honesty, it looked and felt so weird that I cannot really think of a fitting analogy for our appearance. The closest I have managed is hippos drying off after wallowing in an African river. It's not a great comparison as we weren't in Africa and none of us were particularly rotund. However, it was very cool to relax in the sun drinking a beer and gently picking the dried flakes of mud off our faces.

The festival was amazing. All kinds of shenanigans went on in the mud pits. This was especially true as the afternoon wore on and everyone got increasingly drunk. We had mudball fights - like snowball fights but dirtier, gooier and warmer - we had mudslides and there were even a few mud wrestling contests. My personal favourite was doing a giant belly-flop into the mud. There was also a fantastic array of inflatable obstacle courses in which you could slip and slide through and into giant pools of mud.

The mud festival was one of my very favourite days in Korea. It was so much fun. However, it ended horrifically for me. To explain what happened, I probably need to discuss two elements of Korean food culture. The first of these is their love of cooking their own food, even in restaurants. For example, in a kalbi restaurant, the meat is delivered to your table raw and you cook it on a small grill in front of you. As the majority of Korean cuisine is made up of pork based products, you need to be very sure that you cook it thoroughly!

The second element is Koreans' love of eating things that are either still alive or only recently deceased, and certainly not cooked. Back in Taean, Mr Kim was a huge fan of this. Or, to be more accurate, he was a huge fan of getting me to eat things that were still moving when they passed my lips. For example, we often had barbecues on the roof of the school and he loved to bring eels. These would arrive in a plastic carrier bag filled with water and the poor doomed creatures swimming as best they could in the confined space. When the coals were hot enough, he would fish them out of the bag, chop them up with scissors and drop the still moving pieces onto the grill. It was delicious, but the sight of a live eel being chopped up and cooked was not for the faint-hearted.

Similarly, when my mother came to visit, he took us out to a well-known seafood restaurant just outside Taean. It did fantastic fried fish, squid and prawns. However, unbeknownst to me, its speciality was baby octopus … live baby octopus! To serve it, the poor creature was pulled out of a tank next to our table and chopped up on a wooden board before our eyes. Whilst the dismembered creature wriggled around in front of us, Mr Kim told me to eat it quickly as it tasted better whilst it was still moving. Being way too susceptible to peer pressure for my own good, I picked up my chopsticks and grabbed a twitching tentacle. As I popped it into my mouth, Mr Kim warned me not to drink anything until I had fully swallowed it as otherwise liquid could cause one of the suckers to stick in my throat and choke me!

In Boryeong, one of these elements - and I am not 100% sure whether it was eating some shellfish that needed cooking but was not done through or if it simply was eating something raw - gave me some quite spectacular food poisoning. We had eaten at a restaurant on the sea-front that specialised in raw fish and also had oil drums repurposed into rudimentary bbqs, onto which we threw a massive array of shellfish. At the time, whilst I was quaffing large quantities of Korean beer, it all went down beautifully. A few hours later, though, I was in a terrible state. Sadly, the consequences of the meal took the edge off a fantastic weekend and in all honesty, convinced me that some of Korea's eating habits were very much best left to the locals!

ANYON KASEYO

As the previous chapters of this book have conveyed, I certainly had a lot of fun and experienced some weird and wonderful things in Korea. Some of the events mentioned make for fantastic, albeit slightly risque, dinner party anecdotes. Recounting my teammate miming that he had shot a dog in my 'honour' never fails to raise a chuckle and, similarly, describing spending a night surrounded by naked Korean men in a sauna also tends to amuse people.

I also absolutely loved my experience with the kids. I have already laboured the point that I initially moved to Korea as a way to travel and that I never imagined the teaching element of my time there would be life-changing. Yet, that was how things transpired. My experiences in the classroom in Taean were so great that I gave up all notions of returning to the UK and looking for work in order to take up teaching as my life's vocation. Even today, I still recall some of the kids I taught with great affection. I will, most definitely, never forget Sang Min., Whenever I look back on the photos I have from my time at Jung Chul there are loads of little guys - most of whom will be fully-fledged adults by now - who I remember and smile.. However, in truth, despite the wonderful memories I have of the kids, I never really considered staying more than one year.

My decision not to stay beyond the end of my contract was a straightforward but multifaceted one. The first major factor in this was that I felt that my race there was very much run. As I made clear in the previous chapter, I didn't really feel that Korea had too much to offer in terms of travel or interesting places to visit - there were only so many times I could visit the DMZ - and I had grown tired of travelling to Seoul for weekend drinking. Whilst I would miss the kids and miss hanging out with Ossie, I didn't feel another year would be much fun. I felt that if I was going to be so far away from home, I wanted the sacrifice to be worthwhile.

Secondly, my story ended with a bad taste in my mouth. As you may well have noticed over the course of the preceding chapters, my mood in relation to life in Korea began to sour and got progressively worse over the course of the year. The obvious catalyst for this change was the overt racism I encountered on the football field. However, the biggest factor was the deterioration of my relationship with Jung Chul. I am genuinely not sure if the problems I faced were based on racism similar to that experienced with Lee-Wah or if they were motivated solely by cold hard cash… or, as I suspect, a combination of the two.

Most teachers living and working in Korea sign a contract that includes a flight to and from their home country. In most cases, including mine, when the contract is first signed it provides either a one way ticket to Korea or half the price of a return ticket. The ticket home, or a financial equivalent, is paid at the end of the contract. Additionally, most contracts also include a completion bonus - mine was almost one month's salary. This financial arrangement is designed to: i) Stop teachers flitting between *hogwans* mid-contract. As I explained earlier, foreign teachers are hugely popular commodities and opportunistic *hogwan* owners would think nothing of poaching each other's talent. And, ii) Stop teachers jumping on a plane home if Korea didn't suit. These were logical precautions, but they also meant that a teacher reaching the end of his contract cost the school a lot of money. Because of this, some of the less scrupulous hogwan owners tried their very best to force their teachers to quit after ten or eleven months so as to avoid paying out the big money at the end of the year.

Some of the soju-fuelled antics aside, I felt that I got on very well with Mr Kim and I didn't expect to face any of those issues. However, I was wrong. I am not sure what was going on in the Kim household - either there was a major difference in opinion or Mr Kim was using his wife to do his dirty work - but things got quite unpleasant with Christine as she made every effort to get me to leave before they had to pay me. This all started about 9 weeks before my contract was due to expire. A few weeks prior to that, the school had hired a second foreign teacher. At the time, they had explained that he was there as a second teacher on the team rather than as a replacement for me. However, it quickly became clear that Christine saw things differently.

Until that point, I had been Jung Chul's superstar. As the only foreigner, I was rarely not the centre of attention and not the flavour of the month. As I have noted on multiple occasions, nothing happened at Jung Chul without Mr Kim taking a picture of me in the process. A few days after Alan arrived from Ireland, things began to change. Suddenly, my classes went from being 'amazing' to 'completely unacceptable'. I found this fabulously ironic as, by that point, I had actually managed to learn and develop enough to teach some genuinely passable classes - with no help from Jung Chul whatsoever.

My schedule and daily life at school also suddenly changed. As Korean's love early mornings, at no point during the year did I get much of a chance to sleep in and was usually in my classroom well before 8am most days. However, as Christine was trying to push me to quit, she popped a bunch of 6h30am classes onto my timetable. As well as this, she decided to change my classroom. For the first ten months, I was in the school's biggest and most visible classroom - Mr Kim wanted parents of potential students to see me right away. After Alan's arrival though, I was moved out of sight and given a classroom with an old-fashioned blackboard and no tech to help with classes.

It was a really unpleasant little period of time that echoed the horrible feelings from events with Lee-Wah as Christine also seemed to be channeling some pretty deep-rooted racism. Whenever I queried any of her comments or asked why my classes were being changed apparently at will, she would respond, "If you don't like it, you should go back to your country". She would often follow this up with some superb soundbites of nationalistic nonesense, "We do things differently here; you cannot understand. It is the Korean way"

It all left me very sad. I had loved many elements of my life in Korea and genuinely wanted to leave with a smile on my face. I felt that I had made some great friends. There may be moments in the book where I haven't painted either Mr. Jang or Ms. Ahn wonderfully well, I mentioned Mr Jang's punishment of Ka Eun and Ms Ahn's slightly superficial and dated attitude to gender, but I liked them both a lot and enjoyed getting to know them. Similarly, I felt that I had a decent relationship with a lot of the guys I played football with - obviously not the ones who racially abused me. Yet, despite all the positive things, when I left Taean for the final time I couldn't help but feel resentful.

Korea has a very positive image in modern media, both the traditional kind and social media. As I touched on earlier, K-Pop has now reached western airwaves, Samsung is one the world's most powerful global brands and Korean food is becoming increasingly popular in restaurants across Europe and the USA.. All of this reflects the dynamism that was so evident across the country and most obviously in Seoul. However, it overlooks an underbelly of nationalism and racism in the country that is not so pleasant. I was not alone among my *wae gook* friends in being on the receiving end of some blunt and offensive comments.

Despite the unpleasant situation at Jung Chul, I managed to make it to the end of the year and Mr Kim paid me the money he owed me in full. Then, without even the merest hint of irony - as his wife had been attempting to make my life as unpleasant as possible - took me, Ossie and Alan as well as Mr Jang and Ms Ahn out for a lavish dinner and drinks. Christine, on the other hand, was notable by her absence. By the end of the night, we were drinking soju cocktails with a straw from giant punch bowls and Mr Kim could barely speak. In all honesty, regardless of the fraught final few weeks, it was probably a fitting end to my year with Jung Chul.

PART 2: Between Two Worlds

CASTING OFF

My time in Korea ended on a humid evening in September at Incheon docks. For my return to the UK, I had some pretty ambitious plans. I was in Incheon for the first leg of a journey that would, if all went well, take me back home without setting foot on a plane. The plan was to take the ferry from Incheon to the Chinese city of Tianjin - which will feature heavily in the coming pages of this book, although at the time I had no idea it would be a place that would have such a big impact on my life at the time - from which, along with my friend Alana from Seosan, I would travel to Beijing to see some of China's great sights. From there, I would take the train to Ulaan Baatar in Mongolia to revisit the country I had loved so much just over a year previously and then on through Russia to Moscow. After seeing Red Square and the like, I then planned to combine trains and ferries to travel through the Baltic states and northern Europe before catching a ferry from Holland, Belgium or France.

As the ship pulled away from the quayside and turned into the darkness of the Yellow Sea, I was disappointed that we were going to miss what I presumed would be the most interesting sight on the journey. The port of Incheon is located in the northern part of the Republic of Korea, not at all far from the Democratic People's Republic to the north. Having caught a glimpse of the North on my two trips to Imjingang and the DMZ, I had hoped to get a different view from the handrail of the ferry as we would travel along North Korea's west coast for the first part of our journey. Sadly, this was not to be as everything was very dark by the time our mooring lines had been cast off. Therefore, all we managed to see were a few indistinct lights in the distance.

As it transpired, even if we had set off earlier we would not have been able to see too much. Whilst I stood and stared into the darkness I struck up a conversation with one of the crew who explained, in pidgin English, that the lights we could see were the running lights from North Korean fishing boats. When I asked if they sailed past North Korea in the day, he shook his head and explained that they didn't get too close to them when things were light for fear of engaging with any vessels from inside the hermit state.

After we moved away from Korean shores, I began to feel rather contemplative about the year of my life that I had just passed on the Korean peninsula. It was a rather bittersweet moment as, in many ways, I had really enjoyed it and was sad to be departing. The kids had been fantastic and it was a true joy to spend a year with them sharing a small slice of their young lives. Not for one second whilst I was preparing for my adventure did I imagine that I would have enjoyed things in the classroom as much as I did. I had also made lots of great friends. I was travelling to China with Alana and I had big plans to go travelling again with Ossie. I had also seen some cool things and had some amazing experiences: I had enjoyed the bright lights of Seoul, eaten dog and stared at the last vestiges of the Cold War.

As great as some of those experiences were, I was also setting sail for China with a pretty bad taste in my mouth. I had been discriminated against racially on the football field, which was something I was not going to forget in any kind of hurry and my story at Jung Chul had ended badly with Christine either: i) If I am taking a conciliatory view, trying to cheat me financially, or ii) If I am being more cynical, trying to cheat me financially and also throwing in a big dose of racism.

Whatever my take on Korea - whether I focused on the kids and my friends or I focused on the racism - I was very much entering a period of possibility. Even though, on a couple of occasions, Mr Kim had asked me if I would like to stay for a second year - an offer I am pretty sure he knew I would refuse and one which I am sure Christine would have been furious about had I accepted it - I was not really keen on remaining in the country. A second year represented a little too much stasis at that point in my life. At the same time, though, I was not particularly bothered about returning to the UK to find a full-time desk job. The thought of more temping and the prospect of trying to find a job did not particularly entice me. Therefore, not only was I travelling to China for some R&R, but I was also sizing it up as a potential place to live and work.

The ferry to China was actually a pretty interesting experience in itself. As the journey was scheduled to take something between 19 and 20 hours, we had booked a second class cabin - slightly smaller than first class but without an external window - to allow us to pass most of the journey whilst sleeping. The alternatives, the more expensive first class option aside, did not seem particularly inviting. Third class was a series of open bunks near the bow of the ship that seemed to lack any degree of privacy and I imagine it would have been frightfully noisy. Those travelling fourth class just curled up on a pile of newspaper on the floor. With the apparent luxury of a cabin, we planned to hit our bunks whilst in Korean waters and to wake up as we closed in on the Chinese coast. Interestingly, the theme of Korea in the evening and China in the morning was one that actually permeated the whole voyage. As we settled in for dinner in the ferry's restaurant, the menu was in Korean and there were K-Pop music videos playing on the TV mounted on the wall. The following morning, the food was Chinese as was the pop music we could hear. It seemed the ferry company was being nice enough to try to get us ready for our new surroundings.

CHINESE SOIL

Arriving in China took a little longer than we thought it might. I am not 100% sure why, but we spent four or five hours extra anchored outside Tianjin without actually entering the harbour. Because of this, rather than docking in the afternoon as planned, we stepped onto the quayside in darkness. After disembarking, we had a short walk to a very small single-story building where our visas were checked and our passports stamped by a man in full military uniform who had an icey Communist glare. It wasn't the warmest of welcomes! It was also a huge contrast to Korea where, the DMZ aside, it was rare to see such overt displays of authority. Whenever I had done anything immigration related at the local government offices in Seosan, the staff had been very nice.

The rather brusque immigration experience had put us on edge a little, but that was just the beginning. Every element of arriving in Tianjin was a bit of a shock to the system and we felt very much out of our element. We had gone from a country that was in the main modern and democratic to one that in large part was very much not. In Incheon, we had departed from a fully-fledged ferry terminal with shops and restaurants that was connected to a metro system which you could take all the way to the centre of Seoul. When we arrived in Tianjin, we found ourselves on a concrete dockside surrounded by cranes and shipping containers. There was no terminal building, no signs and nobody to answer any questions. The immigration officials spoke no English and, as we have established, didn't seem to be the type of chaps to offer helpful tidbits to random travellers. As we stepped out of the passport office and into China proper, we were greeted not by a modern transit system but a row of rather old and dilapidated looking taxis. We were still in the Far East, but our first impressions of China were that we had travelled back in time.

There was no information in Lonely Planet about getting away from Tianjin docks. The only info it gave was for people arriving in the city by train, by bus or by plane. Therefore, we had no real idea what our next step should be. Was it a case of a taxi directly to Beijing or would we need to grab one to Tianjin train station? If it was the latter, would trains still be running at night? So, with precious little information at our disposal, we approached one of the taxi drivers and asked rather sheepishly if he could take us to Beijing.

It was clearly not the driver's first time dealing with confused arrivals from Korea. He shook his head with great authority and said "Tianjin Zhan". We understood the name of the city, but the other Chinese word meant nothing to us. We shrugged our shoulders and tried to give off enough of a confused expression to show that we had no idea what he meant. In response, quite comically, he made a "Choo choo" noise and motioned his arms like an old-fashioned steam train.

After agreeing that he would take us to the train station, he used a pen and paper to explain that it would take about an hour and fifteen minutes, and would cost about $20. Both of those numbers sounded strangely high. However, we had boarded the ferry to Tianjin without realising that 'Tianjin' was a slightly flexible term. Like both Beijing and Shanghai, Tianjin and the surrounding areas had its own administrative region. Unlike Shenzen and Guangzhou for example, which are part of Guangdong province, Tianjin is part of Tianjin. We weren't aware that Tianjin is a big area and has its own separate port town, Tanggu, which is about 40km away from the main part of the city. This was where we had come ashore. Consequently, we were still quite a way from the city itself.

It would be an exaggeration to say I was hooked on China within the 60 or 70 minutes it took for us to reach downtown Tianjin, but it wouldn't be a huge one. The first forty minutes of the journey were rather nondescript. The one thing I noticed was how much darker things seemed than in Korea. In most Korean cities, even at night things are still bright because of the glow of just so much neon. Even Taean, a small fishing town, thronged with bright light after 8PM. China seemed to be different. We did see plenty of lit up buildings in our first few kilometres in the country, but there were also vast patches of black.

Our taxi journey weaved its way from the port and through a few miles of industrial units before dropping onto a highway that ran towards the city. The highway was dark and populated mainly by large trucks, but once we made it into the suburbs of the city, I was mesmerised. I do not wish to diminish Korea as a country or my own experiences there or to overly romanticize China, but it has a romance and a pull that can grab you within seconds.

I felt myself falling under its spell as soon as I saw all the bicycles. At the first major traffic junction we met, I could scarcely believe my eyes.

As we sat at a red light, I watched hundreds of bicycles go in either direction. It felt like what I had assumed to be the laziest of stereotypes brought into fantastic and gripping reality. It was such a contrast to Korea where junctions in Seoul would see hundreds of sleek Kias and Hyundais zipping through at 70 or 80km/h.

To feed into my romantic notions of China even further, you could actually see couples and even families riding one bike together. We saw scores of bikes being ridden by a man with a woman seated above the back wheel with her feet dangling off to the side, a few of which had the women holding a baby as they scouted by. It was amazing to see and had me feeling unbelievably excited about visiting the country and perhaps coming back to live and work there.

The taxi dropped us off at Tianjin station, where we got our first experience of blunt Communist architecture. It was a hideous looking building made out of huge slabs of concrete. It sat across the river from the main body of the city and dominated the vista, but really not in a good way. However, as hideous as it looked, we were not there for the aesthetics. It was only a staging post on our route to Beijing. Unfortunately, once inside, we soon got another clear example of not being in Korea anymore.

In Korea, the bus stations - I took the train only twice whilst I was there - were bright and modern affairs. Some, in Seoul for example, had clear digital timetables in both Korean and English. As helpful as this was, it wasn't actually a major issue. Korean script is phonetic and relatively easy to read, so I could easily decipher the Korean for Taean, Seosan or Seoul. In Tianjin, on the other hand, we were lost. The cavernous main hall of the train station had a huge timetable above the ticket kiosks, but to us it was all unintelligible. Chinese script is far more complex and there were no English translations. Our only option was to join a queue and see if we could communicate enough to get a ticket to Beijing.

To our surprise, this didn't actually prove to be too difficult. When we got to the front, I just said "Beijing" and held up two fingers. The guy behind the ticket counter nodded and printed us two small pieces of pink paper and passed them under the glass partition between us. Unfortunately, they made no sense at all to us as everything aside from a few numbers were written in Chinese. One of those numbers said

03:45. This worried us as we had arrived at the station at just before 22:00 and we didn't fancy a wait of almost six hours in a plain concrete waiting room in which there were only metal seats and where all the shops and cafes had closed. To be sure, I pointed to my watch and then to the number. The ticket seller nodded to confirm.

The horrid timing of the train knocked the wind out of our sails. We really hadn't envisaged having to take so long to get to our hotel in Beijing. When we bought the ferry tickets, we had been hoping to arrive in China in the afternoon and be in our hotel by 19:00 or 20:00. As we sat mulling the less than ideal situation, the contrast to Korea was, again, unavoidable. Even in a small town like Taean, buses ran to Seoul and other big cities almost every hour. Had we been in a big Korean city like Daejon or Busan, even at 22h00 there would be buses running regularly to Seoul.

Thankfully, a little bit of ingenuity and a slice of good fortune allowed us to avoid the six hour wait. After purchasing the tickets, we wandered out into a large open area outside the station. Our initial plan had been to see if we could find somewhere to get some food as we had not eaten since taking lunch on the ferry. However, our attention was piqued when we saw a line of coaches parked on the road outside the station. We didn't know where they were going, but we had nothing to lose by seeing if one of them might be heading to Beijing..

In contrast to Korea, there were no signs and no waiting rooms. Rather, there was just a small rotund lady carrying a small bag over her shoulder. We asked her "Beijing?". She nodded and wrote "25" on a scrap of paper (25RMB was less than £4). It seemed a bargain as the train tickets had cost us 35RMB, but we were concerned about the timing. So, again, I pointed to my watch. The woman waved her hands as though she were encouraging urgency. We took this as a good sign and jumped on the bus.

BEIJING

The bus dropped us outside Beijing train station around two hours after we purchased our tickets. It seemed odd that the bus operated from train station to train station without there being any actual form of bus station, but that was a technicality for us as we were just glad to get to the Chinese capital and reach our hotel rooms at a relatively sensible time in the evening. Consequently, I woke the next morning and was desperately keen to explore. The first night in China had been about first impressions and comparisons to Korea, but I was excited to go further and get a full-on taste of the country.

Tiananmen and the Forbidden City

We decided to begin on the most obvious of levels by heading to Tiananmen Square and the adjacent Forbidden City. Obviously, when you hear the word "Tiananmen" you think of one event in 1989 and your brain automatically adds the word "massacre" after. However, as you would expect from a totalitarian regime that controls media and communications with an iron fist, there is nothing there to denote that anything like that ever happened. There is no memorial to the man who stood in front of the tank and no museum to detail or explain events. Instead, the machinery of the Communist state still dominates the view.

In the centre is the Mausoleum of Chairman Mao and to the left is the Great Hall of the People where the Chinese government sits. It seemed a pretty ironic name to me as it was heavily guarded and there was no chance any of the people could get at all close to it. At the top of the square is the Forbidden City. Even though it was built centuries before Marx, Lenin or Mao, it also bears the symbols of their repugnant ideology as a giant oil painting of Mao sits above the main entrance.

We had been in China less than a day and experienced barely two hours of daylight, but it was clear to us that the Communist government wasn't shy in stamping itself forcefully and liberally across the city. However, as blunt as they appeared to be, the picture of a Communist leader hung on an ancient imperial palace still seemed to be a bit of an odd juxtaposition. I quickly learned, though, that the location was significant not just for its history as the home of many emperors but also because it was at the front of the Forbidden City that Mao had declared the formation of the People's Republic after his victory over

Chiang Kai Shek's Nationalists in 1948.

The picture itself also seemed odd in that it was, quite literally, a warts and all depiction as it features a large mole on Mao's chin. Even more oddly, the painting gives the impression that Mao was wearing make-up and the mole had been covered by a little foundation. I found it strange that the artist who painted it would create a picture in which it looked, quite obviously, like Mao was wearing make-up. I also found it strange that when creating a picture like that they did not just remove the mole all together. The irony of the situation was that the Chinese government continues to airbrush the massacre, which happened right below where the picture hangs, out of history. It is also happy to forget, literally, the tens of millions of deaths for which Mao was responsible. Yet, they kept the blemish on his face in the picture..

After completing a quick initial tour of the square, we decided to begin by visiting the mausoleum. Truth be told, I had a few quibbles about going to see it. Firstly, a mausoleum is not your average tourist attraction and has a certain macabre element to it. Secondly, Mao was a horrific human being who caused untold suffering. However, Lonely Planet and a few websites that I had visited prior to the trip recommended it because it provided a unique insight into China's recent past. They also explained that the 'Great Helmsman' still casts a huge shadow over the country today and that seeing the mausoleum offers a valuable insight into China's past, present and future.

No ifs, no buts, no maybes, it was one of the weirdest things I have ever seen. The first factor was the queue to get in there and the apparent devotion of those involved. We had to wait about thirty minutes before we could get inside and when we did we were pretty much the only people who didn't either leave a bunch of red roses or prostrate themselves and start whaling. The man was a mass murderer, statistically, arguably the most murderous man to have ever lived. His numbers comfortably outstrip those of Hitler or Stalin. Yet, three decades after his death, people wept for him! I wanted to scream, "Didn't he kill your father, your grandmother or your uncle????"

The second factor was the body itself. It really didn't look real. This was my first mausoleum, so I could not compare Mao's body with others that have been similarly preserved (Lenin, for example). However, it looked more like a wax work to me than it did a real person. There are plenty of rumours that it is actually a replica of the body due to the fact that it took too long to embalm it after he died as Mao had requested cremation but senior figures in the Chinese government argued for several days about whether to follow his wishes before finally deciding to have him preserved. Others also suggest that on certain days of the week the body on show is real, but on others it is a wax work as the body needs maintenance to avoid decay. I am not sure if those rumours are true, but it was a strange and ghoulish sight nonetheless.

The entire trip was made even more surreal when we exited the mausoleum to be greeted by a huge array of stalls selling all kinds of cheap and tacky souvenirs bearing Mao's image. There were hundreds of postcards. There were countless t.shirts. There were thousands of cigarette lighters and cigarette cases.. But, my personal favourite was a wrist watch that did not have a second hand; it, instead, ticked by having Mao's hand make a waving movement. I was genuinely tempted, but I thought better of buying one. It was a fun thing to see, but the Mao supermarket highlighted the existential conflict that was growing in China between having an authoritarian and supposedly Communist regime in power, yet embracing capitalism more voraciously than any other country on earth.

From the mausoleum, we headed to the Forbidden City, which was utterly amazing. Everything we encountered after passing under the mole was magnificent. The scale of the place was fantastic and the pagoda style buildings were just amazing. I am not entirely sure my words can do justice to the scale and beauty of the place. So, instead, I shall just pick out my favourite part, which was a brilliantly old-fashioned fire prevention system. Located outside the great hall were two huge brass bowls, each with a metallic loop on either side. Apparently, these would be filled with water. Then, in case of fire a long piece of wood could be inserted between the loops and the emperor's servants - I imagine it would have taken many of them - could lift the water to pour it onto the fire.

Newer China

Tiananmen and the Forbidden City gave us fascinating insight into Chinese history on both an ancient and more modern level. In one day, it felt like we had experienced more of the past than I did during a whole year in Korea. There was still plenty more to see as well. On our second day, however, we decided to go for a change of pace and to experience China on a more modern and more capitalistic level.

Our plan was to visit the Xiushui Silk Market. I was pretty excited about the trip. This was not because of the shopping opportunities it afforded but more for the evocative name. It sent my imagination back to the era of the Opium Wars and the Boxer Rebellion. I had images of a dark and seedy market located somewhere within a warren of darkened side streets. In reality, I was actually picturing the start of an Indiana Jones movie, but even so, I was expecting something a bit exotic. I could not have been more wrong! The Silk Market was a modern five storey building with huge neon signs all over the facade as well as video screens playing a constant stream of TV commercials on a maddening loop. It was a jolt of modern commercialism and made for a huge contrast to the previous afternoon.

As striking as the outside of the market was, as soon as we made our way inside we got another giant shock to the system. It was just so busy and just so intense. The first two levels were crammed with stalls and salespeople who were frighteningly keen to jump out and sell you all manner of goods. They had almost anything you could imagine on sale. On those first two floors, everything was designer labels and came emblazoned with logos of major international brands. There were Nike trainers, Gucci handbags and Rolex watches. It was an amazing cornucopia. The one common element to all of them was that they were fake. Nothing at all was genuine. The sheer scale of it was unbelievable. It was like a small shopping mall dedicated to knock-off merchandise.

I wasn't really in the market for a counterfeit watch or a pair of dodgy trainers. However, Alana was most certainly keen on a faux Chanel handbag, of which there were thousands on display. So, we headed over to one of the stalls in order for her to buy one. This proved to be a surprisingly lengthy but also fabulously entertaining experience. There were no prices attached to any of the bags. So, Alana asked how much one particular specimen would cost. The price the salesgirl gave was downright ridiculous; it was far higher than that of a genuine version of the bag. We both stared at her with obvious disbelief before thanking her and walking away. This sparked a frenzied negotiation process. The salesgirl grabbed Alana by the sleeve and immediately halved the price. This still meant that it was still quite expensive, but the change in price piqued Alana's interest.

Reaching an appropriate price was a long and drawn out process. After we returned to the stall, we went back and forth between prices. At first the girl was keen to make concessions. 50% soon became 40 and then with a bit more bartering 30. However, after this, she began to dig her heels in and the price dropped by only a few RMB each time. On each occasion when the discussion seemed to be going nowhere, we would shape to leave and she would rather dramatically chase us out of the stall and make a minor concession..

It was a long hard slog but, eventually Alana got the bag for about 18% of the original price. It was a cool and invigorating experience: Part hard-bitten commerce and part theatre. As we walked away with Alana clutching the bag, I was keen to do more!. I didn't want to buy anything myself but, thankfully, Alana had her eye on three or four more bags. So, I would have plenty of opportunity.

Summer Palace

The interlude at the Silk Market was a fabulous experience. However, after a day of commerce in 'new' China, I was ready for more history and another taste of imperial China. It being September, Beijing was stiflingly hot. So, we decided that the best thing to do would be to head out of the city centre towards the Summer Palace, which is located in the northwest corner of the city.

In all honesty, I knew precious little about the Palace before our trip. It didn't have the cache of the Great Wall or the Forbidden City, but the pictures of it in my Lonely Planet guide looked genuinely amazing. So, we jumped on the blue line of the rather clunky Beijing metro and headed away from the centre of the city. The Beijing transit system - just two dated metro lines at the time - was nothing like the super-modern one in Seoul where there were scores of lines and stations on almost every street corner. This meant it took what seemed like forever to get anywhere close to the Palace. However, it was worth the wait.

Before we went into the palace, I stopped to read the information boards that were posted just after the entrance. Along with explaining that it was declared a UNESCO world heritage site in 1992, it gave a short history of the site that taught me some things of which I knew nothing before. Originally constructed in the 1700s by the Qing dynasty, the palace we were about to see was actually rebuilt in the early 1900s after the European colonial powers - with the British chief amongst them - burned the original version to the ground in response to the killing of two British envoys.

The Qing did a fantastic job of rebuilding. The palace was a magnificent thing to see. It was built in the hills on the banks of a lake in order to keep things cool in the summer months. This definitely worked as there was a lovely breeze coming in off the water and things felt much more pleasant than in the centre of the city.. It also made the scenery absolutely magnificent. The main body of the palace rises up through the trees on a small hill that slopes down to the lake. The palace, like the Forbidden City, had wonderfully colourful and ornate eaves that brought wonderfully bright colour that was off-set perfectly by the lush greenery. We were dumb struck.

We had entered the palace grounds at the bottom corner of the lake. To get to the main areas we needed to take a covered and decorated walkway that went along the banks of the lake. On its own, it was a beautiful piece of design. Each of the horizontal beams that supported the roof were decorated with a delicate yet colourful painting. There were hundreds of them. It was a beautiful spectacle, but was also art on a massive scale. However, it was not just the scale and beauty that were impressive. The story behind them was also fascinating. I cannot 100% corroborate the authenticity of what follows as I didn't get the information from a guidebook. Rather, we overheard a tour guide explaining things to a group of American tourists. I am not sure if he was adding a bit of ancient colour to his little routine in order to elicit a slightly better tip or if it was actually the case. Either way, I found what he said to be just lovely.

He explained that each of the pictures on the horizontal beams were not simply stand alone pieces of art done just for the sake of looking pretty. They were, in fact, used as a form of ancient late-night entertainment. Apparently, each evening, the eunuchs at the palace - of which there were many as the Imperial Chinese loved to whip the testicles off - would walk the princesses back to their sleeping quarters along the walkway. When they did so, they would choose one of the pictures along the way and use it as the basis of a story to entertain her and help her feel restful before bed.

As Alana and I followed the walkway - in a rather slow manner as we were stuck behind the Americans - I looked up at each of the pictures and wondered what type of story the eunuchs would pick for each one. It really captured my imagination. I was so lost in thought in fact that I scarcely noticed we were nearing the end of the walkway and reaching the main area of the palace, where the scenery was about to get even more impressive.

The main body of the palace was a fantastic spectacle. It was also pretty hard work. Even though we were in the hills and there was a pleasant breeze from the lake, the weather was still quite hot. This meant that getting up the steps leading to the top of the palace was something of a trial and we were sweating prodigiously by the time we got there. It was worth it, though. The view from the top was fabulous. We got a fabulous panorama of the lake and the surrounding trees punctuated by the occasional pagoda. I was breathless … in more ways than one!

Things go wrong!

I absolutely adored my few days in Beijing. The sites I saw were fabulous and the atmosphere in China was intoxicating. I certainly wanted more and was already set on the idea of going back to work there. However, as time drew on, more pressing matters began to hove into view. I needed to get home and that was going to be a herculean undertaking. Sadly, as may have already become apparent as this book is not about a journey through Russia to Europe, things didn't go at all well. In fact, they went so badly that I didn't even manage to take the first steps on the route I had planned.

To organise my visa to Russia and to get tickets on the Transiberian railway, I had used a Russian travel agency that had organised all the requisite documentation. To get my Russian visa, I needed to go to the Russian embassy in Beijing with an official invitation letter they had issued and sent to me whilst I was still in Korea. The embassy would then process my application and issue the visa. The process felt a bit bureaucratic, but seemed simple enough. The travel agent assured me it should take no more than a couple of days. She was wrong! Badly, wrong!

The Russian embassy was located in the northeast area of Beijing. The consular section was only open in the morning and actually getting to see someone proved to be easier said than done. On my first attempt, I arrived at just after 10am and was met with a queue reminiscent of a

Moscow breadline in the 1980s. I joined it, but as it moved less than a couple of meters in thirty minutes, it became clear I had no chance of getting seen that day. So, I returned before 8am the following day and managed to get close to the front. This was where my good fortune ended, alas, as the consular official told me that as the address I gave on my application was in Korea and I wanted to enter Russia through Mongolia, consequently I needed to get my visa done in one of those countries … not in Beijing. I was mortified. The travel agent had not told me this. If she had, I would have tried to get it in Korea. I had thought of doing that anyway, but, as Mr Kim had been no big fan of giving me time off, I figured it would have been too difficult. Therefore, I had presumed getting it in China would be the easy option.

Ordinarily, the setback should not have been an issue. I was going to Mongolia anyway, so could conceivably have gone to the Russian embassy there.. However, the invitation letter had been issued more than a month before and was valid for only a few more days. My ticket to Ulaan Baatar was for four days later and the journey itself would take over two days. By the time I was scheduled to get there, the letter would no longer be valid. It seemed I was screwed!

I left the embassy rather disconsolately and sat in my hotel room and pondered what I could do. I emailed the agency to see if I could get another letter in time. Sadly, as the embassy wanted an original copy, there was no way it would get to China in time. They suggested I could get to Ulaan Baatar and look for another agency that might be able to issue an invitation. However, I only had three days there, so I was worried that I wouldn't have time to find one, get the letter and then get the visa processed in time to make my train. I Googled to see if I could find an agent online and maybe do some of the process via email to give me a jump on things. To my dismay, though, I only found one company with a functional website and they failed to respond to an email.

As the date of my train drew closer, I pondered what I could do. In my gut, I felt that I would probably be able to find a travel agent that would sort me the documents I needed. Having already lived in Ulaan Baatar, I had an idea where I might be able to find one. But, and there were two really big buts, Mongolia was not a country where things moved quickly and Russian bureaucracy was similarly renowned for its lack of haste. Consequently, my head told me there was a pretty high chance I could miss my onward train to Russia. The fallout of missing that train was costly. I would need to buy all my train tickets again and also pay for accommodation in Moscow - a prerequisite for a visa and thus non-refundable - for a second time as well as at least two extra nights accommodation in Ulaan Baatar. It would come to much more than I could afford.

It was a hugely difficult decision, but I ultimately concluded that I could not risk getting to Mongolia and being unable to make my train. The cost of new tickets would just be too much and I didn't fancy the idea of being left to twiddle my thumbs in Ulaan Baatar. So, I decided to double down on China and both extend and expand my stay. The new plan was to let go of my Transiberian dreams and travel south to Shanghai to get a deeper and richer taste of China. I figured that Beijing had been so amazing that seeing more of the country was a no-brainer.

To get to Shanghai, I had thought about taking the train. However, as I happened to be in China on the weekend of the National Day Holiday, I had trouble finding tickets in the nicer 'soft sleeper' class and I didn't much fancy taking a twelve hour train ride on a stiff-backed plastic 'hard' seat. So, I asked the travel desk at my hotel to see if they could find me a bus ticket - it seemed I would be reverting to Korean style travel. This proved to be much easier and, for less than £20, I would be travelling south for fourteen hours on a first class overnight bus. It wasn't quite the epic journey across two continents that I had been planning, but it wasn't a terrible alternative.

SHANGHAI

I bade Alana farewell as she jumped in a taxi to the airport ahead of her flight back to Auckland and I then strapped my rucksack on my back and took a thirty minute walk south through the city to the bus station. I am not sure what I was expecting in terms of the station itself and the coach I would be taking. I guess I had Korean standards in mind and was, thus, expecting something modern and super-comfortable. As it turned out, I was a little bit shocked at how basic things were. The station was clean but decidedly rudimentary. There were no digital information screens, no Starbucks or Dunkin Donuts and no sleek waiting rooms in which to relax. It didn't compare at all to any of the major stations in Seoul and didn't even compare too well to the station in Taean. It filled me with a little bit of trepidation about what I was getting myself into. A year in Korea had conditioned me to traveling in a certain degree of comfort!!

To my disappointment, the bus was nothing like the super luxurious Korean coaches which often had giant leather recliners and a bathroom nicer than the one in the apartment Mr Kim had provided for me. The Chinese bus was a whole lot more basic. It was clean, but was significantly older and less elaborate. The most interesting facet, though, was that the ticket I had purchased did not provide me with a seat; it entitled me to a bed. This felt really odd as I had never seen anything like it before. The bus had two levels of bunks, one on top of the other that ran in three columns along the length of the bus. Mine was near the front on the bottom level. It was, for someone my height, rather short. However, it was pretty comfortable and came with a crisp white pillow and clean sheets under which to sleep.

As I was new to China, the journey was fun and intriguing. We departed from Beijing late in the afternoon, which allowed me to see a little bit more of the city as we travelled towards the main east coast highway. Just as when we had arrived in Tianjin, I was again drawn in by the waves of bicycles in the suburbs. It had me humming a certain Katie Melua song and thinking just how much I was struck by the country. Then, as the sun began to set, I settled in for a surprisingly good night's sleep after the stewardess - dressed just like a flight attendant on an airline - brought round green tea and a few snacks.

Whilst the suburbs of Beijing with its plethora of bikes had looked pretty cool, the majority of the journey was spent on a highway that for the most part was relatively nondescript. The journey only really got interesting when I awoke the following morning as it got light outside. This gave me my first glimpse of rural China.

If it was at all possible, I was soon even more hooked on the country. It was very lush and very green and, even though the bus did not deviate from the highway, there was just so much to see. We passed countless small towns in which I saw rice fields, small rural farms and scores of farmers pottering along on motor-rickshaws. There were Chinese pop videos playing on a small TV screen at the front of the bus, but I scarcely paid them any attention, the scenery outside was far more gripping; I wanted to get a good look at rural China as it whizzed past my window..

As the sun fully asserted itself and we eased into the morning, the landscape through the window began to change. The rice fields started to fade away and the scenery became decidedly more urban. This excited me. I was arriving in one of the world's great cities - a metropolis that was at the apex of China's growth and transformation and which had a fascinating history - and I was desperate to drink as much as I could. In all honesty, though, the final stages of the journey as we inched our way into the city were a little disappointing. As the bus station was in the northern suburbs of the city, we didn't pass too much of great interest. The panorama was, just as in suburban Beijing, dominated by apartment blocks and bicycles. I would have to wait a little while before I was able to see the wonders of the city.

.

The less than dramatic suburban vista made me much more motivated to get out into the city proper in order to see more. As I dumped my bag in my hotel room, I had two major ideas in mind. Firstly, I wanted to see the glitz and glamour of one of the fastest growing cities in Asia and, indeed, the world. Secondly, I wanted to see a bit of history. Whereas in Beijing the history on show was either Communist (Tiananmen Square and Mao's mausoleum) or much more ancient (The Forbidden City and Summer Palace), in Shanghai there was something different: the colonial element from the turn of the previous century when foreign powers such as France and the UK had taken advantage of the collapse of imperial China to grab parts of Chinese cities along the east coast.

My hotel was located quite close to the old concession areas, so I decided to take a walk to the French Concession - the most well-known, and apparently most beautiful, of the European districts - and grab some lunch. I had heady visions of sitting on a cute little wrought iron table nibbling on a croissant and enjoying a cafe au lait as I might in Paris or Nice. Alas, I was to be disappointed as the tree-lined boulevards had fallen into a state of crumbling disrepair and there were no cute Parisian style bistros or cafes to be found.

Despite the absence of any serious gastronomic options as well as the presence of quite a bit of flaking brickwork and a few derelict storefronts, the style and architecture of the French Concession was resplendent. The roads were wide and lined with large trees that cast some very pleasant shade across the cracked sidewalks. This might sound like a really obvious statement, but, from the aesthetics alone, it really did feel like I was walking around the centre of a small provincial French city. It was genuinely beautiful and afforded the opportunity to visualise what the area would have been like in its 'heyday' - I use inverted commas as an era when European colonial powers basically forced Opium onto the Chinese people and dressed it up as 'trade' really ought not to glorified too much - when it was possibly the most cosmopolitan little chunk of land in the world.

The Concession area was magnificent in its cosmopolitan charm. However, as I have already described, it lacked a bit of the modernisation and gentrification that would have allowed me to sit and have a relaxed European lunch. There were no chic bistros or expensive boutiques - although I imagined it would not be long before that began to change. Instead, it was just Chinese shops and restaurants. This may have left me a little hungry, but it worked as a fantastic juxtaposition. In one way, we had both Europe and Asia as the Chinese shops and signs sat against the European style setting. And, in another, we had an area with fantastic history and without too much development sitting just a few hundred metres from some of the fastest change and transformation in the world.

After a lunch of Chinese food eaten at a disappointingly plastic table by the side of the road, I headed into the main throng of the city. The heart of Shanghai is based around the Huangpo River where, in the colonial period, ships brought in opium and took Chinese made goods away to Europe and America. There were three elements here that I wanted to see: i) Nanjing Lu, a major shopping street that runs at a right angle to the river, ii) The Bund, the near bank of the river that is dominated by powerfully built European buildings, and iii) Pudong the area on the far bank of the river which is dominated by modern skyscrapers. My Lonely Planet and every bit of internet research I did told me that it was an assault on the senses to see history, modernisation and so many people all rammed into a relatively tiny area. It was right!!

I began on Nanjing Lu. My route from the concession area initially took me not to the river but to the metro station at the opposite end of the street about a kilometre away. My plan was to walk down the road to the river soaking up the atmosphere as I went. It would be an experience that knocked me on my ass! It was one of the most vibrant and bustling places I have ever visited. It was almost incomprehensibly crowded and crammed full of shops and stalls with people shouting and screaming to hawk all manner of goods.

Having just come from Korea, I was not unaccustomed to crowds. The metro in Seoul can be a claustrophobically busy experience and areas like Gangnam and Dongdaemun are bustling even in the early hours of the morning. Yet, Nanjing Lu was something else. It was on a completely different level. There was so much more life and more spirit. It was fabulous.

Nanjing Lu genuinely was a sensory slap to the face in it's own right. However, another element of the visit that really struck me was the contrast to Beijing. They were two very different cities. In the capital, Xiu Shui was a fabulous explosion of capitalism. But, that was just one building. The rest of the city did have plenty of souvenir stalls but the majority of the city seemed a bit more political or administrative. There were lots of modern buildings, of course, but there were also plenty of wide boulevards lined by government buildings. It was almost like the Communist Party didn't want its headquarters to be too sullied by the ideology it had battled for half a century but was now beginning to embrace.

Nanjing Lu on the other hand, was a huge fiesta of shopping. For the full length of the road there were shops, street sellers and cafes. You, literally, didn't get a break. There was so much to see on a commercial level. There were two or three buildings that served a similar purpose to Xiu Shui with several floors of fake goods. There were also lots of shops selling Chinese branded clothes, of what seemed to be terribly low quality, at ridiculously low prices. Also, in a different vein, there were also plenty of western brands and stores catering to China's growing nouveau riche.

Not only did Shanghai seem different commercially, but it also looked different to Beijing. Large parts of the capital seemed to be built to just three or four storeys. The Qianmen and Wangufin areas close to Tiananmen were all relatively low.. Only in Jianguomen and Chaoyang - the main business areas - did you see large skyscrapers. Compared to that, Shanghai seemed to be a far more vertical city. The majority of the buildings were higher than in Beijing.

Nanjing Lu was like a steep valley or canyon of shopping. With the huge throngs of people flowing in and out of the buildings, the area felt chaotic and claustrophobic. This feeling grew more and more intense the closer I got to the river. As I neared the end and saw the skyscrapers on either side of me beginning to drop away and the wider panorama of the river loom into view it felt like a giant gulp of air.

Nanjing Lu opens out onto the Bund as the road reaches the Huangpo River. It is glorious. In front of you, there is a large main road but after that there is the bend of the river and on the far side the giant skyscrapers of Pudong. Up until that point, China had matched and surpassed Korea in history and culture but had fallen significantly short in terms of modernity. In one fell swoop, that equation changed. It was one of the most dramatic skylines I have ever seen. To this day, aside from my first impressions of Dubai, I have seen nothing that hits you quite as bluntly and with such great force..

With such an amazing view in my sights, I crossed the road - no easy task as my attention was firmly drawn away from road safety by what lay in front of me - and walked towards the river. I started intently across the placid waters and mused to myself how amazing China was. I had seen imperial and Communist history in Beijing and then colonial history and crazy modernity in Shanghai. It seemed to be such a historically and culturally rich country. At that very moment, just to ram the point home a little bit, a Buddhist monk ambled in front of me and stood at the wall that separated the Bund from the water beneath. The juxtaposition to the modern skyscrapers in the background was simply delicious. It was a scene laced with such metaphor that I couldn't resist taking a photo - it is one I still have today and look at regularly.

As magnificent as the views of Pudong were, they were only the start. The fabulous contrast of old and new continued as I turned around to see the buildings on the Bund. The view changed dramatically. The glass and modernity gave way to imposing colonial era architecture. The buildings were built in the late 1800s and felt like British Victorian institutions. It was a truly fabulous vista and the whole 360 degree panorama seemed like an analogy to the country itself: history and modernity were there to take in simply by turning your head.

As I am sure this section of the book has conveyed, China had a huge impact on me. Both Shanghai and Beijing were fantastic places to visit. This might sound like I am being anti-Korean or trivialising the year I spent there, but it genuinely felt that I had experienced and learned more in ten days or so in China than I had in a year in Korea. There was absolutely no way that I would be going back to the UK permanently. That could wait. It was early October by the time I got home. The plan was to spend the last three months of the year with friends and family whilst also looking for a job in China. I would then be off to Asia once more in the New Year.

PART 3: China

LOOKING BACK ... AND FORWARD

One of the toughest aspects of my time in Korea was spending so much time away from my friends and family. The worst part of this was Christmas. In isolation, passing Christmas Day in Seoul was not too bad. Me and my friends had engaged in a fabulous buffet lunch at a pub in Itaewon where we then enjoyed a very nice selection of Belgian beers. However, as fun as that was, it was not the same as being at home with my mum or my dad and grandad. Therefore, after returning from the Far East, I was really happy to spend the end of the year at home and to enjoy an English Christmas.

Opening gifts on Christmas morning in the UK was fantastic and made me promise myself that never again would I be away from home at such an important time of year. However, once I had rung in the new year, my mind turned back east. The plan was a simple one. I would fly to Beijing in early January where I would rendez-vous with Ossie who would be finishing his year in Korea. From there, we would embark on a tour of the country. We planned to visit Shanghai and some of the surrounding cities such as Hangzhou and Nanjing as well as trying to get to the ancient capital of Xi'an - where we would find the Terracotta warriors. If things went well, we would also have time to go further west and enjoy some of the wonders of the ancient Silk Road.

BACKPACKING

I arrived in China by plane two days ahead of Ossie, who was taking the ferry from Korea just as I had done a few months before. Our plan was to have a couple of nights in Beijing to enjoy a few beers and to catch up before jumping straight on a train and heading to either the glitz and glamour of Shanghai or the ancient wonders of Xi'an. We thought it was a pretty sensible and achievable itinerary. However, our plan was scuppered before we had managed to travel a single kilometre - and before Ossie had even landed in China - as we encountered a situation of unbridled travel chaos caused by the Chinese New Year.

I didn't know it at the time - or at least not until I made my way to Beijing railway station - but the Spring Festival holiday (As Chinese New Year is known in China) is a period of unmatched human migration. In no place on earth and at no other time of year are there so many people on the move. This is because the Chinese government allocates three weeks per year for workers to have public holidays and for production at factories across the country to shut down. These weeks take place at Spring Festival, May Day and the Chinese National Day in October and are often the only time off millions of low-paid workers will get.

The Chinese government introduced the Golden Weeks in 1999 to mark the 50th anniversary of the founding of the People's Republic by Mao Zedong after the Civil War against Chiang Kai Shek's Nationalist forces. In that first year, nearly 30 million people used the opportunity to travel. A huge majority of these were workers who had moved to cities on the east coast from more rural homes in central or western China to find work and better opportunities. It was a great success as they all clearly loved the opportunity to have the time to make the journey home to see relatives. In every subsequent year the number of people travelling has increased. In the mid 1990s there were 28 million migrant workers in China, but by the start of the new millennium that number had grown into the hundreds of millions (By 2018 it was just under 300million). As a consequence, with so many people trying to get home for the holidays, train tickets can be like gold dust.

On my first full day back in China, still in a state of blissful ignorance in relation to the situation around the country, I thought it might be a good idea to try and go to the railway station in order to get a jump on buying some rail tickets. I was under the rather deluded impression that buying train tickets in China was going to be the same as in the UK. I naively presumed that I would be able to leisurely wander into the station and buy a ticket to any destination I might fancy. That was really not the case. Rather than being able to walk into the station building as I would in Sheffield or Manchester, in Beijing I found a giant throng of people outside the station battling to get access to the row of ticket windows in the front of the building. It was 100m wide and 30m deep with, quite literally, thousands of people all pushing and shoving to get to the front.

It didn't look much fun, but as I had no other option available to me, I joined the push and waited. As I was used to the rather genteel British approach to queueing and even the relatively measured approach used by the Koreans, I found it really hard work. The Chinese seemed happy to push, pull clothing and even try to sneak under my armpit to get ahead. After forty brutal minutes, during which I was forced to abandon any quaint notions about waiting politely, I managed to kick, push and elbow my way to the front. My objective was to get sleeper tickets to either Xi'an or Shanghai at some point in the upcoming three or four days. But, alas, this proved impossible. There were no tickets to either city available for the entirety of the following week. Essentially, this left us stranded in Beijing.

Obviously, this unforeseen delay was a massive disappointment. Once Ossie had made landfall and wended his way from Tianjin to Beijing, we had to sit and reassess what we would do. We discussed trying to get tickets on a train to somewhere else and asked the travel agent in our hostel if she could help us out - I really didn't fancy another bout with the crowd outside the station. Sadly, she also came back empty-handed. This meant that we would be stranded in Beijing for a few days and perhaps for more than a week. However, the change in plans actually proved to be rather serendipitous as we got to celebrate the new year in Beijing, which proved to be a truly fabulous few days.

Spring Festival in Beijing

Before arriving in China, the only taste I'd had of Chinese New Year was on TV: BBC news reports or travel documentaries. These always seemed to show a rather cliched view of things. There would be acrobats, paper dragons and plenty of fireworks. Therefore, I had a rather colourful image in my head of what we might expect. However, this was a very westernized impression of Chinese culture. It was the same as thinking that the sweet and sour pork and prawn toast in your local Chinese restaurant was genuinely authentic Chinese food - for the record, I never saw prawn toast or prawn crackers during the four years I lived in China! Consequently, I would not get what I was expecting.

Obviously, in reality, things were always going to be different. As opposed to the UK or US where Trafalgar Square and Times Square are packed with drunk party-goers for western new year, most Chinese people tend to spend the Spring Festival at home with family and friends. This was also the case in Mongolia where I had found Ulaan Baatar eerily quiet as the lunar new year changed. However, despite not getting carpet-bombed by fireworks and not seeing Tiananmen Square full of acrobats and revellers, Beijing provided a fabulous experience.

We had booked a hotel in the older 'hutong' area of the city, which was located in the southern districts just below Tiananmen Square. It was a fabulously interesting and quaint locale. The whole district was a warren of single storey houses built around small central courtyards. In ancient China, either a large extended family or smaller individual family groups would live in rooms on the outside of the courtyard and share a well in the centre. In more recent years, that had evolved to sharing a tap in the centre, but the layout and communal approach remained unchanged.

The hutongs were a great piece of Chinese history. Sadly, by 2006 they were beginning to disappear quickly as China modernised at pace and the more traditional places to live were replaced with high-rise apartments. However, it seemed to us that even though the hutongs might soon be a thing of the past, they provided a fantastic sense of community. Therefore, to enjoy Spring Festival as much as possible, we decided to immerse ourselves in that community. This was never going to be particularly easy as we didn't speak any Mandarin. So, to take things down to the most basic of levels, we grabbed a few bottles of frighteningly cheap beer - less than 30p for 500ml - in the hope of lowering our inhibitions a bit and making interaction a tad easier.

Getting ourselves a little socially lubricated worked an absolute treat. This may sound less than sophisticated, but we basically just started shouting "hello" and "ni hao" to everyone we encountered in the hope of somehow getting involved in some celebrations. It wasn't the most nuanced strategy but the local people seemed to respond very well. Lots of people reciprocated our greetings with a few also joining in with toasts. A few families also invited us for dumplings - the traditional food eaten by people in northern China at Spring Festival - and to share a glass of rice wine as they celebrated. It was lovely.

As cool as dumplings and beer were, the high-point of our time in the hutong came when we bumped into two local guys who were sitting on small plastic stools in the street whilst pounding back the *bai jou* (Chinese rice wine) and seemingly having as much fun as us. After exchanging drunken greetings, we offered them beer and they offered us *bai jou* - they got the better end of that deal as the rice wine tasted like paint thinner. After we had toasted China, England and - with a bit of translation difficulty - Northern Ireland (Ossie is from Derry), our new friends took out the longest set of firecrackers either of us had ever seen. They rolled them out onto the floor where one of them proceeded to take the cigarette out of his mouth and use it to light the fuse - China in 2006 was not a haven of Health and Safety. The ensuing cacophony reminded me of news reports from war zones where you see tracer bullets lighting up the sky. As the hutongs were so narrow and enclosed, it felt like the sparks were bouncing between the walls. We almost felt like we needed to duck and cover. It was amazing!

We really enjoyed our hutong experience, but it ended in bizarre and disturbing fashion. We had wanted a taste of authentic China and at the end of the night ... We got one!!!!!!! As we walked along a deserted hutong, we encountered two men standing in the street covered in blood. Straight away, we feared we had stumbled upon something horrific. A murder? A terrible accident? As it transpired, things weren't quite so bad, but they were far from pleasant. As we approached the men, we discovered that the source of the blood was an animal prone on the ground. On closer inspection, we found that it was a dog. On even closer inspection, we found that it was a dalmation that the men were in the process of skinning. As we stopped and stared, one of them turned to us and said, "dinner". As the previous section of the book detailed, I had eaten dog in Korea. However, the blood and the hands on nature of skinning the animal made it a sight that still haunts me - much more so than the oil drum outside Taean.

Our evening celebrations had been fantastic, but we also wanted to get a taste of what things could be like during the day when we were a little more sober. So, after sleeping off the beer and *bai jou* and then having a rather slow-paced breakfast, we jumped on the blue metro line - which formed a circle around the inner parts of the city - to Ritan Park in the northern reaches of the city. Lonely Planet had informed us that it was a great area for families and young people and was always full of activities during the Golden Week holidays.

As soon as we arrived at the gate to the park, it became clear that it really was a popular spot. It was crazy crowded! The giant sprawl of people trying to force their way inside was certainly off-putting at first, and we briefly considered abandoning the whole endeavour, but we stuck with it as we figured that if so many locals were keen to get inside it had to be worth it. Once we got into the main body of the park, we discovered that whilst it might not have warranted the huge battle to get inside it was definitely good fun.

The first thing that struck us was the fantastic array of paper lanterns on display. There were, quite literally, thousands of them on the ground making beautiful patterns as well as interesting sculptures. They were fabulous in one way as the many paper bodies made up some cool pattern that spread across the park, but it was also amazing as each individual lantern seemed so delicate and intricate. There were also a couple of tunnels made solely from red lanterns attached to metal archways. These looked fabulous. It all felt very 'Chinese' and went some way to satisfying my desire for a 'traditional' Chinese New Year.

The lanterns certainly looked cool and brought some colour to the bitterly cold northern Chinese winter. However, on their own they would not have warranted the journey. They were pretty, but Beijing has a whole plethora of fabulous sites and attractions that are much more worthwhile. But, thankfully, there were also scores of games and activities dotted around the park. In some ways, despite being on a massive scale, Ritan took on the feel of an English village fete. There were plenty of food stalls - lamb skewers and pork dumplings as opposed to Victoria Sponge - and loads of games where you could win prizes. Just as you might find in the UK, there were shooting galleries, darts and basketball throws - although, I was mildly disappointed that there was no hook a duck. It all seemed nice, clean fun and the thousands of Beijing locals seemed to be having a great time.

To get into the swing of things, we decided to try out some of the fun and games. We started with a bit of shooting. Alas, I was utterly terrible. I missed the stacked tin cans with four of my five shots. Ossie did a little better, but neither of us got close to winning any prizes. So, we decided to try something different. Next to the shooting gallery was a stand set up with a large pyramid of cans on a green and rather dirty looking carpet surrounded by white netting, which we guessed was designed to make it look like a football pitch. It looked much more like our cup of tea.

When we got to the stall, there was a Chinese guy having a go at knocking down the pyramid. He was not very good. Two of his efforts clipped the edge of the pyramid and removed a solitary can and one missed altogether. With such an unimpressive precedent set, we figured that at the very least we wouldn't look particularly foolish when we gave it a go. However, things soon got a little more pressured as, seemingly out of nowhere, a huge crowd encircled us to watch our efforts. It appeared that for a large proportion of Beijngers watching two foreigners smashing a football at a pile of rusty tin cans passed for prime time entertainment. This was the first, but absolutely not the last, time we would draw a lot of attention for simply being foreign. Back then, China was a far less international country so exposure to foreigners was much more of a novelty for regular Chinese people than it is today. Therefore, on countless occasions we found ourselves observed even whilst doing some utterly mundane tasks.

With an audience of over one hundred people watching on intently, I stepped up and side-footed the ball into the cans. It hit in the centre of the pyramid and sent the majority of them flying into the air. The success was met with a huge cheer from my adoring audience. After the stall holder cleared things away, we saw that there were just two cans left standing. So, Ossie took his turn and knocked them down. The crowd went nuts again with both Ossie and I getting plenty of high fives and slaps on the back from the onlookers.

As we basked in the glory of our victory, the stall holder came over to give us our prize. This is where things got amusing. With a wry smile written across his face, he sidled up behind us and presented us with a giant pink teddy bear. The large group of Chinese found this hilarious. The sight of two foreigners - one with a giant beard and the other who stood over 180cm with a shaved head - cradling a pink teddy was clearly a break from the norm for most of them. In all honesty, it was for us too!

We really weren't sure what to do with our prize. For a brief second, we entertained the notion of taking it with us on our travels and taking pictures of it on the Great Wall and with the Terracotta Warriors, but quickly dismissed that as fanciful. Not wanting to look arrogant in front of the crowd, we quietly wandered back towards the stallholder to return it. As we did so however, we heard a voice speak out in disjointed and heavily accented English. "Give. It. To. Me". We turned around to see who had spoken and found a young couple looking at us with the girl waving very timidly. It seemed a no-brainer, so I walked over and presented her with the bear. The move was greeted with a cheer and a round of applause from the crowd and filled us with plenty of Spring Festival cheer.

A Food Tour of Beijing

Getting on the beers and dumplings and enjoying the park were big highlights of our Spring Festival. They were great fun and the food was surprisingly delicious. However, as cool as all that was, Beijing is a city full of fantastic culture and history. Therefore, we were really keen to see as much as possible. We had our eyes on several fantastic historical sights such as the Temple of Heaven and the Great Wall. Before we got onto those though, we decided that we wanted to start things off with something of a food tour of the Chinese capital. We had both eaten plenty of sweet and sour pork or kung pao chicken in our day, but we wanted to try some slightly more exotic and unusual dishes whilst we were in the city.

We started our tour in one of the oldest and most colourful restaurants in Beijing, *Tian Hai Can Ting*. This was a small restaurant located in a crumbling building in the hutong area of the city. It was super-cramped and certainly not very clean. The bathroom was, essentially, a hole in the ground that played host to some rather unpleasant odours and horrific stains. The kitchen, which was visible from the main dining area, was also sorely lacking in basic cleanliness. When we peered inside the 'chef' was cooking with a cigarette between his lips and was wearing a filthy white undershirt. Despite the cleanliness issues, though, *Tian Hai* was one of the most amazing places at which I have ever eaten.

I loved *Tian Hai* because it took a wonderfully simplistic approach to Chinese cuisine. Compared to Chinese restaurants in England, it really cut through all the culinary bullshit. My local Chinese restaurant in Rotherham used to include mangetout, broccoli and mini-sweetcorn in their dishes. *Tian Hai* had none of those frivolous niceties. The sauces and ingredients were paired down and came across as simple yet powerful. It was fabulous.

We ate at *Tian Hai* on successive days - it really was that good - which allowed us to really explore the menu. On our first visit, we went for some standard local dishes such as Beijing beef, which was shredded beef in a thick and salty sauce. On our second visit, though, I got my first introduction to Chinese food in its spicy form by trying some of the Sichuanese dishes on the menu. They were eye-wateringly hot. The waiters found it hilarious that our pasty British skin had gone garishly pink after just a couple of mouthfuls. It was hard work, but the food was delicious and really gave me the motivation to visit the far flung corners of China's southwest - an ambition we would fulfill three years later.

Our pink complexions and good custom ensured that we were popular figures at *Tian Hai*. So, before we left for the second time, they offered us a complimentary glass of rice wine ... made with snakes!!! On the bar at the back of the restaurant were three giant jars of liquid each containing all manner of oddities. The first was filled with the type of plants you might expect to find on a riverbed. The second contained a combination of frogs and lizards, all dead of course. The third, and the one our drinks came from, contained two snakes coiled around the inside. It looked like something you would see in one of the Indiana Jones movies .... and seemed a great idea at the time. Sadly, in a similar vein to our earlier night in the hutongs, it tasted like rubbing alcohol!

After *Tian Hai*, we decided that our next stop would be the *Dong Hua* night market, home of some of the most unusual food opportunities in the Chinese capital. Located at the eastern gate of the Forbidden City - *Dong Hua* literally means East Gate - the market sold food on a stick. You could, quite literally, buy almost anything impaled on a small wooden skewer. This started off rather mundanely with small pieces of spiced lamb - which is a dish that originates in the west of China but is a hugely popular form of street-food across the country - and candied fruits. However, as you got deeper into the market, things got crazier and we found ourselves more excited and also more perturbed about what was on offer.

The first stall that really grabbed our attention featured a weird array of creatures that I would not ordinarily even consider to be remotely close to being food. These were - in ascending order of cuteness - giant locusts, scorpions, seahorses and starfish. My thought process as I mused about what to order might sound somewhat arbitrary, but I just couldn't bring myself to order and eat a starfish. The child inside me just wouldn't allow it. I went to and fro on whether or not I wanted to try a seahorse, but decided it was worth a go. So, I ordered a stick with three locusts, one with three scorpions and one with three seahorses.

Things started badly. The locusts were disgusting. They were quite possibly the driest thing I had ever eaten and tasted solely of the fat they had been fried in. Thankfully, the scorpion was a big improvement. It was, as you might expect, extremely crunchy as scorpions are not the fleshiest of creatures. However, they came seasoned with some very nice spices. Interestingly, when I ate the third of the scorpions, my tongue brushed the end of its tail. To my surprise, there was still a bit of sting left and for 20 or 30 minutes my tongue was tingling strangely. The scorpions were pretty good but, to my complete surprise, the seahorses were absolutely delicious. There was a hint of fishiness, but they also tasted oddly sweet. Had they not been such sweet little things - in an aesthetic sense - I would have contemplated eating another stick.

The seahorses were easily the highlight of our culinary exploits at *Dong Hua.* However, there was still plenty more to see, even if some of it was not so pleasant. The first of these was a stall selling only testicles. Its wares were arranged in ascending order of size. On one side of the stall there were sticks onto which four or five tiny spheres of meat were impaled. These were lambs' testicles and were about the size of a glace cherry. They were nowhere near as sweet as a cherry, though. Instead, biting into one brought a rush of salty liquid. It really was not pleasant in terms of taste and also left a small psychological scar as I thought about why they were so salty - it gave me a sudden urge to cross my legs.

As we moved along the stall, the testicles got bigger. The lambs gave way to pigs, goats and rams. Then, at the end, were the bulls' testicles. These were huge. They were so big, in fact, that they needed two sticks to hold them. Against my better judgement, I decided to buy one. It was awful. The texture was horrific. It felt chewy yet was oddly dry and salty. The only thing I could compare it to was blancmange that had been drained of fluid and heavily salted. It was genuinely terrible. I tried my very best to work through it, but by the time I was halfway through I was gagging.

After the testicle stall, there were still more wonders on offer. I had previously thought about lizards and snakes - both of which I would try at a later date and both of which tasted like slightly gamey chicken - but the balls had done for me, so we retired for a beer to wash the hideous taste of residual bull semen away.

The Great Wall

With time to kill in Beijing, taking a trip to the Great Wall seemed like an obvious way to spend a day. So, we started looking into some of the excursions on offer from the hotel at which we were staying. We had briefly considered the idea of trying to get there on public transport. However, this soon got shelved for two main reasons: i) We would face the same issues we had when trying to get to Xi'an or Shanghai: public transport would be difficult to find and crowded, and ii) even the more accessible areas of the Wall are not that close to Beijing or any other major city, so transport options were relatively thin on the ground.

Another major consideration was where we would actually go. It is a common misconception that the Wall is one coherent structure built to keep the nomadic hordes from the North out of China. Both historically and geographically speaking, this isn't really the case. Sections of fortifications were built as early as the 7th century BC. These were only really brought together into a 'wall' during the Qin dynasty around 200BC. Since then different dynasties built upon and expanded the fortifications with the majority of what we now see as the Great Wall being built in the Ming dynasty in the 1600s. This means that whilst there is a general pattern of the wall running from east to west across northern China, it is by no means one unified unit. There are several different sections and off-shoots spread across the northern region.

The sections of the wall closest to Beijing tend to be the busiest. The easiest to reach and the one to which most tourist trips go is Badaling, which is famed for being comically busy. The staff at our hotel warned us that it really wouldn't be worth going because, even in deepest winter, there were likely to be thousands of people there and therefore the chances of seeing any unspoiled and uncrowded sections of wall were slim. Additionally, it had been hugely restored in recent years so we would, essentially, be viewing a replica of the original wall. It sounded like a tourist hell to us, so we opted to give that one a miss. The second option was a little further away and likely to be a little less crowded. The Mutianyu section was also a bit more dramatic as it was on steeper hills that afforded some amazing views. However, the tourist element was still there as you a) could get to the wall by way of a cable car, and b) you could get back down to the coach park on a toboggan.

I cannot lie, the toboggan and the cable car sounded very cool. However, the amount of tourists that we might encounter seemed a bit off-putting. So, we decided to go for the third option: a hike between the Jinshanling and Simatai sections of the wall. We were sold on this one because the guys in the hotel told us that not only were both sections far less busy than Badaling or Mutianyu but that also the 11km between the two are largely deserted and afford some of the best available views of the wall.

As Jinshanling is quite a way from central Beijing, our day began early. We were on a bus - whilst still extremely hungover - at just before seven. However, the early morning headache was absolutely worth it as we arrived at Jinshanling before nine and were alone, aside from the other people on our tour bus. Being the youngest and fittest amongst that group, we struck out quickly and were soon alone on the ramparts. It was fabulous. The Jinshanling section of the wall covers some fabulous rolling countryside with guard towers situated on each of the small peaks along the way. We just loved reaching each of these and then looking down to see the wall bending and twisting along the ridges of each hill. There was not a soul to be seen. It was magical.

There are plenty of myths and misapprehensions about the wall, several of which I laboured under until I visited and then did some further reading. I dealt with one of these earlier by explaining that it is not one coherent wall. It is also not the only man-made structure visible from space. For the record, according to many space expeditions - although ironically not China's first manned space mission in 2003 - it is visible from low earth orbit, but not from the moon. One other myth is that the wall provided a solid defense against rampaging hordes from the North. I was surprised to learn that it was, in fact, surprisingly ineffective. A few years after my trip to the wall, I found a copy of John Man's excellent work, *The Great Wall.* In it he explains that the wall often served more as a comfort blanket than as actual security. He argued that for many of the dynasties - going way back to the Qin who lived in the last two centuries BC - when they were strong, they had no need for the wall as bandits would fear their powerful armies.. However, as they began to get bloated and weaker, which was a common cyclic occurence in ancient China, they built more walls to hide behind. It rarely worked. Possibly the best example of this came with Chinggis Khan and his Mongol armies in the thirteenth century. In 1211, they simply went around the fortifications that had been constructed by the Jin dynasty and inflicted horrific losses.

Interestingly, the wall was perhaps of greater use in other areas. For example, it was used a lot more as a communications conduit than a barrier. With its solid construction and clear direction, it provided a safe and navigable path between towns. This was particularly true in more western regions where roads were remote and less passable. The guard towers and fortresses along the wall also served as an excellent way of regulating trade and collecting taxes - it was impossible to get a cart of goods over the ramparts so they were checked and controlled at fortresses along the wall.

The hike to Simatai was exhausting - 11km up and down big hills was hard work - but when we got there, we were very impressed with what we found. The Jinshanling section and the Simatai section are joined by a small suspension bridge. After that, the Simatai section towers away from you. The frighteningly steep steps seemed to just climb away into the sky. I may be in danger of slipping into hyperbole here, but it almost felt like a stairway to heaven. Having already put 11km of harsh terrain into our calf muscles, we only got a few hundred metres up the Simatai section before we decided it was far enough and the pictures we could snap were of requisite quality.

As we bounced down the Simatai steps and made for the car park, where we were told there was a nice little restaurant where we might find some lunch and a decent cup of coffee, we noticed a sign that ensured that Jinshanling/Simatai was the right choice. Mutianyu might have offered us a toboggan and cable car, but here we were presented with a zip wire that would take us from the wall to the valley bottom below. It was several hundred metres long and started around 80m above the valley bottom. When I look back on it now, I remember how much fun it was and how fabulous the whole scene was, but I wince at the abject lack of safety. I sat on a rickety wooden plank that was attached to me and to the wire by a single carabiner.

Xian

After almost a week of waiting and countless trips to the train station and our hotel's travel desk, we finally managed to secure tickets to Xi'an thanks to some sterling work from the travel agent. However, to catch the train, we actually got a little bit of a surprise as we would not be travelling from the main station in the centre of the city, but from a different station altogether. Ironically, as it transpired, we had been trying to buy tickets at the wrong station anyway! At the time - things have since changed with the expansion and modernisation of China's railway system - trains from Beijing Station tended to operate in the northeast of the country and to the major cities on the east coast. If you wanted to travel to the western parts of the country, the trains departed from Beijing West train station.

Until we got out of our taxi in front of it, I had no idea as to quite how big and crowded Beijing West actually was. It was, in that period, one of the busiest railway stations in the world. During the Golden Weeks, it was busier than almost any other travel hub on the planet - including Beijing's main station - as millions of people were trying to find their way home to provinces inland. When Ossie and I arrived, we were greeted by a scene of unchecked and unfiltered humanity. There were, without a hint of exaggeration, tens of thousands of people pushing and shoving to get into the main building and onto their trains. It made the crowds that we had seen at the main station, which were larger than anything I had ever seen in England and most I had seen in Korea, look tiny and insignificant.

Getting through the crowds and into the main building was a frightening affair. We both had rather large backpacks, so it was difficult to stay balanced as we were buffeted from side to side by the crowds. On two or three occasions, it genuinely felt like we would be knocked off our feet, which could easily have resulted in us being trampled underfoot by the herd. Thankfully, we managed to keep our footing and navigate our way inside the main building. We had initially hoped to sit and relax with a beer or a nice coffee before getting on the train. Sadly, this proved to be totally impossible as the whole station was full to bursting. It looked like a scene from a news report on the aftermath of a natural disaster. Hundreds of family groups were sleeping or squatting on sheets of newspaper strewn across the floor and large groups of workers sat around bundles of luggage playing cards. The concept of a quiet pint or a nice foamy latte suddenly seemed ridiculous. This was a different world for us.

By the time we got onto the train, we were exhausted. We felt like we had had to fight our way through. The state of the station had also left us worried about the train we would be travelling on. Xi'an was in the heart of China, a long way west. Consequently, our journey would be a lengthy one: just over twelve hours, setting off in the evening and arriving early in the morning. Because of this, we didn't really want to find ourselves on a cold, rickety and dirty train. Thankfully, we needn't have worried as it proved to be surprisingly pleasant and comfortable.

At the time, there were four standards of rail travel in China. The first, hard seats, were exactly as they sounded. They were wooden or plastic seats in a cold metal carriage. These were often, by European standards, crazy cheap. But, they could be hugely crowded and frighteningly dirty. Chinese people at the lower end of the income spectrum - such as those we had seen in the station - often travelled for huge distances and staggering lengths of time on these. Some of the slower trains into the central and western areas of the country could take 24 or up to 36 hours to reach their destinations. As 'authentic' an experience as that type of journey would have been, we decided that spending twelve hours in a cold metal box where everyone could smoke and the toilet was a hole in the steel floor was no way to travel. We also opted against soft seats. Again, these were pretty much as they sounded. They were more comfortable, but they had the same issues with smoking, overcrowding and hygiene.

The third class of travel was the hard sleeper. These were not quite as they sounded. The beds, whilst not super comfortable or outrageously wide, came with a soft mattress and clean bedding. They were deemed 'hard' because the bunks did not come in an enclosed cabin. Instead, there were usually six bunks in an open enclave which looked out onto the corridor. It was a much more communal experience than the soft sleepers where you were in a four person compartment with four slightly wider beds and the luxury of a lockable door.

Prior to our travels, Ossie and I had decided that for shorter trips - under seven or eight hours - we would take the soft seats as whilst they might not be super comfy, we didn't really need beds. That was an easy enough decision. However, for longer journeys we were torn between the cost-saving benefits of the hard sleepers and the comfort of the soft sleepers. In the end, for the trip to Xi'an, the decision was made for us as all the soft sleeper berths had sold out. The hard sleepers though, proved to be fabulous. We were lucky enough to be on a very new train. This meant that it was really nice, super clean and surprisingly comfortable: the bunks were small but the mattresses were soft and the bedding crisply pressed.

We were sharing our little enclave - which, unusually, only had four beds - with two off-duty cops who had been in the capital for a holiday. They seemed friendly enough and we chatted in broken English whilst we all ate instant noodles that we had purchased from the food trolley. It wasn't quite the Orient Express, but we felt pretty good. As we moved west into rural China, our travelling companions turned in for the night whilst Ossie and I read up on the sights of Xi'an.

We arrived in Xian at just before 7am. It was a cold and misty morning - it was ten degrees below zero when we checked into our hostel. By the time we had unpacked, we were a bit late to be booking a bus to the Terracotta Warriors for that day, so we decided to walk into the city itself. That might sound like a relatively obvious thing to do. However, the city of Xian is widely ignored by a large proportion of tourists who often tend to fly or take the train in, see the warriors and then leave. The joke is on them though as there is plenty of fabulous history to be seen. The city walls were built in the fourteenth century and extend unbroken for 14km around the inner city area. We wrapped up warm - very warm - and trudged our way around the whole 14km. It was a fascinating little walk. I enjoyed it because you could stare down the roads that stretched away from the walls towards the city centre. It genuinely felt as though we were peering deep into the heart of the city.

As the city is seen - and has been for thousands of years - as the gate to China's West, there is also a little bit of Muslim history in the city. China's western regions are home to the country's Islamic population. In proportion to the rest of the country, that population is small. It represents only about 3% of the total (In 2009, the CIA estimated the raw number to be somewhere around 21million). The majority of Muslims live in the western provinces such as Gansu, Qinghai, Ningxia and Xinjiang. It is Xinjiang, China's most western province, where there are significant issues with the local Uighur popluation - which is Muslim - striving for separatism and to be free from government repression.

The mosque in Xi'an is located in a warren of small streets in the older section of the city. A large chunk of those were given over to the sale of the type of fake goods that I had found at Xiu Shui in Beijing a few months earlier. However, after we had navigated our way past the knock-off Rolex watches and imitation Ray-Ban sunglasses, we found a fantastic building that blended Islamic architecture with that of ancient China. Imagine mixing the Forbidden City with the Blue Mosque in Istanbul and you get something of the style, albeit on a far less dramatic scale. This was set in a beautiful garden and was punctuated by a series of small pools. It was a really pleasant place to spend the afternoon.

The walls, the mosque and other parts of Xian were interesting but, if we are honest, we had only headed west for one major reason: the warriors. At the time, I must admit that I did not know too much about China's most dramatic ancient attraction. Consequently, much of the information I am about to put forth was accrued in subsequent years. However, I would argue that my ignorance of the history and significance of the warriors probably helped bolster the sense of pure unadulterated awe I would experience when I first set eyes on the spectacle that unfolded in front of me.

The warriors were the brainchild of Qin Shi Huang, the man after whom China is named, at least if you use the English word for the country. The Chinese themselves actually call their country *Zhong Hua*, which literally translates to Middle Kingdom - back in imperial times, they basically believed their country was the centre of the Earth. The Chin in China, though, comes from Shi Huang as the Q in his name is pronounced Ch. Qin played a pivotal role in Chinese history by unifying five warring kingdoms into one empire that he ruled until his death in 210BC. It was only from then on that China as we see it today could be seen as one country.

Along with the warriors, he is credited with some other pretty impressive achievements. Many historians credit him with standardising Chinese script so that everyone in the newly united country was writing in the same way. I also heard a fantastic story about how he standardised measurements around the country. Apparently, he sent bells to his local governors and leaders that could be used for ringing in order to grab people's attention - in the same way a town crier might have worked in Medieval England I would presume. However, when these were turned upside down, they could also be used as a standard measure for rice. He is also renowned for beginning the Great Wall of China, although back in the Qin period it was more a series of large earth embankments than the magnificent creation that still exists today. The project he started bore little resemblance to the towering steps we had trodden at Simatai.

The Terracotta Warriors were his final and greatest legacy. There are over 8,000 individual soldiers, all with different facial features and uniforms, as well as an array of chariots and horses. These were all there to guard Qin's mausoleum - which has never been opened - that supposedly contains a huge amount of mercury. Apparently there are rivers of the stuff running beside his body. One of the theories surrounding the history of the warriors is that as he grew older Qin was drinking mercury in order to remain youthful and cheat death. The consequence of this was that he was said to be going insane as he aged and the decision to build a lavish tomb and an army of soldiers to guard it was the last bewildered desire of a deranged mind.

No matter what the motivations or causations for the warriors, they were a truly amazing sight. When we visited, only 1,000 of them were visible. The rest were still left buried as the Chinese authorities didn't have the resources to work on preserving all 8,000 of them at once. Irregardless, the size and scope were still amazing. The building in which they are housed is the size of two football pitches. Walking in, you are blown away by the scale of everything. The perspective is simply fabulous. Each row, containing hundreds of bodies, stretches away into the distance seemingly narrowing away to nothing. Again, I will skirt dangerously close to hyperbole, but it is genuinely breathtaking. It is easy to draw an analogy to the Pyramids of Giza when you think of the age of what stands before you - well over 2,000 years - and the scale of what you are seeing and the work needed to build it all. You cannot help but beg the question "How could they do so much with so little technology?"

Even though the scale of the warriors was magnificent, they were also amazing on a micro rather than macro level. As we walked around the perimeter, we looked into the pit and admired the subtle differences between each of them. Some of them had thick bushy moustaches whilst others were clean shaven. Some had different kinds of headwear, whilst others were showing off their locks. It was also really interesting to see the armour they were wearing and the weaponry they were carrying - although some of this was wood and had eroded to nothing. Some had swords, others spears. It really was amazing to see the juxtaposition of the massive scale with the intricate detail of each individual.

Yinchuan

With Spring Festival having passed, we were not expecting to face too many travel problems as we moved on from Xi'an. However, sadly, this would not be the case as the Asiatic winter weather had other ideas. Our initial plan was to head west towards the cities on the ancient Silk Road. A few years before, I had read Peter Hopkirk's fabulous book *Foreign Devils on the Silk Road*. It deals with the period in the early twentieth century when, as China opened to the outside world whilst the final imperial dynasty collapsed, a series of foreign explorers travelled to the country's remote western regions to explore the wonders of the ancient Silk Road. This began with the Swedish naturalist Sven Hedin. His motivations were relatively pure, but he was followed by a collection of opportunists who plundered many of the ancient relics that had rested beneath the sands of western China for thousands of years. It was a fabulous read and it really whetted my appetite for some of the more remote locales in China.

There were three or four places along the Silk Road that we were very keen to explore. About 1,700km northwest of Xi'an was the city of Dunhuang in Gansu province. It is home to the Mogao Caves, a system of 500 temples built around what was formerly an oasis frequented by Silk Road travellers hundreds of years ago. The Chinese tourist board - always a reliable source of unbiased and entertaining information - claimed, rather mathematically, that you could fill 25km of gallery space with the statues and frescoes inside the caves. This sounded fantastic. However, as Hopkirk detailed, the caves also played host to a piece of more recent Silk Road history, one which meant the gallery would not be quite the spectacle it could have been.

Like the majority of the old Silk Road, the caves lost much of their importance and were frequented less and less by travellers as traffic going between east and west began to dwindle when the Ottoman empire cut trade links with the East. At some point in the late 1300s or early 1400s, the caves were abandoned and, with nobody there to maintain them, disappeared under the shifting sands of the surrounding desert. They were rediscovered in 1900 by a Chinese abbot living close by. Over the subsequent 20 years, a series of European 'explorers' came to the caves and pilfered a huge quantity of the statues and frescoes. The Hungarian-born British explorer Aurel Stein arrived first and hacked the majority of frescoes off the walls of the main caves and carried them off on a pack of camels to the British Museum. Despite the shameless theft, there was still plenty to see at Dunhuang as the complex itself was huge and even the lesser treasures that remained were very much worth visiting.

Along with Dunhuang, we were also keen to go further west to another ancient oasis, Turfan. There we would find the Bezeklik cave system which, like Mogao, housed a fantastic array of statues and frescoes. These were located close to the Flaming Mountains, a giant rock formation that stretched around 100km into the desert and which rises up into the air in a series of reds and oranges that inspire its name. It sounded dramatic and seemed unmissable.

As cool as both Turfan and Dunhuang looked, they were actually down the list when it came to attractions in the far west of China. Our dream destination was the remote city of Kashgar, which is located at China's most western tip in a region nestled amidst the borders with the Central Asian states - there are frontiers with Tajikistan and Kyrgyzstan close by - as well as Afghanistan and Pakistan. It is seen as the heart of China's Muslim Uighur population. As it is 4,000km from Beijing and even over 3,000km from Xi'an yet just 600km to Tashkent in Uzbekistan and 800km to Kabul in Afghanistan, it is supposedly a unique cultural experience - it is in China but not necessarily of China.

Or at least it was. At present - the time of writing is 2020 - the Chinese are doing all they can to oppress the Uighur population. This, allegedly, includes a huge system of detention camps as well bulldozing much of the old city and replacing it with the same modern concrete skyscrapers you would find in most Chinese cities. The government in Beijing is also building road and rail links that reduce the travel time to reach Kashgar dramatically and, in so doing, taking away distance as Kashgar's primary form of cultural defense. There are also reports of the government offering large subsidies for ethnic Chinese (Known as 'Han') people to relocate west and, in so doing, make the Uighurs a minority in their own land.

In 2006, though, much of Beijing's plan to subjugate Uighur culture was still a while away. It was rioting in the provincial capital of Urumqi in 2009 that really kicked things into gear. Therefore, 2006 would have been a perfect time to visit. So, the day after our trip to the warriors, we headed to the train station looking for tickets west. For the second time in a few days, I was met by a giant rugby scrum of people. Unlike in Beijing though, this crowd was genuinely impenetrable. We waited and jostled for 30 minutes but managed to get no closer to the ticket window. So, we went back to the hostel to use its ticket booking service - it would cost us an extra 10% in commission, but we had no choice. When we asked the girl behind the desk for tickets, she shook her head resignedly and informed us that there were snow drifts on the tracks and all trains west had been cancelled indefinitely. When we asked how long she thought that might mean, she whistled gently to herself and guessed at two weeks, minimum.

With the option of going west no longer on the table, we thought about our alternative options. There were plenty of choices if we wanted to go back east as there were scores of trains to either Beijing or Shanghai and the tracks were clear of snow. However, as we were already in the west, we thought it would be a shame not to see some of the more remote areas of the country. So, we pulled the Lonely Planet out of my backpack and began to look for alternatives.

It was not quite as easy as we might have expected to find somewhere interesting to go. Whereas the eastern parts of China are densely populated with many big and interesting cities dotted along the coast, the central and western regions of the country are far more open. After twenty minutes gawping at the map of China and flicking through the book to find information about different cities, we settled on heading north to the city of Yinchuan in the sparsely populated province - for China at least - of Ningxia. However, we faced a familiar problem. No train tickets.

At this point, I made one of the most foolish mistakes of my life. I asked, "What about the bus?" No problem said the girl at the ticket desk. The fact that tickets for the bus were readily available for that very evening should have been a massive red flag. However, our naivete and desire to get moving got the better of us. My naive outlook in regards to taking the bus in rural China - which in 2006 remained one of the most impoverished parts of the world - stemmed from my experiences when I had visited China the previous year and took a bus from Beijing to Shanghai. Whilst it hadn't quite measured up to what I had experienced in Korea, it had been pretty nice. There were bunk beds, there was a stewardess - just like on a plane - and we were served snacks and drinks for the duration of the trip. I figured that if the bus from Xian was anything like that, we would be fine. To our utter dismay, it would be nothing like that. Not even close.

The trip started badly. At the bus station, we boarded a vehicle that was significantly older and dirtier than the one I had travelled on a few months previously. As we departed, we settled into our bunks and inspected the less than pristine whites of the sheets. I apologised to Ossie and admitted it may not have been my finest piece of decision making. Little did I know that things would shortly get worse, much worse. An hour's drive outside Xian, the bus stopped at a motorway service station and we were ushered off the bus towards another that was parked a few metres away. We were given no reason for the change. We were just presented with a fait accompli.

Whereas the first bus was maybe not the cleanest, the second was downright filthy. It could best be described as a hovel on wheels. The bedding was soiled and smelled of stale sweat, the windows were cracked and one of our fellow passengers had feet that stank so badly that the driver made him wrap then in plastic bags. We would, ordinarily, have simply got off the bus and tried to make alternative arrangements. However, we were in the middle of nowhere and it was minus fifteen outside. We really didn't want to travel further but we felt we had no choice other than to hold our noses and head north.

The journey was horrific. It proved to be fourteen of the most uncomfortable hours of my life. It was a toss up between the biting cold and the terrible hygiene as to what made the trip worse. The temperature in Xian had been around ten degrees below zero, but as we got into the mountains en route to Ningxia, the mercury dipped even lower. It was so cold that ice formed on the inside of the windows and my water bottle began to freeze. To keep everyone warm, the bus company had provided quilts for each passenger. Ordinarily, this would have been great. However, they were filthy. They were covered in some very very dubious stains and we were justifiably worried about fleas or bedbugs.

We had begun our journey at around 18h00. By 21h30, we were really getting sick of the squalid conditions on the bus and were desperate to have a break and to get a breath of much needed fresh air. Therefore, when the bus pulled into a rest stop we were delighted and were amongst the first passengers to force our way off. We were high up in the mountains between Shaanxi and Ningxia, so the air was clear, crisp and extremely cold.

The frigid but pristine air was a blessed relief, but apart from that the rest stop was almost as horrific as the bus. One of the first things we wanted to do was go to the bathroom. This proved to be a traumatic experience as the toilets were one of the least hygienic places I have ever encountered. I use the word 'toilets' but in all honesty this is too grandiose a term for what we found. There were no cubicles, no urinals and no partitions. Instead, all we saw was a low brick wall and then a giant pit full of faeces and urine. This was truly disgusting, but we were grateful for a couple of small mercies. Firstly, because we were there at night, the temperature was a long way below zero, so the majority of the contents of the latrine pit were frozen solid and less aromatic than they would have been in daylight hours. Secondly, as the 'toilet' was not lit, the darkness meant that we didn't see some of the evils contained within the pit - I dreaded to think what type of vermin were scurrying around below us.

After making our way back from spending a penny, we headed to the rest stop's small canteen. We were hoping to get a good and hot meal. However, the level of hygiene was not dissimilar to that in the toilets and the prospect of getting food poisoning whilst on our bus from hell was too much to risk. So, we decided against hot food and instead opted for a packet of instant noodles and some boiling water. It was a pathetic little meal, but, in all honesty, we were just happy to be off the bus as we knew that we had another ten hours or more of discomfort before reaching our destination.

When they finally drew into view, the neon lights of Yinchuan's long distance bus station were a truly wonderful sight. It was barely 8am when we descended the steps from the bus, but we immediately headed off in search of a hotel so that we could change our clothes - which stank from the squalor of the bus - and to have a hot shower in order to fully resanitise ourselves and to thaw our frigid limbs. After that and catching up on the sleep that we were unable to find on the bus, we made a beeline for Yinchuan's main train station in order to book soft-sleepers to our next destination in a few days. There was no way on earth that we wanted to get stranded for a third time and would certainly not be travelling by bus again!

We had chosen to visit Yinchuan in order to see two historical sights: i) The Xi Xia tombs, and ii) The Twin Pagodas of Baizokou. Two years before arriving in China, I had lived in Mongolia for four months and in doing so I learned quite a lot about Chinggis Khan. Yinchuan was therefore historically fascinating as, just over 1,000 years ago, he almost totally eradicated an entire civilisation that once occupied the region. The story is a medieval 'classic' of betrayal, revenge and unimaginable brutality. I had read about the fate of the Xi Xia civilisation - often also known as the Tanguts - in Lonely Planet and in a couple of books I had read about Chinggis. Therefore, I was keen to see the remnants of the civilisation and perhaps gain a little bit of insight into a passage of history that, perhaps due to the startlingly wide range of savagery associated with Chinggis, has largely been overlooked by historians..

Things began in the early thirteenth century as Chinggis commenced his expansion south from Mongolia into northern China. In 1209, fearing attack - and in all probability annihilation - from the Mongols, the leader of the Tanguts agreed to become a vassal of Chinggis'. As part of the agreement, Chinggis received a supply of camels and horses, as well as the daughter of the Tangut king as a wife. This little setup seemed to work well for a decade or so. Chinggis had his camels and his wife, and the Tanguts could feel safe from the brutality that had been inflicted on other groups and would tear a swathe of horror across Central Asia and into Eastern Europe.

Perhaps though, the leader of the Tanguts grew a little too comfortable and underestimated who he was dealing with as, in 1219, he made the mother of all mistakes. At that point in his reign of terror, Chinggis was attempting to spread his empire into the Middle East. He would, ultimately, succeed and a few years later his son would create the largest pyramid of human skulls the world has ever seen from the rather unfortunate citizens of Baghdad. The Tanguts made their fateful decision when Chinggis was in the process of attacking kingdoms in what is now modern-day Iran. To smooth the process of conquest, he requested that the Tanguts provide him with troops. Foolishly, they refused. Even more foolishly, their king decided that it was an opportune moment to question Chinggis' authority and suggest they review their agreement.

Revenge was not a dish served quickly by Chinggis. He still had more pressing issues in the Middle East, which held his attention. However he had not forgotten the Tanguts' treachery and eight years later he returned to northern China. This time he was in no mood for truces, nuptials or camels. Instead, his forces ransacked Yinchuan and in doing so slaughtered almost the entire Tangut population.

To see the Xi Xia tombs, which are the last remnants of the Tangut civilisation, we hired a local guide with a 4x4 as both the tombs and the pagodas were about 20km away from the city and the roads were covered in ice. After our journey to Yinchuan, we were in absolutely no mood to take any chances with public transport and had not found a single taxi driver willing to venture so far out of the city. So, we ignored the cost and opted to travel in heated comfort.

Each of the tombs was built in the form of a small uneven pyramid, about 20m high, fashioned from the surrounding earth. Most were dusted with a gentle covering of snow and the areas surrounding them were carpeted in crisp winter white. As the whole area was pretty much deserted, everything was deathly silent. The only real noise came from our boots crushing the previously unspoiled snow underfoot. It all felt very ghostly. It was an interesting feeling and, as we walked back to the car, Ossie and I debated why it felt like it did. Was it just because we were miles from nowhere and the ground was covered in virginal snow? Or, was there a macabre presence hanging over the place?

After the tombs, we sat in the 4x4 enjoying a sachet of Nescafe coffee made with hot water from our driver's flask - we were a long way from the closest decent latte - to warm our frozen bones. We then drove for 30 minutes across the frozen plain in the direction of the Helen Shan mountains, which separate Yinchuan from the Gobi desert to the north. It was a bleak and featureless panorama in which we saw not another vehicle for miles. We cut through the frozen plain in the direction of the mountains at the foot of which we would find the pagodas.

The Pagodas of Baizakou are a truly fantastic visual spectacle, albeit not much of a historical one. They really looked genuinely stunning. The photos I took that day are some of the most impressive from any of my travels around the world. The pagodas were both about 50m high and 2m or so wide. They were decorated with bright tiles and ornate little carvings. The gravelly slopes of the Helen Shan, which were bereft of any plants or greenery, loomed up over the turquoise tiles and decorations to create a fabulous juxtaposition of harsh deadened landscape and bright delicate architecture.

As beautiful as the pagodas were, and they really do take your breath away, there was almost nothing to learn in terms of history. At the time, Lonely Planet had precious little to say about them and my subsequent research also found little of note aside from the fact that they were 13 and 14 storeys respectively and were built in the late Xi Xia period. So, with some impressive photos stored on the memory card in my camera but minimal new information learned, we made our way back to the city.

We departed Yinchuan the next day on the morning train to Beijing. We were kind of retracing our steps but, as Ningxia is so far north, it didn't have too many trains heading south whereas getting to the capital would be quite easy. We planned to stop off briefly to grab a few beers and get our laundry done at our hotel. After that, we would head south to Nanjing, Shanghai and Hangzhou. Thankfully, as our train to Beijing was heading east and with the Spring Festival holiday behind us, the journey would prove to be a simple one, albeit taking a lengthy 19 hours.

Even though the final hours of the trip would drag - 19 hours on a plain bunk in an open carriage can be quite dull - it started hilariously. The train was one of the more rural green versions that tend to i) be cheaper, and ii) serve some of the smaller cities in the country. Whereas our train to Xi'an had cabins, the one from Yinchuan was much more open and had a far more communal feel. There was precious little privacy. This meant that the two *laowai* (Mandarin for 'foreigner') got plenty of attention. I seemed to garner the most of this and also created quite a bit of mirth amongst the Ningxians.

As we waited for the train to depart, Ossie went in search of a toilet and I sat cross-legged on my bunk reading Lonely Planet and boning up on what we might find in Nanjing. As I did so, I noticed a large crowd beginning to form in the corridor adjacent to our compartment. They were all peering intently at me as foreigners clearly weren't always a particularly common sight in Ningxia. In fact, during our time in Yinchuan, we had seen no other westerners. However, the attention I was getting seemed to be a little more intense than the usual whispered "hello" that we had experienced in Beijing and Xian. So, I glanced up, nodded and said "Ni Hao". This met a hushed silence, until a middle-aged man shouted - at an uncomfortably loud volume - "Buddha"! With others following suit, "Laowai Buddha". It appeared my shaved head and body language was a big hit.

The Yangtze: Shanghai and Nanjing

To get to the central part of China's east coast, we took a train from Beijing to Shanghai. However, as I had visited the city just a few months before, we decided to use it mare as a jumping off point to explore the surrounding region rather than a destination in itself. Before we jumped on a train to Nanjing though, we did have one thing that we really wanted to do in China's business capital: Take a boat trip.

As the city is located on a bend on a river, there were plenty of opportunities to get out on the water. The majority of these tended to be short affairs on the Huangpu with small boats doing circuits that took in the colonial splendour of the Bund and the modern skyscrapers of Pudong on the opposite bank. I am sure those would have been nice and would have afforded the opportunity to take some amazing photos, but we had our eyes on something more dramatic.

When I was in China the previous year, I had seen publicity for a river cruise that went from central Shanghai along the Huangpu to the point where it flowed into the Yangtze. It sounded amazing and conjured up some very evocative images of one of the world's great rivers. The Yangtze emerges into the Yellow Sea to the north of Shanghai after undertaking an epic journey through the southern half of the country. It rises deep in the mountains of Tibet before winding its way through the southwest - including through the mega-metropolis of Chongqing - before heading gradually northeast towards the dense population centres on the east coast.

On a cold and wet Tuesday morning, we walked down the gangway of a small boat that, for some reason, was decorated to look like a paddle steamer on the Mississippi. After casting off, we got a fabulous view of the delights of Shanghai. The city certainly looked amazing from street level, but being on the river gave a whole different physical perspective. The old British buildings on the Bund looked much more imposing as we stared almost directly up at them. On the other side, the skyscrapers in Pudong towered away and gave us a pain in our necks as we strained to look up almost vertically at them.

We took plenty of amazing pictures in the first few minutes of the journey and felt that we had seen something magnificent. However, things quickly got far less exciting. Within one kilometer, the amazing sights of central Shanghai gave way to a far more industrial landscape. The banks of the river were soon taken up by dock areas full of barges and small container ships that were bringing in raw materials and taking away finished goods as part of China's huge export trade. It was not much of a spectacle. We had been hoping to see some slightly more rural scenery and to get a glimpse of a bit of nature. We were to be massively disappointed. The journey to the Yangtze took just under three hours at no point did the industrial feel to the landscape give way. We simply sat and played cards waiting in vain for things to change. If nothing else, it painted a stark picture of China's manufacturing might.

Many of the pictures or videos of the Yangtze that I had seen were of tree-covered mountains dropping down to beautiful green water. As we neared the mouth of the Huangpo, we began to understand that these were from areas far inland and that we would be experiencing nothing of the sort. The water in the final few kilometers was a sickly brown colour and the left bank was dominated by a series of slightly rusty looking Chinese naval vessels. Once we passed these, the banks seemed to melt away and the waters of the Yangtze asserted themselves. It was a huge expanse of water, so much so that we could see nothing on the far side. Instead our view was dominated by hundreds of container ships moving east to the sea and west to ports inland such as Nanjing where we would be heading the next afternoon.

After our brief trip to Shanghai, we bought tickets to Nanjing, a four or five hour ride to the northwest. Our main plan was to see the Nanjing Memorial, which commemorates the period in the 1930s during which the occupying Japanese forces ran amok in an orgy of violence that became known as Rape of Nanjing. We rolled into Nanjing station in the early evening and checked into a hostel that we had booked online whilst in Beijing. Just as with our bus ride to Yinchuan a few days earlier, we should have seen the warning signs. When we lugged our backpacks into the lobby, we were greeted by a young woman wearing a hat, gloves and an overcoat. It really should have been a clue. Sadly, we failed to take note and soon found that our room was bitterly cold. The windows were single delicate pieces of glass and there was a huge hole in an outside wall at the side of the air-conditioning pipe. We pondered the idea of looking for somewhere else. However, a quick glance at Lonely Planet - this was pre Google Maps, remember - revealed no budget options anywhere close to us. So, we decided to put up with it for one night and to minimise the impact of the cold by going out and getting nicely beered up.

Putting away several bottles of Yanjing beer helped us cope with the cold. It also meant that we were a tad groggy as we jumped into a taxi and made our way to the memorial the following morning. However, it really didn't take long for us to be feeling horrifically sober. Prior to visiting Nanjing, the majority of memorials that I had visited - mainly for WWI or WWII - had always been sober and understated affairs. The Chinese though, had taken a far more direct and blunt approach to dealing with events in Nanjing. I had never really seen anywhere that put the horror and suffering of war so bluntly and directly in front of you. It was jarring and disturbing but also delivered supremely unfiltered reality.

The first jolt to the system came as we entered the main courtyard. Emblazoned across the main wall in giant concrete lettering was the number 300,000. This referred to the number of people thought to have been killed between December 1937 and January 1938. (The figure is the number provided by the Chinese government and primary sources from the time. The International Military Tribunal held in Tokyo in 1946 put the number at 200,000, but the Japanese still, to their detriment, put it far lower). It was a bare statistic, but it got the message across profoundly. However, it was nothing compared to what we encountered when we stepped inside.

The first major room inside the memorial stopped us in our tracks and left us sick to the stomach. We found what was, essentially, a giant collection of bones. The room was presented as though we were walking through an exposed burial ground. There was earth - and the bones contained within - up to around chest height on either side behind glass walls. There were, quite literally, tens of thousands of bones. They filled our field of vision and gave us simply nowhere else to look. The sheer scale and volume was certainly disconcerting, but perhaps most disturbing was the subtle detail of the exhibit. On each bone, there was a small pastel coloured ribbon. I forget what the actual colour scheme was, but the use of delicate yellow and pink was a jarring juxtaposition to what they represented. Each colour stood for a differentiation in age or gender. The different shades showed that men, women and children were all heavily represented, but the quantity of kids' remains was horrific.

The bone room was sobering and a little frightening. It had an almost hypnotic effect and we found it very difficult to drag ourselves away and to head into the main body of the museum. When we did, we again faced a full-on assault to our senses. Whereas the bones were a brutal yet simple view into the tragedy, the museum emphasised the brutality by delving into graphic detail. There were a huge amount of photos, videos and testimonies of the atrocities. They all told terrible stories of rape and killing. We saw photos of mass beheadings and rows of severed heads lined up on a wall. We read testimony from western diplomats and medical workers who saw women and children raped and then bayoneted by Japanese soldiers. We watched videos of bodies being flung lifelessly into large pits. It was all horrific and made for one of the most chastening afternoons of my life.

As we rather solemnly made for the exit, I noticed a small panel on the wall containing a quote - from whom I cannot recall - that brought a tear to my eye. The exact wording escapes me, but it went something along the following lines: "The tragedy of Nanjing was that not only were so many people killed, but also that they died in such appalling and humiliating fashion"

The trip to the memorial really knocked the wind out of our sails. We spent the rest of our afternoon ambling around the city centre and a couple of parks on the outskirts with no great direction or purpose. To drag ourselves out of our malaise, we decided to do a couple of things. First, we opted to collect our bags from the freezing confines of our hostel and find a nicer place to stay. And, second, we made plans to go to a hotpot restaurant for a super spicy dinner that we intended to wash down with more Yanjing beer. It would prove to be an eventful evening.

We managed to find a reasonably priced business hotel a couple of kilometres from the frigid hostel - more on the significance of that later - and then headed out on the tiles. It didn't take us long to find a restaurant serving something we were really keen to try and which we quickly termed yin and yang hotpot. This was a metal pot, split in half like the aforementioned Buddhist symbol with half containing a spicy red liquid infused with chilies and the other holding a simple vegetable broth. Feeling hungry after a long day, we sat down ready to eat. Unfortunately, though, we soon realised that we faced a bit of a problem. The menu was only in Chinese.

If you were to visit a major Chinese city today, it is unlikely you would be unable to find an English menu or at the very least a menu with pictures. However, back in 2006 it was a very common problem. To fix this, we decided that our best option was to take a very physical and also interactive approach. We stood up, grabbed our waiter by the arm and started to take a tour of all the tables in the restaurant. We looked at everybody's pots and started pointing at the foods we thought would be good for our own.

I found the whole passage not only fascinating but also a lot of fun. Had the roles been reversed, a Chinese person pointing at my food in an English restaurant, I would not have been at all impressed by the intrusion. The Chinese, on the other hand, seemed to welcome it! Several families invited us to their tables and showed us what they were eating. It was fantastic and felt very communal. There were lots of delicious looking things that we told the waiter to add to our order, but a few others that looked a tad odd and we thought - like the testicles in Beijing - were best avoided.

The upshot of our little tour was that i) we got a fantastic array of food, and ii) everyone was very interested in whether or not we were enjoying our meal. We were. It was fantastic. The red hot half of the pot was super spicy but really tasty. I love food with a bit of a kick, and I really love food with a bit of kick washed down with cold beer. So, things were looking good. However, under the watchful gaze of our fellow diners, I probably got a bit overconfident and neglected the calmer side of the pot. This was an oversight I would come to regret a few hours later.

After dinner, we popped a few more beers away before making our way back to the hotel. We were planning to turn in, but before I could grab my pyjamas I found myself facing a little bit of gastric discomfort. With undisguised haste, I made for the bathroom … where I lost the contents of my bowels rather quickly and, not to be too blunt, rather explosively. As I sat there, I began to regret paying so little attention to the milder side of our meal, which might have helped to calm things down

As mentioned earlier, we were staying at a "business hotel". We didn't really understand at the time, but this term doesn't always mean the same thing in China as it does in the UK. In China, particularly at the time we visited, "business" hotels were synonymous not only with accommodation for guys travelling for work … but also with sex work. Over the subsequent four years in which I lived in China, I would often stay at such hotels - for work; not for sex tourism - and would regularly find cards on the coffee table offering 'special massage'. This was the environment Ossie and I had unintentionally entered. When we checked in, things had seemed fine. But, as I sat rather gingerly on the toilet, we began to experience the seedy side of our accommodation.

Whilst I was befowling the bathroom, Ossie was sitting on his bed reading Lonely Planet - and I presume holding his nose. However, his reading was interrupted by a phone call. Apparently, on the other end of the line was a young Chinese lady. At first there was a distinct lack of communication as Ossie's Chinese was pretty rudimentary and the girl didn't speak much English. Consequently, things didn't move on so easily. However, she managed to get her point across by dropping what was presumably one of her few English phrases: "Make love". Ossie seemed pretty freaked out by this, so he hung up the phone. Five minutes later, though, we got a knock at the door. As I was still indisposed, Ossie answered and was greeted by a young Chinese woman. The offer of 'love' was again made and again declined. When I finally managed to escape the bathroom and gingerly make my way back to my bed, Ossie informed me that the girl had left our door with a look of pure disgust at the smell emanating from the bathroom.

Our trip to Nanjing had a certain comic element to it in parts and so too did our departure from the city, even though it was also slightly disconcerting. We left for Hangzhou - a four hour train ride away - in the early afternoon. We arrived at the station nice and early. Again, unfortunately, any notion of enjoying a nice cold beer or a coffee before we got on the train was dispelled by a giant crowd waiting at the front of the station and a similar throng in the main waiting area. So, to kill time before we got on the train, we dropped our rucksacks on the ground to use as seats and started to play cards.

During our travels, we had been playing a series of games of rummy - which, to my frustration, Ossie generally won. So, with half an hour to kill, we thought it would be cool to continue the duel. Much to my dismay, Ossie won again. When we were done, we packed up the cards and got ready to jump on the train. At that point, I casually glanced up and noticed that we were not alone. In fact, we were surrounded by a crowd of around 50 Chinese men staring at us. It was a freaky and disconcerting experience. When I looked up, I made eye-contact with a few of them who just stared rather blankly at us. It took me a couple of seconds, but I managed to realise that they were trying to figure out what kind of game we were playing. With no way to explain the rules in detail, we just sheepishly grinned at them all before we rather awkwardly picked up our bags, slid them on our backs and headed for our platform.

Hangzhou
Nanjing had been a fascinating place to visit, but we still had plenty to see in the central area of China's east coast. Next on the list was the ancient city of Hangzhou. As we boarded the train, we reflected that aside from the troubles we had faced in being able to get train tickets,

our explorations across China had gone unbelievably well. We had seen some genuinely awe-inspiring sights, had some cool adventures and met lots of interesting people. Sadly, our luck did not hold for the last leg of our journey as things ended in something of a damp squib, quite literally, in Hangzhou.

As the journey was not so long, we took soft seats from Nanjing to Hangzhou. On the train, as we had been accustomed to, we quickly became the centre of attention. Nobody was calling me Buddha this time, but lots of our fellow passengers were really keen to say hello and ask us questions. At first, this was all good fun and we enjoyed engaging with local people as we had throughout our travels. However, on this occasion things went beyond friendly conversation as it just didn't stop and the questions got less and less conversational and more and more like an interrogation. After a few gentle openers, we got:

"How much do you earn?" (None of your business)

"How old are you?" (26. Again, though, none of your business)

"Why don't you have any hair?" (Not sure how to answer that, but it is really not a nice question to ask!)

"What is the average salary for a worker in England?" (I am not sure how to answer that. We don't really call people 'workers' in England like you do in China. Salaries differ from job to job)

"How much is a kilogram of rice in England?" (Errr, I have no idea as I don't ever cook rice)

"How many people live in your apartment?" (I am travelling at the moment, so I don't have apartment)

"At what age do people stop work in England?" (65, but I am not sure why you need to know that)

"Do you know David Beckham?" (No! For God's sake)

By the time we neared Hangzhou, we had really had enough of the inquisition and were desperate to get a bit of peace and quiet. So, when we pulled into a station where we saw the Chinese characters for Hangzhou, we jumped off with a sense of relief. That emotion was short-lived though as: i) Almost as soon as we left the station it began to rain, and ii) When we emerged onto a quiet suburban street rather than a large urban square as is the norm outside major Chinese train stations, we quickly began to realise that we had alighted from the train at the wrong station - rather than the main station, we were at a much smaller one in the outskirts of the city. As the rain softened the pages of our Lonely Planet whilst we tried to figure out where the hell we were and how on earth we could get to our hotel, we decided that our only option was to jump in a taxi and hope that a) The driver could find our hotel, and b) It wouldn't be too expensive.

The taxi wound up costing significantly more than the train tickets. This pissed us off quite a bit on its own, but things got really bad when we realised that the address we had for our hotel - copied from the website we had booked on - might not have been correct. The taxi driver assured us that we were in the location that we had given him, but there was simply nothing there. Not a single building. All we could see were trees and some street lights. We trudged a few hundred metres in one direction and then back in the other but found nothing. By this point, the rain was pounding and we were soaked to the bone. So, we felt that there was nothing else for it but to jump back in the cab and look for alternative accommodation.

By the time we had checked into an overpriced and decidedly uninspiring tourist hotel, it was getting late and we were ravenous. Unfortunately, the rain was still falling pretty heavily, so we were not so keen to venture too far for fear of getting soaked again. This meant our dining options were sparse at best. We had wanted to eat local food, but every Chinese restaurant that we found was closed - it is not uncommon for restaurants in China to be shuttered by 21h00. The only places we could find were Pizza Hut and McDonalds. Neither of us were keen on either option, but we had no other choice than to sit and eat bad pizza whilst hoping that the weather would get better in the morning.

Things didn't get better. We woke to a thick blanket of cloud shrouding the city with the rain falling as a heavy mist. Visibility could not have been more than 40 or 50m. This was a huge issue as Hangzhou is a city in which you need to be able to get a good view. The city's main attraction is the West Lake, a giant freshwater lake that is ringed by mountains on three sides and is crowned by some beautiful causeways, bridges and pagodas. It is a fantastic place to put your camera on panorama mode … or at least that is what I am told.

With the clouds hanging low over the city, we could scarcely see 40m across the lake, let alone to any of the mountains in the distance or the pagodas on the far banks. We walked along the western edge of the lake hoping that as the day wore on the skies would clear. They didn't. So, after two hours of fruitless wandering, during which we got unbelievably wet, we decided that our sight-seeing cause was lost. Feeling drenched and unmotivated, we sat down in a restaurant to have a spot of lunch. Whilst we ate, one of the waiters told us that lots of tourists liked to spend time out on the lake by renting a boat. Obviously, the weather was not ideal but we figured that a boat might allow us to get a better taste of the lake.

We had visions of striking out into the water in a solid and sturdy rowing boat. As the lake was 2.7km wide, we felt that getting a long way out into the water to see a bit more was not an unrealistic proposition. Yet again, we were to be disappointed. There were no rowing boats. All we were able to find was a small battery powered craft that was, if we were honest with ourselves, designed for kids. It was tiny, but we hoped it might be able to ferry us a good distance out into the water. Alas, we were wrong. The boat had a maximum speed that was significantly less than walking pace. To make things even worse, almost as soon as we had cast off we discovered a series of small buoys connected by thick ropes barring us from going more than 50m into the lake.

After pottering around the banks of the lake for a few minutes and being overtaken by elderly Chinese couples and mothers pushing infants, we decided that it really was time for us to call it a day and give up on Hangzhou. As I was just a few days away from having to say goodbye to my buddy and start my new job, Hangzhou would be our last stop. It felt sad to end the trip in such circumstances, but we had enjoyed our travels immensely.

DAWUFENG

Teaching in Korea had been, in many ways, a massive challenge for me. It was my first time working with kids and Mr. Kim gave me precious little training. I also had to worry about four year olds trying to stick their fingers up my bum! However, in others, it had been a bit of a cakewalk as I was well paid, the school was modern and the kids were used to working with a foreign teacher. Therefore, when I started looking for work in China, I decided that I wanted a change of pace, something that would be more of an experience. So, I took a job in a small town on the outskirts of Tianjin - a metropolis around 80km southeast of Beijing with a population of around 12million and, purely coincidentally, the city where I had arrived with Alana a few months before. It would prove to most definitely be an 'experience'.

The town in which I would work was called Dawufeng. It was located on a highway between downtown Tianjin and the port town of Tanggu, which was one of the biggest transport and logistics hubs in northern China and the place where the ferry from Korea had deposited me 6 months or so before. Dawufeng was a very industrial little town. There were a variety of factories surrounding the town, but it was dominated by a giant production plant that churned out gigantic oil and gas pipes.

Tianjin Pipe Corporation was first formed in the 1980s as part of Deng Xiaoping's Eighth Five Year Plan through which the country was tentatively beginning to get involved in international commerce. However, in the 1990s as China opened itself to trade with the west, it began to operate quasi-privately. Unlike many formerly state-owned corporations, which were often mired in corruption and inefficiency, it was doing rather well. In fact, it was doing so well that it employed more than half the people who lived in Dawufeng.

Whilst TPCO was a very modern facility, the town of Dawufeng was anything but. The vast majority of the buildings - including the apartment block in which I lived and the school at which I worked - were built in the late 80s and early 90s in conjunction with the development of the pipe factory. They epitomised everything that was wrong with Communist architecture, design and construction. They were all made of brutish grey concrete and, despite being barely 15 years old, were dilapidated and crumbling.

I arrived in Dawufeng on a cold and misty Tuesday evening. The agency who had arranged my employment sent a driver to collect me from the bus station - I had taken a bus from Beijing, the opposite service to the one Alana and I had taken a few months earlier - and to take me to my new apartment. Unlike my arrival in Korea, there was no comfortable sedan and no western music on the stereo. The car was a cold and rickety Chinese-made rust bucket. The driver seemed friendly enough but spoke very little English and chain smoked from the moment we got into the car until we reached Dawufeng. As the car was a product of Communist industry, we did not really get much speed up. So, the journey was not a quick one.

It was still light when I climbed into the car. However, as we clanked and crunched our way through a series of anonymous suburban sidestreets in the direction of the highway, the last embers of daylight disappeared. As we dropped onto the highway, I was grateful that the new-found darkness provided a small degree of cover from the terror-inducing driving habits on show. The majority of the traffic was made up of giant trucks heading towards the port in Tanggu. Their drivers seemed to pay scant attention to either traffic laws or basic road safety as they careered along at frightening pace whilst weaving indiscriminately between lanes. As the car into which I was crammed had the structural integrity of a rusty tin can, I was left wincing and praying for the journey to end.

When we pulled off the highway, I breathed a huge sigh of relief. However, once I had finished counting my blessings and feeling grateful that I had survived the journey to Dawufeng intact, I quickly wanted to see what my new hometown would be like. Disappointingly, as there were very few street lights - or, more accurately, few working street lights - I was left peering into blackness to try to make out any details of the town. When we pulled into the courtyard of the apartment block in which I would be living, it was still shrouded in darkness. There was no lighting in the courtyard; the only illumination came from lights in the apartments above. To get inside and up the stairs, the driver had to take out a torch and guide us slowly up four flights of darkened stairs - there was no lift - until we reached a giant and rather rusty steel door.

My new apartment showed me that if I was looking for a major challenge, I had certainly found one. The apartment Mr. Kim had provided me in Korea was by no means luxurious as it was metallic and very badly insulated which meant that it was swelteringly hot in the summer and bitingly cold in the winter. However, despite those obvious shortcomings, compared to what I discovered in Dawufeng it was positively palatial. Prior to the trip, my recruiter had told me that they had found me one of the nicest apartments in town. It was not nice. Not nice at all. Either my recruiter had been rather economical with the truth in order to get me on board, or the accommodation options in town really were terrible.

In all honesty, Chinese recruiters are never famed for their honesty and transparency. The situation in China was like that in Korea in terms of supply and demand of teachers, but on a far bigger scale. There are, literally, thousands of schools in China that want English teachers and a relatively small supply of foreigners wanting to come to China - particularly to places outside of Beijing and Shanghai. On top of this, there is also the financial issue. Schools in Korea - and also Japan and Taiwan - offered far higher salaries, which meant teachers were far less likely to head where salaries were very low. Therefore, Chinese recruiters will often lie, cheat and deceive in order to get teachers in. However, based on what I would see in Dawufeng in the subsequent weeks, on this occasion, he was probably telling the truth. When the driver opened the door, I was greeted by a dirty and frighteningly basic home. It looked like something you would expect to find in the UK in the 1970s.

At School in Dawufeng

Settling into my apartment had given me a very clear picture of what I would be dealing with in Dawufeng. But, I got a fuller glimpse into the town and its rather bitter reality when I made my way to work the next day. The school was a short walk - over a small industrial wasteland - from my apartment. It looked like a prison. The exterior had a solid concrete face punctuated with a series of very small windows and the doors were covered with large metal bars. Inside, the institutional feel continued. The corridors were also plain concrete, painted the palest and most sterile of greens, and smelled vaguely of disinfectant. It really didn't feel like a place that would stimulate young minds! Quite soberingly as well, there was a painting of Chairman Mao and a surprisingly well-stocked selection of Communist flags in the lobby.

The teachers' room for the English department, which I would share with four colleagues, felt like something from the 1950s. It was a big shock compared to what I had experienced in Korea. Back in Taean, we had computers and comfy sofas, and the team - Mr Kim excepted - spoke great English. In Dawufeng, we had cheap wooden desks and rickety wooden chairs. There were no computers - the school was not even connected to the internet - no TV or radio and just one internal phone line. Of the four teachers in the team, only one of them actually spoke any English.

The lack of tech in the school was not a great surprise. Dawufeng was a very poor town - which was something I knew before arriving there - so I was not expecting too much. I was pretty clear when I took the job that I would be working with old school blackboard and chalk rather than interactive whiteboards and computer software. However, it was a major shock to find that I would not be able to communicate with the majority of my colleagues. As a consequence, neither on that first day nor in the subsequent three months did I really manage to get to know any of them very well - there would be no team nights out to the sauna or the karaoke room!

Mrs Li, who was the most vocal of the teachers, did speak decent albeit heavily accented English. So, at first, I thought I might be able to get to know her a little. However, this was not to be. As she rarely got the opportunity to speak to an actual English speaker, she was keener to practice her language skills than to actually get to know me. Just as on the train to Hangzhou, conversation wasn't really a two-way process. Rather, she either bombarded me with questions or jumped into monologues where she could practice specific vocabulary.

"Where is your hometown?" (Sheffield)

"What is the primary industry there?" (Err, traditionally steel, but not so much anymore)

"What is the salary of an average worker?" (I really have no idea)

"How much does it cost to rent an apartment?" (I don't know, maybe £500)

"Oh, so expensive. I imagine people earn much money there. Here we do not. My salary is only Y1,500 per month. I think that is less than £200. But, here the cost of living is lower. You can buy a kilo of rice for Y30. How much is a kilo of rice in Sheffield?" (I really have no idea)

Once the questions about Sheffield and the UK had been exhausted, she would switch to her favourite subject, money.

"How much do you earn?" (Errr, well, in England it is not polite to talk about money)

"Ok, I see. Do you know how much I earn?" (Yes, you told me)

"Ok, do you earn more than me? (Like I said, we don't really like to talk about money in England)

"Ok, sorry. Where do you live in Dawufeng?" (The school has rented me an apartment)

"Ah. How many rooms? Do you have a washing machine? Do you have a TV? Do you have a rice cooker?" (Two bedrooms. Yes, there is a washing machine. Yes, there is a TV but it is very old. No, there is no rice cooker)

"You have two bedrooms and you are single?" (Yes)

"Oh wow. You are very lucky. My apartment has one bedroom but I live there with my husband, my son and my husband's parents" (Ok, right)

I didn't know what to say about the apartment. I felt bad that I considered the apartment the recruiter had organised for me to be awful when Mrs. Li was clearly living in far worse conditions. I also felt bad because I was, to all intents and purposes, viewing my job in Dawufeng as charity work because the salary was so low, yet I earned three times my colleague's salary. 'First World Privilege' wasn't really a phrase used at the time, but it probably best described the situation.

With all that in mind, it didn't feel like it was too much of an ask to devote a bit of time to allowing her to practice her language skills. But, yikes, it felt so intrusive! One small mercy in the teachers' room was that my recruiter provided me with an assistant/translator. These usually changed from one week to the next, so I never really got to know too many of them but at least I had someone to talk to.

Once I was over the initial shock of being part of an English department where almost nobody spoke any English, I thought I ought to ask a pretty pertinent question: "How on earth do they teach English if they cannot speak a word?" I thought that was a sensible thing to wonder. Apparently, though, the situation was a really common one in China as there was a huge lack of English-speaking teachers. Anyone in China who spoke decent English was much more likely to be attracted to a job in the business sector where language skills were also at a premium but salaries were much higher than that of a teacher in a small town. Therefore, the kids had to 'learn' by chanting English words read to them by an English teacher who could neither understand nor pronounce the vocabulary in question.

Because of this situation, the kids in Dawufeng were i) very eager to see me, but also ii) kind of freaked out by the giant bald *laowai* who had just walked into their lives. In Korea, I was something of a novelty, but the kids had taken classes with a foreigner a few weeks before I arrived and foreigners were a relatively common sight in Korea, even somewhere as small as Taean. In a small Chinese town like Dawufeng, my arrival was akin to an alien casually ambling into their lives and starting to teach them some basic vocabulary.

My first week of classes was a whole lot of fun, but also proved to be very hard work. In Korea, I was used to having small classes with less than twelve kids in a classroom that was brightly decorated and equipped with a PC and TV. All the kids had modern American textbooks and even mini computer dictionaries. China was a different story. The smallest of my classes had 37 kids. Almost all of the classes had at least 40 students and some of them had over 50 kids. The facilities were also very basic. The rooms had bare concrete floors and walls, with just a large desk and blackboard at the front. The kids didn't have books. Instead, we had a more extreme version of Mr Kim's Magic Foreigner Syndrome. In Korea, at least Mr Kim gave me books and resources; the Chinese were hoping I would get 50 kids speaking English with just a piece of chalk. I was, quite literally, left totally to my own devices. There was no direction, no syllabus, no objectives.

Despite the paucity of equipment or any guidance whatsoever on what the school wanted me to do with the kids, the first week was great. The majority of classes were just introductions. With the help of my assistant, I taught some basic greetings such as "Hello" or "Nice to meet you". It was super fun. I must have said 'hello' to almost 1,000 kids. Some of them were crazy excited to meet their new teacher and were almost screaming, "Nice to meet you!!!". Others seemed almost petrified and refused to make eye-contact. They just stared at their shoes and tried to mumble their hellos.

The majority of those early classes went really well. However, there was one that really did not go to plan and still sticks with me today. I will attempt to get my defence in early by establishing a couple of important facts before I recount the story: i) Instead of a formal school uniforms, Chinese children usually wear cheap tracksuits that are all identical and, ii) Many Chinese kids, even girls, often sport short and rather utilitarian hair-cuts. In short, I don't want to generalise, but many Chinese kids do not look hugely dissimilar. Those points notwithstanding, I still deeply regret the unfortunate - and I must admit, in a way, rather humorous - incident.

It was a secondary school class with kids of around 12 or 13 years of age. My assistant and I were assigning English names to the kids - just as in Korea, a hugely common practice in China - before doing some introductions. I had taken a rather binary approach by writing a list of boys' names in blue chalk and a list of girls' names in a shade of red chalk that looked kind of pink. Things started off swimmingly and we had got 30 students in when I invited a large and heavy-set young person to the board to choose a name. Based purely on body shape - which I concede was ignorant on my part - I ushered the child to the names in blue. As I stood waiting, I heard a mumbled, "I'm a girl" and the young lady shuffled over to the names in pink. The rest of the class burst into raucous laughter at their new teacher mistaking a female student for a male one. I went pretty red in the face and the girl seemed close to tears. I wanted the ground to swallow me up.

The first few weeks of teaching in Dawufeng were crazy. I did some introductions and then tried some basic stuff like age/numbers, hobbies, jobs or food. As fun as this was, for the most part it was almost impossible for me to get beyond the excitement - and in some cases nervousness - about the *laowai* who had come into their lives. No matter how much I tried to focus on a lesson plan or keep the kids on a specific track. All they wanted to do was play and shout, "Hello". Despite my best efforts, we didn't get very far.

I probably shouldn't have been too surprised at the reaction I got in the classroom as not just the kids but the entire town was slightly mesmerised by my presence. This was made clear at the end of each school day. After finishing a hard shift at the coal face, I would usually leave through the same door as the kids. Without fail, as my bald head emerged from the door, the parents and grandparents who were waiting for their kids would halt their conversations and stare intently at me as I emerged from the school and walked towards them. It was freaky. My appearance was enough to render a crowd of forty or fifty people collectively mute. The occasional old lady might whisper "hello", but generally I managed to generate an eerie silence when I appeared.

There was one particular occasion that epitomized this situation perfectly. As I walked to school one bright Wednesday morning, I bumped into Amy, one of the better students in one of my junior school classes. She already spoke some English before I arrived at the school - her aunt worked in a company where she spoke English regularly and had taught Amy a bit of language - and always wanted to chat. She was walking with her mother eating something from a paper bag. I asked her, "Amy what are you eating?" She looked down curiously at her hands, clearly not sure what to call the snack she was holding. She thought about it for a while and said, "Breakfast". I smiled and responded quickly, "I know, but what is it?' She smiled to herself and gently shook her head to show she didn't know the word. I told her that in England we called it a 'wrap'.

I always loved to talk to my students outside the classroom. It is something I still do today whenever I get the opportunity. So, for me, the interaction was totally normal. Amy didn't seem to be too flustered to be chatting to her teacher in the street either. Her mother, on the other hand, looked as though she had been turned to stone. She simply stood and stared at us in disbelief like she was witnessing a murder or seeing Chairman Mao come back from the dead. To try and ease the awkwardness, I smiled at her and went for a polite "Ni hao", but I didn't really succeed. She tried to smile back but managed only an uncomfortable grimace.

One of the things I had loved about working in Korea was getting to know the kids and getting an insight into their daily lives. It was great to talk to them in and out of class, to go with them on trips and to understand what made them tick. Naturally, I wanted to do something similar in China. My first step in doing this was to ask some basic questions in class about subjects like parents' jobs and favourite foods. In no way was I expecting the kind of blunt picture of life in China that I got. Even though Korea is not a country renowned for flair or individuality, I still managed to get plenty of different answers. In China, on the other hand, I was shocked at the violently flat uniformity of the answers I received to almost every question.

One class that always gave me lots of fun answers in Korea was when I covered food. When I did this in Taean, I always got one clear answer first: "My favorite food is Kimchi" (A fermented cabbage dish that Koreans eat with almost every meal). For Koreans, this was almost like a pledge of national allegiance. However, after we had got that one out of the way, the kids talked about loads of different foods. They liked burgers, ice-cream, fried chicken and pizza! In China, because Dawufeng was not a well-off town, I was not expecting such diversity. Nevertheless, I started class by drawing a few different foods on the board in chalk. I put up sketches of burgers, pizza and chicken legs. I needn't have wasted my time or effort. Out of a class of 50, I got only two answers when I asked about favorite foods: rice or dumplings. .

I encountered a similar albeit also slightly disconcerting situation when we tried to teach jobs. In Korea, even though Taean was a small fishing town, I still got a lot of variety in the answers I received. As you might expect for a coastal town, there were plenty of dad's who worked in the fishing industry. In fact, it was pretty common for kids to bring in trays of seafood as a gift for the teachers. However, there were lots of other jobs on show too. I had plenty of kids whose dads were police officers or soldiers, I had a few whose dads were farmers and a few whose dads were bank managers or office workers. As a quick caveat to this, I don't wish to appear sexist as I also asked what their mums did but invariably got the answer, "housewife".

Upon starting a similar class in China, I sketched a few pictures of different jobs - doctor, nurse, teacher etc - on the blackboard along with the spelling and had my assistant write the word in Chinese next to them. Just as with the food, I needn't have bothered with such variety. In almost every class, I got only one answer from 95% of the kids: "My father is a worker". To a degree, this response might have reflected the kids limited linguistic ability. The vast majority were beginning English from scratch, so "He works manufacturing seamless oil pipelines" was probably a bit of a stretch for them. However, it also said a lot about Dawufeng and also about China on a wider scale. In 2006, China was growing like crazy and that growth was based heavily on cheap labour. Therefore, the majority of the country's labour force did basic manufacturing jobs.

With some of my groups I also did classes on colour. Again, the Chinese students showed a remarkable degree of uniformity in their answers. However, compared to jobs and food, this one was far more sinister. In Korea, there were always lots of answers when I asked about favorite colours. Most commonly, I got blue for boys and pink for girls but there were plenty of others. In China, things were different … very different. There was generally only one answer, regardless of gender. Everybody liked red. Perhaps that shouldn't have been too much of a surprise as China is a Communist country - it was, after all, known as 'Red China' back in the 50s and 60s - but it felt quite shocking nonetheless.

The element that struck me with greatest ferocity was the fact that the kids weren't really thinking for themselves in the choice of their own favourite colour. In Korea, the kids often liked a particular colour because of a cartoon character, such as pink because of Hello Kitty or blue because of Astro Boy. There was certainly never a political element to their answers as was the case in China. To put this into context, in Korea the classrooms were painted in bright pastel colours whereas in Dawufeng they were just bare concrete with the only splash of colour coming from the Chinese national flag or the flag of the Communist party. On top of this, if a child did well in class, they were rewarded with a red kerchief to tie around their upper arm. Essentially, the kids were being bludgeoned, bullied and indoctrinated. If the only colour in your life was the red that was forced upon you, what other colour were they likely to like? It all seemed bizarrely Stalinist to me and saddened me immensely. I could kind of get my head around the idea of having that type of scenario with adults. If the only colour in an office or factory was the red flag it would not make for a great environment but at least adults could maybe make their own decisions. But, for kids, it felt dirty. They didn't know any better!

As I explained at the start of the book, I made the decision to move to

Korea not so much because I saw teaching as a great vocation but because I saw it as a means to an end that would provide the opportunity to see an 'exotic' country and get paid whilst doing so. Despite this, as I detailed in the first section of the book, teaching the kids there was a fabulous experience that I genuinely enjoyed. However, as fun as it was, I would be kidding myself if I thought I made a life-changing difference to those children. Even though they liked Paul sonsangnim's classes - I hope - speaking to me was no great event for them. Jung Chul had employed foreign teachers before me and when I left there was already another in place. It also had Korean teachers who spoke excellent English and were great at their jobs. As well as this, Korea had a super modern education system and thriving economy. In short, they probably had a good shot at a decent life no matter what I did in the classroom.

Dawufeng was a different kettle of fish altogether. Not only was I the first foreign teacher the kids had ever worked with, for the majority of them I was also the first foreigner they had ever met in real life. As I have already explained, their Chinese teachers spoke no English at all and they were in classes of 40 or more. At the time, China was a land of huge opportunity - as the later passages of this book will certainly attest - but that opportunity was not always easy to access. The country had an economy that was growing faster than almost any in recent history thanks in huge part to its massive supply of cheap labour. However, to get ahead and to earn more than $100 per month, education was key. Learning English was a massive advantage. With all that in mind, I was desperate to make a tangible difference in the kids' lives.

After the initial shock and euphoria of the first couple of weeks when English names had been assigned and we had done our classes on jobs and food, I decided that it was time for me to start making a difference and helping the kids to acquire the language skills that might take them beyond an entry level job on the production line at the pipe company. It was at that point that the enormity of the task in front of me became clear. Basically, if they were keen on improving their English, I was their only shot. Maybe it was the exuberance of youth or a degree of professional naivety - I still only had one year of teaching experience - but I was ready for the challenge.

When I kicked things off in week 3, I was determined to move things forward and make progress with every kid in each of my classes.

Maybe I was away with the fairies, but I firmly believed that I would be able to transform their lives with a piece of chalk, some rudimentary grammar knowledge and whatever charisma I could muster. I would only be satisfied if the kids started to sound fluent and confident in English. It was a noble objective but, my goodness, I was kidding myself! By the end of week 6, I was exhausted and seeing things very differently.

I had assumed that things would be plain sailing, but there were a whole variety of issues that got in my way. The first major issue that I faced was a pure numbers game. With almost all of my classes having 45 or 50 kids, it was never going to be possible to spend quality time with each of them. In Korea, there was a maximum of twelve kids in a class which meant I could spend time with each one and help those that struggled with a word or piece of grammar. With classes lasting just one hour in Dawufeng, I scarcely had time to share more than a few words with each of them.

The second problem that I had to address was the kids' pre-existing language level. As I have already made clear, a huge proportion of the kids were absolute beginners and needed to be taught such basics "Hello", "thank you" etc. Whilst others, like Amy who I mentioned earlier, had some words and phrases. A third problem that blended in with the language level was that of reaction to meeting a foreign teacher. Consequently, there was a whole matrix of students to deal with: Kids who spoke no English and were frightened of the new foreigner; kids who spoke no English but were super excited to meet me; kids who spoke a bit yet were still afraid of me; and kids who spoke some English and were ready to talk.

It was pretty much impossible to balance all the different types of students. In some classes, where there were lots of kids with very basic levels, I was drawing apples, balls, cats and dogs on the board to do ABCs. Yet, there were kids in there whose parents had decent jobs at the pipe factory and had taught them some English. Those kids sat there hugely bored. If I changed things in order to keep them feeling engaged, the other kids were lost. In an ideal world, I could have used a photocopier to make worksheets or activities to give the higher level kids something to work on whilst I did ABCs. Unfortunately, the school had neither a photocopier nor the paper to go in it.

It was really hard to make any significant progress with the majority of kids. Nonetheless, I put in huge amounts of effort to try to make a big difference for them. In truth, we did make a bit of progress. I got a few of them to recognise English letters and understand some basic verbs but the speed of their learning was pretty much glacial. I found that hard to deal with. My one job was to help those kids develop a valuable life skill and I was coming up short. So, I decided that I needed to reassess things. As I had so many kids and so few resources I decided that I perhaps needed to redefine what success would look like. All the kids speaking fabulous English was clearly a pipe dream.

I started by thinking about what I could do with the kids who were afraid of me. I had managed to get a few of them to make eye-contact and exchange some words with me, but the majority were still limited to monosyllabic phrases or pained silence. With those guys, I decided to shift my focus to showing that I did not bite and was nothing to be afraid of. I figured that if I couldn't get them speaking fluent English, I could at least help them to feel less afraid of foreigners. It was not always easy. But, by walking amongst the desks and crouching down to make eye-contact at a nice low level, I started to break a few barriers down and managed to generate a few smiles. It wasn't much, but at least I was getting somewhere.

I also decided to fall back on some tried and tested techniques from Korea. The first one was candy. Just as in Taean, I adopted the technique of shameless bribery and it seemed that nationality wasn't an issue in that regard: Chinese kids loved being rewarded with sugar as much as Korean ones did and I quickly became a far less intimidating figure to many of them. The only difference between the two countries was that I had to buy a far bigger bag of candy to reward five classes of 50 kids! I also dropped in a few simple praise techniques such as high-fives and fist bumps - the kind of thing their Chinese teachers would never have considered - if the kids got an answer correct. This too seemed to lighten the mood and get the kids feeling comfortable with me.

It was really interesting to see what happened next. It was, in many ways, a carbon copy of the reaction in Korea. After school on a Tuesday evening, my recruiter gave me a call to say how delighted the school was with the classes. Apparently, they thought the kids were making great progress. On a purely objective and linguistic level, this was absolute nonsense and was perhaps another reflection of Magic

Foreigner Syndrome. However, on a more subjective level, there might have been something to the argument. If the kids were no longer freaked out by the very concept of someone from another country, then that was progress of a sort.

Life in Dawufeng

I enjoyed teaching at the school in Dawufeng. It was a fabulous experience. Had the working environment been my only consideration, I may have stayed there beyond the three months of my contract. It would have been nice to see if I could have had a bigger impact with the kids and to develop closer relationships with them. However, I never seriously considered staying longer. Everyday life in my little industrial town was nothing to be savoured and I knew I needed to move somewhere with a better quality of living. The entire atmosphere around town felt almost Dickensian or even dystopian. By the time Spring was in full bloom, I was looking for my next job in China.

There were many things wrong with life in Dawufeng. However, I will start with the biggest and most challenging of them: health. This proved to be a constant struggle and had a big impact. Perhaps the best way to illustrate the effect that life in small town China had on me can be found with the weight loss I experienced and with an example that came just a couple of weeks after I left Dawufeng and moved to downtown Tianjin for a new job (More on that in the coming pages). Two of my buddies from the UK had come to visit me and they were struck at how gaunt I looked - "Bacon, you look like you have got AIDS" were the exact and rather insensitive words they used. They couldn't believe the difference between my regular frame and the almost emaciated figure that greeted them at the airport.

Part of the weight loss was due to the fact that the stores in Dawufeng sold little more than rice, strange Chinese vegetables and weird sauces I didn't recognise. Getting fresh meat was impossible. There was a meat section in the small convenience store in town, but it was not refrigerated and the meat never looked either fresh or palatable. The local outdoor market seemed to have slightly fresher fare on offer but the hygiene levels, or lack thereof, totally put me off shopping there. In neither of those places were there any western foods. Consequently, getting good quality food that fit my palate was really difficult. To get pasta, cereal or even just tomatoes, I had to take a one hour bus ride into the city.

As inconvenient as the shopping situation was, it was not my biggest issue. The main reason I looked as I did was that, over the three months I spent in Dawufeng, I was constantly sick. To be slightly more graphic than some readers might ordinarily prefer, I could probably count the number of solid bowel movements I had on one hand. Diarrhoea and stomach cramps were a nightmare that stayed with me for the entirety of my stay. I put this down to the horrific environment around me.

There have been countless stories published about the ecological disasters inflicted upon China in the past two decades as the country has prioritised economic development - and production of low-cost products we in the UK and US buy on Amazon or in Primark or Wal Mart - over environmental sustainability. Dawufeng was, sadly, a classic example. It was by far and away the most polluted place I have ever visited. To illustrate this, I will go back to my first few days in town. The first full day I spent there had been rather sunny - what the Chinese optimistically described as a 'blue sky day'. However, after that it seemed like the town was gripped by a period of prolonged winter weather. There was no rain and no snow, but it seemed to be cloudy almost every day for the next two or three weeks. Being from the north of England, this just seemed normal at first. But, after a while, I began to realise that Dawufeng wasn't in the midst of an usuallyy long spell of foggy weather. Rather, the air quality was so poor that the sun was unable to break through the layer of smog above the town.

A clear illustration of the impact of the pollution came on the football field. Once or twice a week, I would step out onto the sports field behind the Secondary School area and play a casual match with some PE teachers from school and a few workers from TPCO. The majority of them didn't speak English, but it didn't matter so much as it was a good source of exercise and a fun way to pass my lunch break … and, to my delight, I wasn't racially abused once.

However, it proved to be really hard work for my lungs. At the end of a forty minute game, I would be wheezing like an old man and on occasion I would blow my nose at some point after playing and find the tissue filled with frightening black mucus. As the winter gave way to spring, I also noticed the air pollution in another way: I didn't need sun-cream. Since I turned 20, whenever I have played sports outside, I have had to lather my bald pate in cream to stop it burning. In Dawufeng, I didn't have any but never found it an issue. The smog simply stopped the sun getting through.

For months after I left Dawufeng, I still found myself coughing more than I ordinarily would and blowing darkened mucus out of my nose. It really was an alarming situation. Yet, nobody in town seemed concerned. Or, perhaps more realistically, the majority of them didn't care as the industry that caused the problems also provided their jobs. So, whenever I mentioned air quality, they just laughed and said, "Don't worry. Dawufeng is a foggy city.' It seemed such a shame to me as so many young kids were breathing in horrific levels of pollutants.

Air pollution was a horrific problem, and continues to be a significant issue around China. However, of more concern to me was the water supply. TPCO and other facilities close to the town took a particularly nineteenth century approach to dealing with their waste: it all went directly into the local waterways. Whenever I would get off the bus after going to downtown Tianjin, I had to cross a bridge over a small irrigation channel. Each time I did this, I would play a little game with myself by guessing what colour the water would be that day. We got through reds, yellows and one disturbingly fluorescent shade of green. It made me worry about the water that was coming into my apartment.

Even from my first day in town, I never drank it. That would have been foolhardy. But, at first, I did use it for brushing my teeth and cooking. After a few weeks though, I began to realise that my stomach issues may have been linked to this. So, by the time I left, I was cooking, brushing my teeth and even washing dishes in bottled water. It helped, but even with that measure, I was never hugely healthy.

The environment certainly left me feeling worse for wear. Thankfully though, there were no long-term effects on my health. However, that might not have been the case for all the residents of Dawufeng. I was not privy to any of their personal medical issues, but there was one very alarming sign that was clearly visible in the classroom: the number of identical twins. In total, I had about fourteen classes in Dawufeng - with maybe 650 or 700 kids in total - and out of those there were seven sets of identical twins.

When I asked one of my assistants and Mrs. Li about this strange phenomenon, they treated it in the same way as they did the air quality by shrugging it off as a quirk of daily life in Dawufeng. I couldn't really agree with their rather laissez-faire attitude and felt that it couldn't possibly be a coincidence that such a virulently polluted town would have such statistically anomalous birth patterns. Mathematically speaking, identical twins (monozygotic twins to use the technical term) account for three births per 1,000. Therefore, seeing one or two sets might well have been normal, but seven seemed excessive.

After I did a bit of digging on the subject of twins, I discovered that I might not have been wrong to think things were a bit off as not only had scientists in Germany established a link between pollution and multiple births but there were also other examples in China. Apparently, there were plenty of villages and small towns across the country where twins were surprisingly prevalent. For instance, I read about a village in Sichuan province where a huge amount of twins were being born each year. The locals attributed this to the well in the centre of the village, which they believed - much like the water in Dawufeng - had been contaminated.

The air and water quality in Dawufeng were issues both for me and the town as a whole. Conditions in town were just awful. However, on a more personal level, I also found my apartment to be a very difficult place to live. Even though my recruiter continued to assure me that it was amongst the nicest in town, it was a hovel and a very depressing place to return to after a tough day in the classroom.

First of all, the furniture and decor was old and dilapidated. However, this was the least of my concerns - I could have lived with some cracked tiles and rickety chairs. Instead, the biggest problem was the cockroach infestation. They were everywhere. I would often sit on the toilet - and, as already discussed, the poor water quality in town ensured that I needed to do that a lot - and, rather than read a book as I ordinarily would, I amused myself by watching the cockroaches running around the light fittings above my head. The fitting was bowl-shaped. Therefore, some of the weaker specimens would get stranded in the bottom and die. Each morning, as part of my daily routine, I would not only brush my teeth and make my coffee but also empty the dead insects out of my light before taking my shower.

The health and environmental issues I faced in Dawufeng made my life particularly unpleasant. However, they were not alone in contributing to my poor quality of life. They were ably supported by the all-encompassing boredom I faced and the creeping loneliness that began to set in. The big problem with living in a small Chinese town was that there was absolutely nothing for me to do! The first part of this was the absence of people to do anything with. Unlike in Taean where I had Ossie and other expats close by, in Dawufeng I was the only foreigner within a 30km radius and there were very few people in town who spoke any English. This meant that it was up to me to fill the long evenings in isolation.

Just as in Korea, TV was not really an option as almost all of it was in Chinese. The antique Chinese-made set in my apartment showed a few local channels and the state-run broadcaster CCTV. Thankfully, there were two channels it broadcast that were relevant to me. CCTV9 was the English language station, which was generally as bad as you would expect from a Communist propaganda tool, but had the occasional show that was watchable. CCTV5 was, on occasion, my saviour as it showed sport. The highlight of my week quickly became Saturday evenings when I was able to watch football matches from Europe. However, to my disappointment, for the rest of the week the sport on show was distinctly Chinese. There was plenty of volleyball, lots of badminton and prodigious amounts of table tennis.

To try to keep in contact with the outside world and to give myself some distraction, I asked one of my assistants to go with me to the local office of the Chinese state telephone company to ask if I could get the internet installed in my apartment. I am not sure if it was because I was a foreigner and they were freaked out by i) my very existence, or ii) the fact I was asking for a commodity that is unbelievably tightly regulated in China, but I was totally shut down. I got the steeliest of refusals. No details, no explanations, just a flat 'no'. When I returned to the school, my assistant asked the rest of the staff if they had the internet at home. None of them did and all seemed to think that I was asking for the world with such an apparent luxury - it seemed that the people of Dawufeng had no need for such frivolities.

As there was no internet at work or at home, my only option was to go native and use the local internet cafes. I say "go native" because, in 2006, the vast majority of Chinese people accessed the web in internet cafes. This was the case for a few reasons. Firstly, with many Chinese workers earning less than £200 per month, a computer - even a cheaply made Chinese model - was massively beyond their means. Secondly, as thousands of people migrated to big cities to find work they often lived with several people in a tiny apartment. Therefore, the idea of having the space and privacy for a computer desk was fanciful.

There were two internet cafes in Dawufeng. Both of them were horrid places. They were both always extremely busy and filled with cigarette smoke. The clientele were predominantly male and seemed to pass their time by watching pirated movies and TV shows or playing online games. I faced a difficult dilemma with the two cafes. They were my only access to information and communication with friends and family as well as being a way of keeping myself entertained. However, even spending just five minutes in either of them left me stinking of cigarette smoke to such an extent that I needed to take a long and thorough shower to get the stench off my skin. I would also have to throw all of my clothes straight into the laundry basket.

Things in Dawufeng were so tough that even getting something to read proved to be hugely difficult. There was no chance of finding anything in English in town. The local shops only had Chinese newspapers. In downtown Tianjin, which was over an hour away on the bus, things were better … but not by a huge amount. There were a few shops that had copies of China Daily, the Communist Party's English language mouthpiece. As that was generally unreadable, I gave it a wide berth. There was a large book store in the centre of the city that did have some books in English, but these tended to be Chinese editions of very old classics. I managed to pick up a couple of volumes of Hemingway and a copy of the Great Gatsby, but after I had finished those it was slim pickings. Therefore, if I wanted to read something modern or exciting, I had to go all the way to Beijing, which was an eight hour round trip at minimum.

Escaping to the Country
Despite the issues I faced, Dawufeng was an enthralling experience. However, because of the demanding classes, the near squalid conditions and the creeping loneliness I was growing increasingly tired and frustrated with life as I neared the end of my stay there. My employment contract finished at the end of May and I was planning to leave after that and find another job in China. Before I could do that

though, there was the May Day Golden Week holiday. This provided six days off. The idea of staying in Dawufeng for that length of time without anything to do utterly appalled me. So, I decided that I needed to make a break for it and do a bit of travelling. My objective was the city of Datong 450km northwest of Tianjin.

Datong was an ideal choice because it was relatively easy to get to - it was eight hours away on a train running during the day or a 14 hour overnight sleeper - and because there were some really cool things to see. There were two major attractions that had captured my attention. These were the i) Yungang Grottoes, a series of caves and carved Buddhas dating back over 1,500 years, and ii) The Hanging Monastery, which was basically what it said on the tin: a monastery hanging off the side of a mountain.

As it was a Golden Week, it wasn't so easy to get a train ticket. I had hoped to save money on hotels - the school in Dawufeng didn't have internet or paint on the concrete walls, so they were not paying anywhere near as much as Mr. Kim had - by getting sleeper tickets in both directions. This would have allowed me to arrive early in the morning, see the attractions and then leave late that night. Sadly, this was not to be as the sleepers on the outbound leg to Datong were all booked up, so I had to take a day train instead. As I was alone and didn't have my buddy for support and distraction, this proved to be a long and gruelling trip.

Just as when the two of us had taken the soft seats from Nanjing to Hangzhou, I quickly became the centre of attention for my fellow passengers. This time, though, things were worse and far more intrusive. I had started the journey wearing headphones to listen to music, but this proved to be no deterrent as a middle-aged lady seated opposite me reached across and poked me in the leg. This began an interrogation that the Stasi, Securtate or indeed the Chinese secret police would have been proud of and which managed to involve everyone within a 10m radius of my seat. The middle-aged lady kicked things off herself:

"Where are you going?" (Datong)

"Why are you going there?" (To see Yungang and the monastery)

I had hoped that maybe someone around me would jump in with some advice or insight on my trip, but instead they just powered on with the questions.

"What is your job?" (Teacher)

"How much money do you earn?" (Sorry, that is none of your business)

At that point, she threw in some that were similar to the trip to Hangzhou such as a worker's salary and the cost of basic commodities in England. She then briefly went quiet before her neighbour asked a question in Chinese, which she then translated to me:

"How many rooms do you in your apartment" (Two bedrooms and a living room)

This response solicited the same type of response as it had from Mrs Li. They were astounded that I had such a big place to myself and quickly began telling me how small their apartments were and how many people they shared them with.

"Where in England are you from?" (Sheffield)

"Do you know David Beckham?" (Oh for God's sake!)

Eventually, after what felt like several days on the train, I arrived in Datong just as the sun was beginning to set. Despite my best efforts whilst still in Dawufeng, I had been unable to book a hotel in advance. At the time, there were no places to stay listed on any hotel booking websites. When Ossie and I were backpacking, we had generally been in bigger cities and were able to book somewhere to stay in advance - the one exception had been Yinchuan which was also pretty remote. Consequently, when I emerged from Datong train station my first objective was to find somewhere to stay.

There were a couple of hotels close to the station that, from a distance, didn't look terrible. However, on closer inspection, neither of them looked particularly inviting and both had clearly noticed that I was a foreigner - I appeared to be the only one in town - and adjusted their prices when I got close to their respective lobbies. Not wanting to pay upwards of $100 for a dirty and dated room, I made my way back into the station where there was a small tourist office. The lady there spoke very little English, but she did understand the word 'hotel'

As it was pretty likely that I would be the only overseas tourist arriving that evening, she closed the office and guided me out into the city. We took a short walk down a couple of side streets before she ushered me through a rather nondescript looking double door - had the girl not been there to help me, I would have had no idea it was even a hotel. In truth, the word "hotel" was perhaps a little bit generous. It was more a dormitory than anything else. I spent just under £4 for a bed in a clean but very spartan shared room. I was fortunate that of the five beds in there only two were occupied - by a Korean couple who were already asleep when I arrived.

I was up early the following morning to board a minivan tour to the grottoes and the monastery. The Chinese are huge fans of starting tours at crazily early times in the morning and ours, which included me and the Koreans, left just before 8am. At first, I tried to catch up on some of the sleep I felt I had missed. However, this proved almost impossible as the roads in Shanxi province were simply awful. It wasn't just the roads that were awful though, the whole area was pretty depressing. In fact, it actually reminded me a lot of Dawufeng!

Unlike Dawufeng, where the Pipe Corporation dominated the local economy, in Datong coal was king. Mining dominated the city, which was home to China's third largest mining company. The panorama through the window of the minivan was a clear reflection of this. The city reminded me of a T. S. Lowry painting, albeit in a far more Asian setting. It seemed that the whole city was dusted with coal and that there was a layer of grime covering everything. Just as with Dawufeng, it was a pretty depressing vista.

Even though the area looked pretty bleak, I was actually quite interested to get a glimpse of China's coal belt. Part of this was just idle curiosity as I am from a part of the UK where coal mining was a huge industry before the mid-1980s. The other reason was that, at the time, the coal industry in China was often in the global spotlight due to its horrific safety record. The year before, just shy of 6,000 miners were killed in mining accidents. In 2006, there were four separate accidents in Shanxi province alone in each of which between 20 and 50 miners were killed. The average daily death toll amongst coal miners in China was 13.

I was on a trip to a major tourist attraction, so I was not likely to see too much in relation to mining. However, just by looking out at the surroundings, I could understand why the industry was so dangerous. The most obvious example of this was the men we saw either walking by the side of the road or being bussed around in flat-bed trucks or dilapidated mini-buses. To a man - and they were all men - they were filthy and dressed in what could best be described as rags. From their appearance, you really could not believe that they were working in conditions where safety was given any kind of importance.

I was still staring at the miners and the surrounding landscape when, to my surprise, we pulled into the Yungang parking lot. This was a bit of a shock as I expected it to be a bit further out into the countryside and not to be nestled between huge mining works. It seemed rather sad in itself and also a tad counter-intuitive when it came to attracting tourists. This was, though, a perfect reflection of the Chinese economy at the time. Tourism was starting to become big business, but manufacturing across the country was also huge which meant that fuel was desperately needed. Consequently, the two had to live side-by-side. The dingy surroundings notwithstanding, I was really keen to see Datong's most impressive attraction. A bit of coal dust was not going to minimise my enjoyment.

The Yungang Grottoes are a genuinely fabulous thing to see. They were built around 450AD with the whole site comprising 53 caves and over 51,000 individual statues of which some were 20m or 30m in height and others that were mere centimetres. From a distance, the grottoes are not especially dramatic or spectacular as they could best be described as being 'veiled'. In front of large areas was a layer of rock with a series of holes carved out. As I approached this gave the slightly odd feeling that I was playing a game of peek a boo with Buddha. It was only as I got really close and could fully see through the gaps that I really began to get the splendour of the grottoes.

I gravitated towards one of the larger Buddhas and stared through the gaps in the stone. It was mesmerising. On the way to the grottoes everything was dirty and dingy, but when I looked at the Buddha I was gripped by the most hypnotic shade of blue. Around his forehead was carved a headband that almost glowed like a sapphire that had been struck by direct sunlight. It captivated me. I was struck at the contrast of the bright colour before me and the almost monochrome landscape through which I had just travelled.

Moving on from the Blue Buddha - this was not its actual name, just a moniker I bestowed upon it - things got much more delicate. Behind the veil of rock I was suddenly seeing tiny statues in long rows or in geometric patterns. The detail was astounding as the majority of them were individually painted and carved. It was unbelievable to think that they were over a millennium and a half old. I had seen similarly tiny figures at the top of the Summer palace and, at the time, was blown away by the detail and intricacy. That was a completely legitimate reaction as they were a fabulous sight. However, when I thought that they were 'just' one hundred years old, it really put Yungang - 15 times older - into perspective.

The Grottoes were amazing. They made the horrific train ride worthwhile and made me unfathomably glad that I had succeeded in escaping Dawufeng for a few days. They also really whetted my appetite for more. After having lunch close to the Grottoes, we would be heading back out into the industrial dystopia before winding our way to more rural climes to visit the Hanging Monastery. The photos of the monastery I had seen in Lonely Planet and on the internet were spectacular. It was a temple built with the same classic Chinese architecture as the Forbidden City and Summer Palace, but instead of being constructed horizontally along the ground, it was built vertically up a cliff face.

The monastery is located about 65km from downtown Datong. Thankfully, this meant that we spent some time in an area of nice clean countryside. After nearly three months in Dawufeng and the morning in Datong, this was a very pleasant change of pace. I enjoyed the drive tremendously, but it was nothing compared to Jinxia Gorge where we would find the monastery. On its own, it might well have been worth the visit just for the geographical spectacle. However, once my eyes fixed on the monastery itself the gorge was small potatoes. The monastery was an amazing sight. At first glance, all I could think was that it genuinely was 'hanging' from the cliff face and could plummet to earth at any moment.

The monastery could easily be an optical illusion. I found myself looking at it dumbfoundedly asking "How does it stay up?" It seemed to be a pretty tricky question to answer. Firstly, it was built on a series of ledges - barely a meter wide - that ran at an angle along the cliff face. The majority of the structure was supported by long wooden pylons that reached down and rested on lower parts of the cliff. It was a tremendous feat of design and construction, but it really didn't look either safe or sustainable. The phrase that sprang to mind was "perched precariously".

I was hugely impressed with the view of the monastery from the valley. I had seen nothing quite like it before. In truth, I have seen nothing so architecturally unique since either. In actuality, I probably would have been better served staying there and enjoying things from a distance as the interior of the monastery proved to be a massive letdown. Until that point in my Chinese adventures, I had succeeded in avoiding the nightmare crowds that can often be found at Chinese tourist attractions - there are well over a billion people in China so it stands to reason that things can sometimes get a bit cramped. Ossie and I had visited much of Beijing in the dead of winter to avoid being jostled around the Forbidden City alongside giant tour groups and had chosen the most remote section of the Great Wall that we could find in order to enjoy it in isolation. Things at the monastery were to be different, though. The crowds were huge and took almost all of the joy out of the experience.

Part of the problem was that the monastery clings delicately to the cliff face. Consequently, it is not very wide - if it were, it would be in even greater danger of collapsing down the cliff face. Unfortunately, because of this, there was literally no space in which to stand or move around. We were crammed together like sardines in a can. I had read that the beams used to build the skeleton of the monastery were a marvel of architectural innovation in how they were laced and fixed. However, I had no chance to look at them in any great detail as I was being nudged and bundled forward by the swathe of people behind me. I wasn't even able to get a picture without dozens of people in the foreground. It was a rather disappointing end to a fascinating day.

TIANJIN

As I hope the previous chapter conveys, whilst my experiences in Dawufeng were neither comfortable nor easy, they were certainly unique and gave me a fabulous insight into life in China beyond Tiananmen Square and the Great Wall. Even though I didn't love the diarrhoea and the achingly boring evenings, I certainly do not regret my time there and feel that it gave me a taste of China that few westerners have had or will ever have. However, as the weeks in smalltown China drew on, I also began to feel that while I was getting a very authentic taste of 'real' China, I was simultaneously missing out on some of the rather more exciting changes that were happening around the country.

At that point in its history, China was a country of great inequality and disparity. In fact, some of the cities on the east coast represented a completely different world to small towns like Dawufeng. Consequently, I started looking for a job that would maybe offer a bit more excitement and more of a taste of the new and emerging China. At first, I looked at the possibility of taking a summer job in a big city like Suzhou, Hangzhou or Guangzhou. However, a piece of pure chance steered me on a very different course.

As the previous chapter emphasised, my free time in Dawufeng was not always particularly exciting. Therefore, after a couple of months, I was going a little bit stir crazy. I was desperately keen to get out and have some social interaction. To do this, I started Googling expat sports teams in Tianjin in the hope that I would be able to enjoy some outdoor action and maybe meet some other foreigners. As this was before social media was really a thing, I got precious little in terms of results, which was disappointing. So, with no other real option, I decided to widen my search to Beijing, which brought a lot more success. After finding a website for an expat football league and exchanging a couple of emails, I was soon signing up to play for a team of expats in Beijing the following weekend.

Never in my sporting life have I travelled for so long for 90 minutes of action. The game was in the middle of the afternoon, but I was up and out before 8h30. The first leg of my journey was a twenty minute walk to the TPCO light rail station from where I would ride on the line that links Tianjin and Tanggu for around 25 minutes to get to the city centre. In a piece of slightly odd and monumentally short-sighted urban planning, the tracks stopped about 3km short of the main train station, which meant that I then had to take a short cab ride. At the train station, I then bought a hard-seat ticket - the soft seats had all gone - to the capital.

I had about forty minutes before the train departed. So, I had some time to kill. I am not proud of what happened next. Living in Dawufeng, there was not much access to good coffee, which was a massive pain in my ass. This might sound like a hugely first world issue and it may appear that I am being outrageously precious, but it was a big problem for me and left me groggy and unsociable in the morning. The only product available in town that even resembled coffee was a sachet of Nescafe that came with a synthetic creamer and sugar mixed in. My colleagues at school considered this the height of western sophistication and always took pride in offering me a sachet and a paper cup of hot water. It was pretty awful, so I always tried to make up an excuse if they offered me a cup.

When I saw that the McDonalds on the train station concourse had freshly brewed ground coffee, I jumped in. After such an early start, it was too good an opportunity to miss. To my regret, whilst I was ordering my coffee, I thought about how I had really struggled to get western food in Dawufeng and had not had a burger in months. Despite knowing I was making a terrible decision, I ordered a Big Mac and a double cheeseburger - hardly the best prep for ninety minutes on the football field.

My junk food binge did nothing for the health of my arteries but it did usher me into a deep food coma which ensured there was, mercifully, no repeat of my previous railway interrogations en route to Hangzhou and Datong. The two and a half hour journey passed quite pleasantly as I slumbered gently on my hard-seat. When I arrived at Beijing station, I still had a bit more travelling to do. So, I battled my way to the metro and jumped on line 2 to take me to the Chaoyang area of the city. By the time I got to the match, I had been travelling for more than four hours.

The team I found was the perfect antidote to my loneliness in Dawufeng. There were players from all over the world. I had teammates from England, Scotland, Ireland, Australia, France, Japan and Singapore. I was happy to get onto a football field for the first time since Korea, but it was also great fun just to spend time with people who spoke English. However, whilst getting some football in and doing a bit of socialising was a very welcome tonic, it was a conversation with the team manager that really changed things for me.

By pure chance, he was from Sheffield, literally a couple miles down the road from my house back home. After spending three months with barely any contact with non-Chinese people, it was weird but very welcome to meet someone from the same city as me. As I had been starved of such contact, I was keen to chew the fat and we were very quickly onto our second post-match beer. It was as we progressed onto our third that the conversation turned to work - until that point, the subjects had been mainly football related. I explained that I was a teacher and was about to finish my job. As I did so, his face lit up and he explained that his company was looking for a Business English teacher in Tianjin. He suggested that I should speak to his boss.

The World's Fastest Growing Economy

My recruitment was really smooth and easy. I met the boss for dinner and drinks in Tianjin a couple of times, we seemed to hit it off, and very quickly I was in. I genuinely couldn't quite comprehend my good fortune. They were happy for me to start a couple of days after I finished in Dawufeng and even gave me a very nice apartment - one which had a modern TV and which did not have cockroaches scurrying around the light fittings - to stay in temporarily until I could find a place of my own. On top of this, they were nice enough to triple my salary.

I was surprised by the ease of everything. However, in hindsight, I perhaps shouldn't have been quite so shocked. This was China in 2006. It was a period of unprecedented growth and change. Few places in world history have seen such a transformation as the one that was underway when I arrived! In 2005, annual growth was around 11% or 12% and in 2006 it was pushing 13%. To put that number into context, in the same period both the UK and US had annual growth of less than 3%. That was all part of a transformation that was seeing hundreds of millions of people being lifted from the most abject of poverty: In 1990, 66% of Chinese people were living on less than $1.90 a day; 90% were living on less than $3.20; and 98.3% were living on less than $5.50. By 2010, those percentages had fallen to 11.2%, 28.5% and 53.4% respectively. In that context, my change in jobs was hardly dramatic. In fact, it was merely a reflection of how things in China were developing at the time and how much opportunity there was.

The company I would be working for was also very much of its time and place, and was a perfect embodiment of the opportunities on offer at the time. It had been founded in 2001 by a Brit in his late 20s and an Aussie in his 30s who had spotted a huge opportunity. With China growing so fast and with the cost of labour so unbelievably low, hundreds of multinational companies were relocating their operations to the Middle Kingdom. Without doubt, this was great for the companies' bottom lines - although obviously, not so much for the workers who lost their jobs in Europe and the US - but it also presented them with a bit of a problem: Chinese workers were certainly cheap, but they usually didn't speak great English. My experiences in Dawufeng, where almost none of the English department at the school actually spoke the language, was testament to the difficult situation. This meant that there was a huge demand for professionally done Business English teaching.

In just over four years, they had built a diverse and impressive portfolio of major international clients who needed them to teach their staff to be able to give presentations, participate in meetings and write emails in English. It was massively impressive, and from the outside it also felt a little bit intimidating. They had a wide range of shiny catalogs and glitzy leaflets, all of which featured teachers - professionally photographed - wearing sharp suits and looking like they possessed a wealth of experience. With only a year and a half of teaching behind me, all of which had been with children, I wasn't sure if I would be able to fit in. However, as it turned out, I really needn't have worried.

Getting a job for which I was patently lacking in both qualification and experience reacquainted me with a familiar theme: as a foreigner in Asia, it was ridiculously easy to get well-paid work. Just as with Korea two years earlier and as in Dawufeng, where admittedly the cash on offer was not so plentiful, just being white and having a university degree was enough to get me through the door. Just as in Korea, I felt lucky to have found the opportunity but also in another way a little bit guilty. As I was so inexperienced, I felt like a bit of a chancer. However, when I started teaching classes at a large pharmaceutical company on the outskirts of Tianjin, I began to see that the situation was also the same for many Chinese people: there were plenty of young people whose careers were developing far faster than would have seemed logical.

From the 1950s through to the rise of Deng Xiaoping in the 1980s, China was a chaotic mess and education was either ignored or mired in a climate of political insanity. This meant that the country lacked a well-educated workforce, particularly on the older end of the spectrum. The vast majority of workers with any kind of technical or linguistic skills had been educated in the 1990s or after as the education people received in the 60s and 70s wasn't really worthy of the name. As a consequence, the country's talent pool was young but very shallow. Because of this, big companies were fighting a rather brutal war for talented workers. If you were young and had a marketable skill, you could basically demand whatever salary you desired - if one company didn't pay it a competitor would! It was not uncommon to meet Chinese workers in their early 30s who were on their fourth or fifth major company as they had been poached on multiple occasions.

Over the three and a half years that I would teach business English in Tianjin, I worked at a variety of different multinational companies. These included a software support company, a cement producer and two major pharmaceutical firms. It taught me so much about China and its development. The first of the two pharma operations was a joint venture between a state-run Chinese company and a global pharmaceutical giant. It was a modern well-equipped facility that really hammered home the juxtapositions inside China as it was a million miles away from life in Dawufeng or Datong.

When I arrived on site to begin classes, the HR manager gave me a brief tour of the offices and the production area. It was all very hi-tech and amazingly clean - as I guess you would expect from a company making medicines for the global market! It was my first exposure to a big international company and it was really interesting to see. For example, their logistics department was a thing of wonder. The warehouse, which in true Chinese style was huge, had spaces that were measured to the centimetre to ensure that workers knew exactly where each raw material or finished product was stored and had full digital listings to ensure the manager knew how much was in stock down to the gram or individual pill.

In a really interesting contrast to this, I was also shown a fascinating display about the company's history featuring photos of the very early stages of the project in the 1980s. The display gave a background of the company, but in so doing it also said a huge amount about China's recent past. In the thirty years between Richard Nixon visiting Beijing (1972) and the early part of the new millennium, the country changed beyond recognition. It had gone from being rural and backward - the world's 32nd largest exporter - to being the world's fastest growing economy. The big push for this change came in the 1980s when Deng Xiaoping moved to open the country to western investment and to focus on becoming a major exporter. In 1986, he declared that, "To get rich is glorious" and in so doing set off a tidal wave of growth and development that has still yet to break on the shore.

Whilst I was only six years old at the time and, unsurprisingly, didn't really grasp the significance of what Deng was saying, it was a major moment in global economic history. This was a guy who wore a Mao jacket, had taken part in the Long March and would later order the tanks into Tiananmen Square to crush pro-democracy protests. It was a weird contrast, the hardline Commie sparking the greatest push of capitalism the world had ever seen, and it defined China perfectly … even 20 years later. The country was going nuts with growth and opportunity yet was still a one-party state, albeit one that did not really look too similar to what Mao Zedong originally had in mind.

Only a year after Deng's declaration, the joint venture in Tianjin broke ground on the plant at which I would be working. Even with China's new aspirations for wealth, it was still a pretty guarded time in the Middle Kingdom. Therefore, investment was most certainly not allowed in unchecked. Consequently, most western companies looking to tap the billion-strong market had to buddy up with a local - state-owned - partner. The photos of the groundbreaking ceremony in Tianjin made China in 1987 look a very bleak and cheerless place, much closer to Mao's world than to that of Hu Jintao's in which I lived. The images showed Chinese party members in Mao jackets and with frighteningly solemn expressions shaking hands with foreigners in very expensive suits while hundreds of cold and rather dirty looking workers watched on with blank expressions. The contrast to the air-conditioned lobby in which I sipped a latte macchiato from the machine upstairs whilst perusing the display could not have been starker.

The working environment at the pharmaceutical company was just fabulous. It is a ridiculously obvious fact to state that it was in huge contrast to the China of 20 years before. However, in all honesty, the site was also shiner and glitzier than any office I had ever worked in the

UK! As surprising as that was to me, perhaps the most pertinent comparison I made at the time was to my experience in Dawufeng. Things were hugely different and really highlighted the inequality that was growing within China.

The vast majority of the workers in my former hometown were classic examples of China's vast supply of cheap labour. They would have earned less than $100 per month and, whenever I saw them walking home from the TPCO facility, looked world-weary and bedraggled. It was a sad sight. Even the teachers at the school earned less than $200 per month and, according to one of my assistants, the headmistress probably only made $250 per month. I may well have been viewing things from an extremely western perspective - for many of the workers there, jobs at the pipe company would have been a huge step up from the abject poverty they were born into - but it felt like a town that locked hope and had a real Dickensian feel about the place.

At the pharmaceutical company, things could not have been more different. Whereas at the school I sat in the teachers' room on a wobbly wooden chair and prepped my classes using a notebook because I had no textbooks and no internet access, in my new job I had an ergonomic office chair at a desk in the HR department with a superfast internet connection that I could plug into my work issued laptop. And, whilst I got ready for my classes, I was able to sip on a latte or cappuccino made with freshly ground beans, which was a massive and beautiful contrast to the nasty Nescafe sachets I had in Dawufeng.

When I started teaching business English, I was very nervous. Part of this was completely expected as it was a big change of pace and change of environment for me. I had never taught grown-ups before and both the *hogwan* in Korea and the school in Dawufeng were a world away from a training room in a Fortune 500 company. However, another element was the level of expectation. For the most part, in both Korea and Dawufeng the expectations that greeted me were not so great. In both places my big task was to be a real life *wae gook* or *laowai*. If I helped to improve my students language skills, fantastic, but I was there more to provide the kids an experience than anything else. In corporate China, they were looking for something more. As these were major international companies, the majority of the employees were no strangers to seeing foreigners. So, it was not a case of walking in and wowing everyone with my general foreignness. I was going to have to actually teach them something. This proved to be an interesting challenge!

When I arrived on site and saw how modern the offices were, I assumed that all of my students were going to be able to speak good English and my task would be to build on that.. This assumption was solidified when I met some of the members of the HR team with whom I would be sharing office space. My desk was next to a lady called Winnie who, on my second or third visit, engaged me in a long and extremely detailed conversation about finding a good private school for her son. She was worried about the Chinese education system's rather large class sizes and didn't want him spending his days sharing his teacher's attention with 40 other kids. She described it all with vocabulary that was almost as good as mine. Similarly, the HR manager, Frank, also made a strong impression. It was he who gave me my initial tour of the facility and showed the photos of the groundbreaking in the 1980s. On the way back to the office, he asked me:

"Paul, what is the British perspective on joint-ventures like ours? Do you see them as a good way to enter an emerging market like China or do you worry about losing control of brand integrity?"

That knocked me off my feet! He got a very spluttered and slightly incoherent answer. Nothing in my career up to that point had prepared me to answer a question like that!

When I actually got into the classroom, my initial assumptions were both confirmed and challenged as I saw the duality of modern China played out in the microcosm of one company. Several of my classes were with employees from areas such as R&D, Quality Control and I.T. I even had one lady from a department known as Pharmacovigilance, which was a new word for my vocabulary (She was responsible for dealing with any side-effects people might get from medication produced by the company). These guys gave me a great view into the new China, a China that was as modern or even more modern than my previous life in the UK.

For example, before one of my classes, I was sitting with one of the R&D team and struck up a conversation about her weekend. It was quite an illuminating chat. The first thing that struck me was that she informed me that she lived in Beijing where she spent Thursdays,

Fridays and the weekend before travelling to Tianjin for three days. Having spent large amounts of time on the train to go to play football or buy books in the capital, I expressed surprise and commented that it must have been a pain in the ass to have to use the train twice a week. She laughed out loud at me:

"Oh my God!" I don't take the train. I drive. You're right, though, that would be horrible to do twice a week".

She went on to discuss her weekend and to explain that on Saturday evening she had gone to a wine bar with her boyfriend and then spent a "lazy Sunday morning" at Starbucks drinking green tea frappuccinos.

Teaching students like that was a big change of pace for me. In my career until that point, I had only taught lessons where I was the focal point and had to explain basic language. Suddenly, I had a whole other challenge to face. Whereas in Dawufeng my only objective was to get the kids to say something - in some cases short phrases or basic sentences were a big win - in the corporate classroom it was all about limiting my own speaking in order to give everyone in class the opportunity to express their ideas and opinions.

In all honesty, those classes were a refreshing change of pace! However, as I have already noted, the educational situation in China was a long way from perfect. My school, with its gigantic class sizes and rudimentary facilities, was unlikely to produce highly qualified and creative thinking young workers ready to add value to a developing economy. This was, no doubt, also the case for thousands of schools in the less developed areas of the country. Therefore, at the lower end of the corporate pyramid, things were a bit different. I encountered a lot of students with very basic levels both in English and in their general education. These were usually people that were working on the factory floor. Doing that type of lesson was the closest I would come to the classroom experience I already had as I was mainly dealing with basic vocabulary, very simple grammar and helping them to be able to hold a basic conversation.

Generally speaking, these classes were easy to teach as it was simple language we were dealing with and I was familiar with classes like that. However, some of the students weren't particularly cosmopolitan or westernized in their approach to learning. In the higher level classes, the majority of my students were used to speaking with British or American managers or technical staff and, consequently, had no problems debating and discussing in class. So, when I asked questions like: "What do you think?" or "Tell me about that" they were happy to chime in. With some of the lower level workers, it was a different scenario. We often faced a couple of issues that stopped them contributing to class and made it difficult for me to get much interaction going.

The first was the Chinese attitude to authority, where workers generally tend to defer to the senior person in the room. So, when I asked a question to the group when doing a large class, invariably the majority of the class would sit silently and wait for the boss to give an answer or an opinion first. This meant I was forced to actively call on individuals to answer questions. With some students this worked. However, with others, even this was not enough as I fell foul of an ancient Confucian trait that still permeates Chinese culture: the idea of 'mianze', which can be best translated as 'face'. The basic concept here is that to make a mistake can be a source of shame, therefore it is better to avoid doing anything that could cause one to lose 'face'. The upshot of this was that a lot of older Chinese students would rather say nothing in the classroom than run the risk of getting something wrong and in so doing lose face. It made things hard work.

I had one student at a second pharmaceutical company who epitomised the frustrations of dealing with 'mianze'. His name was Tao Cing and teaching him was like pulling teeth. For example, I would often start a class by asking everyone "What did you do at the weekend?" He never answered. Not once. He would just sit there and shrug. If I pushed him, he might shrug and say, "Nothing". After several frustrating classes, I asked one of his classmates what she thought the problem was. She explained that because he didn't know the words for some of the things he did, Tao Cing didn't want to answer. When I asked her why he didn't just ask me to help him with the vocab, she explained that he didn't want to show people that he didn't know and didn't want to look ignorant in front of a foreigner. Sadly, I never managed to get through to Tao Cing. It seemed to me that the whole concept of education was rather alien to him.

The pharmaceutical company was located in downtown Tianjin. However, many of the other companies I worked with were located in TEDA: Tianjin Economic Development Area, a giant sprawl of factories and production facilities located close to the port of Tanggu - where I had arrived in China with my friend Alana from Korea - which operated as a free trade zone. This area was hugely popular with western companies moving into the region.

The 1980s and 1990s saw a huge influx of multinational companies into China. However, with an autocratic Communist government, this was not always easy. As with the pharmaceutical company, to get access to big markets such as Beijing, Shanghai or Chongqing they usually had to get into joint-ventures with badly-run and often corrupt state-run companies. Things had gone pretty well in Tianjin at the site at which I worked, but others did not go quite so well.

Teaching Business English meant that I had to get *au fait* with the Chinese business world. Because of this, I became very familiar with several examples of foreign companies getting burned in the Chinese market, such as the case of GM and Chery, which was a classic example of a major multinational really regretting getting into bed with a Chinese government company.

GM was looking to crack the China market with its smaller cheaper vehicles such as the Daewoo Matiz. To this end, it partnered with Chery, a Shanghai-based producer. The plan was for Chery to produce the Matiz and other models for sale in cities like Beijing or Shanghai. Unfortunately, things didn't go well. In 2002, GM executives began to feel perturbed when Chery began clandestinely producing their own version of the Matiz and rather less clandestinely selling and marketing it as purely their own creation - it was known as the QQ - at a much lower price and with far greater success. It resulted in a huge court case that GM eventually won, but not until the QQ had sold in the millions and the Matiz had floundered.

With such precedents in mind, it was easy to understand why some companies would not fancy going down a similar road. Therefore a lot of companies felt more comfortable in free trade zones like TEDA where they could operate alone. It was only when I started to make the trip to TEDA that I really began to see and understand the sheer scale of things in China. TEDA was genuinely massive. It was like a small city in itself. There weren't a huge number of apartments or houses because the vast majority of people who worked in TEDA lived in Tianjin proper and were bussed to TEDA every day. It was pre-planned commuting on a massive scale. There were, literally, hundreds and perhaps even thousands of buses shuttling workers between home and work..

Two or three of the campuses I worked at really highlighted the size of things. For example, at a second pharmaceutical company, the HR manager warned me that I needed to arrive early for classes because it was a brisk ten minute walk from the front gate to the building I would be doing classes in. After the aforementioned class, we broke for lunch. The canteen wasn't just bigger than a shopping mall food court, it was bigger than a small shopping mall. Thousands of workers had their lunch in a genuinely huge open space. They also had a game room with ping-pong … twenty ping pong tables. Similarly, at an American chemical company, one of the students met me at the gate in a golf buggy because the journey to her office was too far to walk. I once even went to a client meeting at a giant steel producer where they had a bus service to cover the massive distances between different parts of the plant. The place was so big that it seemed to stretch away over the horizon!

Changing jobs from Dawufeng and the antiquated state school to the super modern corporate world was a major change in my professional life. However, it was nothing compared to the change in my everyday life. The first example of this was where I lived. I found an apartment in the Hedong district of Tianjin. This might sound like a ridiculous piece of exaggeration, but I felt like a castaway returning to civilization. In Dawufeng, I was a one-hour bus-ride from good quality fresh meat and vegetables. In Hedong, I was a five-minute walk from a giant Wal-Mart that sold fresh fruit and veg, fresh meat and even some western treats such as cheese and frozen Italian meatballs. It was not like a Marks and Spencer's food hall or an organic farmer's market but it was a huge improvement for my diet and health. Being able to make a chicken sandwich with lettuce and tomatoes might not seem luxurious, but to me it was fabulous and really helped to settle my delicate stomach.

My apartment too showed such a huge difference to what had gone before. Despite being significantly - almost ridiculously - cheaper than anything I could rent in a major city in the UK. It was large, spacious and hugely comfortable. It was in an enclosed community, with a guard at the gate, that sat in a rather pleasant garden area. There were no cockroaches anywhere, the furniture that came with it was modern and it was easy to get the internet connected. To top things off, the water that came out of the taps was not drinkable - none of it in China was - but it didn't smell and it was clean enough to use for cooking and to brush my teeth.

The disparity in my living conditions between those in downtown Tianjin and those in Dawufeng were symptomatic of a wider pattern in China, where the quality of life and level of economic opportunity are significantly higher in the major urban centres than they are in more rural areas. Dawufeng was no countryside hamlet - it was just an hour away from the big city - but the difference was massive. The further away from the huge cities on the east coast - Beijing, Shanghai, Guangzhou, Tianjin and many others - you get, the greater the income and wealth disparity you find. Because of this pattern, China is a country of epic migration, as I explained at the start of the book when I discussed Ossie and I backpacking around the country and how we found it difficult to get train tickets. Between 1979 and 2009 there was an increase of almost 440million in the country's urban population as workers flocked in from the rice fields of the internal provinces in what was probably the greatest internal migration the world has ever known.

My example, whilst being completely atypical in one key regard as I was not Chinese, actually followed the greater pattern within the country pretty closely. Firstly, I was bang on the nose in terms of demographics as I was young and unmarried like the majority of Chinese who headed to the cities. Secondly, there was a clear economic motivation for the change. Whilst money wasn't the major factor in my decision to move to a small Chinese town, the teaching job in Dawufeng paid a pittance by British standards. As costs were so low there, I was able to live comfortably, but if I had wanted to go home in the summer or at Christmas, the trip would have wiped out anything I might have saved. Therefore, the salary available by moving into the corporate world made a huge difference to me. This was also true of all those moving from the provinces to the big city. In 2009, urban Chinese earned 3.33 times more than their rural counterparts. Those numbers explain exactly why it had been so difficult to get train tickets during the Spring Festival holiday!

My job continuously brought me into contact with clear examples of the huge migration around China and the inequality between city and country. For example, just before the October National Day holiday, I sat chatting with a student named Oliver prior to our class starting. He had moved to Tianjin from the far north of China close to the Russian border - where the winters are very cold and Siberain tigers still roam the countryside - to take a job for a software support company. He was desperately trying to find tickets for the 32 hour train ride that would get him home for the holiday. It was proving difficult for him as all he could find was a hard seat to the city of Harbin (16 hours away) and then a standing ticket for the rest of the trip. With such a horror journey in the offing, I asked him why he didn't just fly. He laughed and told me that he was supporting his parents and grandparents - there were no brothers or sisters to aid in this because of the one child policy - and he wanted to save the money he made in the big city.

Oliver's example was far from unique. I saw similar scenarios at all the companies in which I did training. I often started a new course by asking the question. "Where are you from?" I would almost always get a whole myriad of answers. The pattern was even visible in my own company. In fact, one of the sales team in Tianjin with whom I worked really closely was a classic example of China's new found mobility. She was originally from Henan deep in the heart of the country's interior. After doing well in high school, she was able to find a place at a university in Qingdao on the east coast. After graduating, not for one second did she think about going back home. Instead, she doubled down and decided to move to an even bigger city.

When she first started with us, she looked a little bit like she had just stepped off the train from her hometown. The clothes she wore for her initial interview were clean and were evidently her best threads, but they had the feel of the late 1970s about them. We did the first interview in a Starbucks in central Tianjin and she was clearly wowed by the offer of a drink - this was relatively understandable as a large coffee cost 25rmb whilst a worker in Henan would expect to earn 400 or 500rmb per month and at the time, she was living in a tiny apartment - that was similar in standard to my old one in Dawufeng with four other girls in dormitory style bunk beds.

Barely one year later, the change we saw in her was dramatic. She was clearly really grateful for the opportunity to work with a foreign company and deal with big international groups, so she worked unbelievably hard and unbelievably conscientiously. As a result, she did very well in selling our services across the city and pulled in some nice bonus payments. As she was a really lovely girl and worked so hard, I was delighted for her. By the end of the first year, she was transformed. She was dressed in much more stylish outfits and had banished the country girl image to blend in with the big city folk. She had also moved to an apartment of her own, about which she was clearly extremely proud. Interestingly, one of the first things she did was give her sister the opportunity to follow her by sending her a train ticket and allowing her to move in with her.

Life in the City

Moving to downtown Tianjin allowed me to get access to better food and move into a far more liveable apartment. However, it also improved my social life immensely. As opposed to cities like Beijing and Shanghai, where there are very large expat populations, Tianjin had a small and very close-knit expat community. In Beijing, the Sanlitun district of the city was always full of foreigners, often to the point where they were in the majority. On a Saturday evening, bars like the Den and Rickshaw would be heaving with *laowai* putting away hugely overpriced beers and perhaps consorting with some young Chinese ladies whose services were available for the evening. The area was not as rough or as seedy as Itaewon in Seoul, but at times it had a similar feel. Tianjin, on the other hand, really only had one bar for foreigners: Ali Baba's.

The following statement may work to make me sound as though I were something of an alcoholic - that ship may have already sailed based on some of the earlier chapters in the book - but Ali Baba's became a second home. Despite the beer being ridiculously cheap, over my time in Tianjin I must have spent a small fortune there on Tsingtao beer. However, even though the beer was inexpensive, I didn't go to Baba's for the prices. Rather, it was for the mix of people I could meet there. Whereas the bars in Beijing and Shanghai tended to be populated by white English speaking men, in Tianjin there was a really diverse population of foreigners. Amongst this group, I made some fantastic friends with whom I did a lot of really cool stuff. The following passages will detail some of my adventures and experiences in and around Tianjin.

One of the major benefits of moving to a big city was the opportunity it provided to access culture. Whilst Tianjin had nothing like the Louvre or the British Museum, it did have a huge museum located just outside the city centre. It was a relatively worthwhile attraction in itself, but I also found it an interesting reflection on architecture in China and the aesthetic transformation that the country was undergoing. From the founding of the PRC in the 1940s through to the 1980s and early 1990s, the artistic style of choice for Chinese urban planners and architects was brutalist concrete. The vast majority of apartments and offices were drab and gray. For a country that had produced the Forbidden City and Summer Palace, it was a major fall from grace.. However, from the 1990s onwards, things had begun to change as China modernised and said goodbye to Communist design. Cities like Beijing and Shanghai were transforming rapidly with scores of shiny new skyscrapers springing up. The early part of the millennium was a gold rush for foreign architects as the skylines of every major Chinese city changed beyond recognition.

There were some amazing and staggeringly ambitious buildings that appeared whilst I lived in China. However, my favourite was one of the oldest 'modern' buildings in the country, which stands as a symbol of China's rapid growth. The Oriental Pearl was the first major structure to be built in Shanghai's Pudong district on the modern side of the Huangpo River. When it first went up in the 1990s, it was something completely unique in China. The country had seen nothing of the like before. Without a doubt, it was bigger and more outlandish than any other building in the country. It was a giant spike of concrete that towered up from the river and was punctuated by a series of huge pink spheres. Like the Space Needle in Seattle and the CN Tower in Toronto, it contains no offices or apartments. Rather, it was built solely to be tall and as a statement. The photos of Shanghai in the early 90s show the spike alone and resplendent in Pudong surrounded by open space, a symbol of the country's emerging strength.

Today, the Pearl stands out for its unique design, but shares the Pudong skyline with scores of other buildings. Jinmao Tower and the Shanghai World Financial Centre are both taller and also contain offices, apartments and even a hotel. The Pearl is an amazing building, but it is also a symbol of the speed of China's growth. When it was built it was awe-inspiring and unprecedented. It, quite literally, stood alone. In scarcely more than a decade it had become old news, eclipsed by bigger and fancier buildings as the country's economy and global vision expanded almost exponentially.

The top observation sphere on the Pearl provided magnificent views across Shanghai, but it and the other wonders in Shanghai were by no means the only fabulous new buildings in China. The 2008 Beijing Olympics also brought some amazing design work. The "Bird's Nest" Olympic Stadium - where Usain Bolt cantered to victory in the 100m final - was perhaps the most famous example of this. But, I much preferred its neighbour: the National Aquatics Centre. The "Water Cube", as it is more commonly known, is a giant rectangle of the most stunning shade of blue. During the Olympics it hosted swimming and diving events. However, its sporting function paled compared to the visual effects it offered. This was particularly true at night when the blue shone out into the darkened skies of the Chinese capital.

In the run up to the Olympics, the more I read about the Water Cube, the more I became obsessed with it. I found some of the design quirks to be fantastic. Apparently, the external shell was not only designed to look like water bubbles but also to capture and conserve 80% of the rain that fell upon it so that the water could be used in the bathrooms and other functions inside, although not for the pool. The blue exoskeleton was also made partially transparent so as to allow heat and light to permeate through and thus reduce energy costs by 30%.

Tickets for the Olympics were ridiculously scarce. No matter how big the stadiums, when you have hundreds of millions of potential spectators, lots of people will be left disappointed. I did try to get some for the football preliminary rounds which would be hosted at Tianjin's own modern new stadium. It was known as the Water Drop because, apparently, it looked rather like a raindrop. I never actually felt that comparison was apt and agreed with the majority of locals who called it the sea turtle … because they thought it looked like a turtle. However, getting tickets involved applying for a lottery system through which lucky people were selected at random to ensure fairness. Sadly, I was not selected.

Interestingly, one of my students had far better luck than me. Leo, who worked at a software support company, had been ambitious and applied for tickets for the athletics, which were hugely popular. He was fortunate enough that his ticket out of, quite literally, tens of millions was plucked from the hat. He was extra lucky as it happened to be for the day of the 110m hurdles final when Chinese World and Olympic champion Liu Xiang would be competing. These were, perhaps with the exception of China's matches in the basketball competition where NBA star Yao Ming would be playing, the hottest tickets in the whole games. Leo was, understandably, chuffed. However, this was more for the fact that he could resell the tickets at a 1000% mark-up and pocket over a months' salary in the process. He was even more chuffed when I saw him the Monday after the event as Lou Xiang had failed to carry the weight of the expectations of over a billion people and limped out of the competition. His coach cited an achilles injury but many Chinese thought he had simply buckled under the unimaginable pressure - a billion people expecting you to win might do that to an athlete!

Even though I was unable to get tickets for any actual Olympic events, I did manage to get a tour of the Water Cube a few months later. Interestingly, by that point - about four or five months after the games - other Olympic venues had already been abandoned and were falling into some pretty chronic states of disrepair. The Bird's Nest had been used only once since Usain Bolt blasted to victory and it was starting to look like it needed a few licks of paint. Similarly, the baseball venue, where I had watched a Major League Baseball exhibition match a few weeks before the games, had been totally ignored. It appeared that after the final inning of the games, people had just walked away and left it. The grass was overgrown and the metal stands were gently rusting away.

To my delight, the Water Cube was still in perfect condition.. I visited on a particularly gloomy Beijing afternoon during which the city's smog was at its thickest and a blanket of grey blocked out the sun almost completely. Because of this, the outside of the cube looked nowhere near as vibrant as it did on TV and in the newspapers. However, once inside, it was fantastic. The blue roof allowed light through, which created a truly fabulous visual effect. It genuinely felt like we were immersed in warm tropical water. Despite the hordes of Chinese visitors, it felt beautifully relaxing.

The Oriental Pearl and the Water Cube were fabulous pieces of architecture and genuinely brightened up Beijing and Shanghai.

However, Tianjin was not behind the door with innovative design and the city's museum was at the forefront of this. It was a visually stunning spectacle. It featured a long covered walkway that led into a large crescent-shaped building with a glass facade that sloped away backwards. I am told that the design was intended to create the image of a swan spreading its wings. I am not sure it quite achieved that. To me, it looked more like the moon or a spaceship from Star Trek (A Ferengi Marauder for those wondering). Either way, it looked cool.

The exterior of the museum looked amazing. However, for the most part, the contents were rather disappointing. I visited it for the first time just after I moved downtown and was 100% underwhelmed by what I found. There were three floors, one of which was dedicated to traditional Chinese ceramics and another that was focused on Chinese calligraphy and artwork. It was all the type of stuff you would find in the Asiatic department of most museums. The only area that I found really interesting focused on more recent history, more specifically the turn of the last century when Tianjin was divided up amongst colonial powers into nine different concession areas.

In the latter half of the 1800s as the corrupt and inefficient Qing dynasty - the final emperors of China - began to lose its grip on power, foreign nations such as Britain, Germany and the US shoved and pushed their way into the previously closed borders of Imperial China through a combination of brute force and heavy-handed diplomacy. In a position of terrible weakness, the Chinese were forced to grant concessions in cities up and down China's east coast allowing the foreign powers access to harbours, railways and coal fields. Some of these were granted as early as 1849 and many lasted until WWII. Because they were there for so very long, they grew into almost self-contained cities with their own identity.

Probably the two best known examples of concessions in China are in Shanghai and Qingdao. Between 2006 and 2010, I saw a lot of the French area of Shanghai. I first got a peek of it on my brief visit to China at the end of my year in Korea and then again when Ossie and I were backpacking around the country. On those early visits, it was looking rather dilapidated and as though it had seen significantly better days. Many of the buildings were gorgeous and would not have looked out of place in small towns in Provence, but their shutters were broken, their paint was peeling and their lines were cracked. The majority had been built in the 1800s or early 1900s, but since 1947 and the arrival of Communism they had, essentially, been left to rot. Neither Communist philosophy nor architectural theory were big on French decadence, so the wonderful buildings had to endure 60 years of neglect.

Thankfully, over the time I was in China, things changed and the area got a fabulous second wind as companies began to rebuild and revamp some of the older buildings. The crumbling shells became trendy boutiques, expensive bars and well-appointed cafes. My own company's head office was also located in a fabulous old villa with wooden shutters and an elegant garden.

I also spent a very interesting weekend in Qingdao, which 100 years previously had a large German presence. In truth, there wasn't a huge area of older architecture remaining, but there was a fabulous cathedral that looked quintessentially German. It had two giant towers at the front that were topped with triangular turrets that set me in mind of central Munich. It had the very German combination of being large and imposing whilst also looking like it could have been pulled out of a children's fairytale. As it was set in a small tree-lined square on a hill, it looked so very unChinese, yet you only had to walk 100m and you were back amongst the glass and concrete of a modern Chinese city. It was a fascinating juxtaposition.

The cathedral was fabulous, but it very much played second fiddle to the city's main tourist attraction: The Tsingtao brewery. Set in a stout building with a strong Bavarian feel, it churned out hundreds of bottles of China's best known - but, interestingly not most popular - beer, which you can find in Chinese restaurants around the world. It was founded in 1903 and used German techniques to make some excellent brews, which it has continued to do ever since, albeit having been nationalised by the Communists in 1949 and then privatised again in the 1990s.

Even though Shanghai and Qingdao were the cities most famous for concession history and architecture, Tianjin actually had far more diversity in its colonial history. As with the other cities, it had a French and German area but it also had a British/American concession and ones for Belgium, Japan, Russia, Italy and Austro-Hungary. By the time I became a Tianjin local, quite a bit of the architecture had been lost to neglect and Communist bulldozers. However, plenty did remain. For example, less than 500m from my apartment was the Italian area, which had some genuinely gorgeous buildings that looked as though they had been transported straight out of Rome. There were some fantastic old villas that were slowly being rebuilt and revamped.

Interestingly, just like in Qingdao, Tianjin also had its own German beer. Although it was a far smaller operation and the beer was nowhere near as good as Tsingtao. Irregardless, the Kiessling bakery and brewery was a fascinating piece of history. Like Tsingtao, Kiessling was founded by Germans around the turn of the last century - 1906 to be precise - as a bakery and cafe that served beer that it brewed itself.

The first half of the last century was a turbulent and frightening time in China. In 1912, the final imperial dynasty fell and was replaced by the Republic of China. However, from 1927, the Nationalist government forces were locked in a brutal civil war with Mao's Communists. This conflict was put on hold in 1937 as the two sides joined forces to fight the invading Japanese. After the Japanese were finally vanquished, the conflict resumed until Mao came out victorious over Chiang Kai Shek in 1949 and formed the People's Republic of China.

There were very few constants during that period as Chinese and global politics went through a massive period of flux. However, for foreigners living in Tianjin, Kiessling was one element of life that did not fluctuate, almost like an old-time version of Ali Baba's. It stayed in place until 1949 when the Communists took over. In twenty-first century Tianjin, a new incarnation of Kiessling was again selling pastries. Sadly, these were Chinese made ... and genuinely awful. It also did European food - or at least a Chinese take on European food - and served beer brewed on the premises. I never really liked the food or beer, but it was a cool place to visit as the architecture of the cafe was fabulous and the interior could easily have been as it was 100 years before.

The concession area display in the museum didn't really do justice to the depth of Tianjn's colonial past, but it was still the permanent exhibition that was most worth seeing. However, the most interesting day I ever spent there came when I went to see a fascinating temporary exhibit that focused on some of China's more ancient history. As the early pages in this section of the book explain, from the moment I arrived in the Middle Kingdom I was desperately keen to visit the cities in western China that were part of the ancient Silk Road. However, as those earlier chapters detailed, I was scuppered by the huge demand for tickets at New Year and by some horrific weather conditions.

I had hoped to visit the ancient desert oases of Kashgar and Turfan, both of which are in the modern day province of Xinjiang, as there was a huge air of mystery and romance about them. One area in the west that, sadly, was not as attractive as it could have been was Dunhuang. As I discussed earlier in the book, I had first learned about the story of Dunhuang when I read Peter Hopkirk's magnificent book, *Foreign Devils on the Silk Road*. It details the impact of foreign 'explorers' who plundered some of the ancient wonders that had been hidden under the sands of western China. Dunhuang was one of the focal points of the book. It discussed the Mogao Caves which were home to some of the finest scrolls, manuscripts and frescoes in Chinese history. The caves were first carved out of the rock in 360AD and housed artefacts dating from the 4th to the 13th century.

As the old Silk Road fell out of use, the caves were abandoned during the Ming dynasty (Sometime after 1400) and, ultimately, disappeared from view under the shifting desert sands. They were rediscovered in the early twentieth century by a Taoist abbot named Wang Yuanli, who found the caves and appointed himself as *de facto* guardian of the treasures. He didn't do the best of jobs. In 1907 - during the same period of colonial exploitation that created the concession areas - when the Hungarian-born British archaeologist Aurel Stein came calling, Wang allowed him to remove a large quantity of ancient manuscripts and some of the finest frescoes from the cave walls. In exchange for the selection of priceless relics, Wang received a 'donation' to the restoration fund he started. Sadly, by the time he and the foreign explorers were finished, there was precious little remaining to be restored. In 1908, Stein was followed by the French orientalist Paul Pelliot, who took some of the most significant manuscripts back to Paris and then by Japan's Olani Kozui and Russia's Sergei Oldenburg.

Because of the foreign exploitation, the majority of the treasures from Dunhuang have been housed in foreign museums for over a century. As you can imagine, the absence of the ancient artefacts is a pretty sore spot for the Chinese who would very much like to have their treasures in their own museums. The situation is rather like a Far Eastern version of the Elgin marbles. The tension is exacerbated by the fact that the foreign museums, such as the British Museum in London, have much of their collections hidden away in storage gathering dust.

To give Chinese people a chance to see the wonders of Dunhuang, there was a fabulous exhibition that featured a detailed reconstruction of the caves. I visited the exhibit with some Chinese friends and was absolutely blown away. It recreated each of the caves and the artwork inside. The frescoes looked absolutely amazing. It showed the amazing detail in the paintings and the fantastic design from the 6th, 7th and 8th centuries. It was just unbelievable, but it felt so sad that it was impossible to see the real ones in their original location. Since my visit to Tianjin Museum, the situation has improved a little with the creation of digital versions of many of the manuscripts and databases of the artefacts. There have also been tours where the real-life artefacts - as opposed to the recreation I saw - have been displayed in cities like Los Angeles, although not yet in China.

Not all my adventures in Tianjin and around China were quite so cultural. I spent many evenings in Ali Baba's enjoying copious amounts of the Tsingtao beer I had seen produced and bottled in the Bavarian-style brewery in Qingdao. I absolutely loved this. However, I certainly didn't limit myself to the smoky confines of Ali Baba's. I also liked to get out and about in Tianjin and Beijing to enjoy all the socialising opportunities on offer. The following anecdote details one of those opportunities in Tianjin. I have included it firstly because I found it amusing and, secondly, because just like some of my experiences on trains going around the country, it highlighted the ideas and attitudes of normal Chinese people - particularly those from small towns - to foreigners.

It all took place at the Tianjin Beer Festival, an event that my friends from Ali Baba's and I were very keen to experience. Located about 2km from the centre of downtown Tianjin is Shui Shang Park, a fabulous array of lakes and small islands that offer peace and relaxation in the middle of a giant urban sprawl. It made for a fantastic location for the festival, which was a superb event. There were stalls from all the major beers in China - and some small ones too - dotted around the park on the different islands.

As China is the most populous country in the world - the Chinese beer market has grown to almost twice the size of that in the US - it stands to reason that its beer companies would shift plenty of bottles. However, the vast majority of the top brands to be found in China are virtually unknown outside the country. For example, the world's most popular beer - in terms of volume sold - comes from China and outsells Budweiser two to one. Snow Beer is produced in Liaoning in the frighteningly cold northeast region, hence the name, and is popular for two major reasons: i) It is light and relatively low in alcohol - it is also horrifically low in any form of flavour if you ask me - and is therefore, supposedly, great with spicy food, and ii) It is ridiculously cheap. A 500ml bottle costs less than 40p. In all honesty, you get what you pay for. I found Snow to be rank!

Like Tsingtao, Snow had an interesting colonial history. The modern day company was founded in 1993 and was, at the time I lived in China, owned by the multinational beer company SABMiller. However, the beer's history actually went a long way further back. It all started in the 1930s when the Japanese occupied the northeast area of China - a period known as the Manchurian Crisis in the west. In 1934 the occupying forces established the Manchuria Beer Company as a joint venture between two of their own breweries: Kirin and Dai Nipppn. After the war, the Communist government seized control of their brewery and operated it under state control with the first bottles of Snow appearing in 1957.

The Northeast was a hugely productive area for Chinese beer as one of the country's - and, consequently, the world's - other most popular brands was also founded in the frozen north. Harbin Beer was far superior to Snow as it was crisp on the tongue but was also bursting with flavour. It also had a long history, but with a far less aggressive colonial past. It dates back to 1900 when Jan Wroblewski, who was born in Prussian Poland, started a brewery to supply thirsty Russian labourers working on the Trans Manchurian Railway - the railway line that still links Russia and Beijing. It went through a few different phases of ownership, including Czechs and the occupying Soviet Union after the end of the war, before it was returned to the People's Republic in 1950. It is now owned by Anheuser Busch.

Even though Snow had a huge bar area complete with free gifts and dancing girls, we decided the bad beer just wasn't worth it. So, we opted for a few Tsingtaos and a couple of Harbins before going into the park to sample some of the lesser known brands on offer. It was as we went in search of something slightly different that things got really interesting. After trying a couple of brews that tasted like slightly inferior versions of Tsingtao, we chanced upon a small stand promoting beers from a small company in Shandong province.

For the sake of honesty, I must admit that we were not drawn to the stand by the delicious looking beer. Rather, we were pulled in by the sight of beer girls in mini-skirts pulling free glasses of beer. Who could resist? As we were the only foreigners at the stand, we drew plenty of attention, so much so that within a few minutes we were joined by a smartly dressed young woman who spoke good English and worked as the company's marketing manager. She asked whether we would mind her taking our picture whilst drinking one of their beers. As there was plenty of beer flowing our way, we were happy to oblige.

We were very happy with our little arrangement. However, things moved to a whole new level when the owner of the company appeared. He seemed genuinely thrilled to see a bunch of *laowai* enjoying his product. Apparently, there weren't too many foreigners keen to enjoy a beer in small-town Shandong! As is often the case with older Chinese businessmen - he was a stout guy in his 50s - he was keen to get the booze flowing. As is also often the case with many older Chinese businessmen, he couldn't hold it at all well. Therefore, within a few minutes, he was rip-roaringly drunk and was proclaiming his enduring love for us via the translation of his hugely embarrassed marketing manager. He then decided that he wanted his photo taken with me and Ossie (He also moved to China, roughly a year after our backpacking adventure). So, the dutiful marketing manager snapped a quick shot. When she showed it to him, he shouted out loud in pleasure and slapped us both on the back before sending one of the beer girls for more bottles.

It was a great evening and we had so much fun with our new-found buddy from Shandong. However, I haven't included this little anecdote simply as a way of recounting drinking exploits. Instead, it is in here more for what happened next. The events that followed paint a fantastic picture of China as an emerging nation. They tell of opportunism and of how many people in the country hadn't quite got their heads around being part of the global economy and still saw foreigners as massive novelties.

When I woke the morning after the festival - it was probably early afternoon if I am honest - my recollection of what had gone before was pretty hazy. However, the beer owner had clearly remembered our encounter better than us because, a few days later, I received an email from the marketing manager. I had no memory of giving her my card, but apparently I had done so as I was looking at a website - written all in Chinese - proudly featuring a photo of Ossie, me and the company owner clinking bottles of beer together. We all looked decidedly worse for wear. As beer advertising goes, it wasn't quite up there with the Budweiser frogs, but it made me chuckle: We had become the unwitting faces of a Chinese beer company.

A major philosophy of mine is that, no matter where in the world I have lived or travelled, I have always tried to visit unusual places and see sights that are a bit different. Consequently, whilst I loved the Great Wall and Summer Palace, I also wanted to see some slightly more different sights. Without doubt, there were plenty of unusual things to see in China, one of which also gave me the opportunity to engage my passion for Communist history. I have had a fascination with the subject since I watched the fall of the Berlin Wall as a nine year old at home with my parents. This interest was fuelled further by living in Mongolia and seeing North Korea, albeit from a safe distance. As this book details, I saw plenty of things that related specifically to Chinese Communist history - Mao's mausoleum that I saw with Alana for example - but close to Tianjin there was also an example that had a far deeper past.

Let me begin this particular anecdote with a little bit of military history. In the late 1960s, as the Cold War arms race escalated to its peak, the Soviet Union under Leonid Brezhnev decided that it needed a fleet of aircraft carriers to compete with the United States. The first fully-fledged one of these, the Kiev, was commissioned in 1975 and was followed by three others in the same class. These all remained in service until the Soviet Union collapsed in on itself in the early 1990s. Strapped for cash, the newly independent former Soviet Republics embarked on something of a fire sale. For example, one of the Kiev's sister ships, the Baku, was refitted and sold to India by the Russians. However, the big buyer for much of the old Soviet hardware was China because, just as the Soviet Union was fragmenting and collapsing, China was beginning to grow and exert its fledgling global influence.

The biggest, starkest and most complex example of the post-Soviet panic-selling came from the Ukranians. In 1985, in Mykolaiv (What was then a Soviet Black Sea shipyard but is now in present day Ukraine), work began on a giant Kuznetsov class aircraft carrier to be christened the Riga. However, the Soviet empire disintegrated before the Riga - which was renamed the Varyag after unrest and calls for independence in the Baltic states in the late 80s and early 90s - could be completed. In 1991, the vessel was only around 70% complete. There was a hull and basic superstructure, but little more in terms of internal fixtures and fittings. The newly independent Ukranians had no use for an unfinished aircraft carrier but, with economies across the former Soviet region in tatters, they had a great deal of need for cold hard cash. So, the Varyag was put up for sale.

Unfortunately for the Ukranians, there weren't many countries on the lookout for a huge rusting aircraft carrier. There had, for the previous 30 years, only been two countries capable of producing such immense ships and who actually had any need for them ... and the Americans had ships of their own. Unable to find a buyer for several years, the Varyag sat rusting away. That was until 1998, when a new player in the geo-political game came calling. The Chinese purchased the Varyag for the comparatively paltry sum of $20million.

What follows is a tale of scavenging and repurposing of the highest order and which - just like the earlier example with GM and the QQ - shows how the Chinese were keen to beg, steal and borrow knowledge from anywhere they could find it in order to grow as quickly as possible. It begins with the Varyag's bizarre journey to China. In June 2000, it was towed away from Ukraine towards the Bosphorus. However, the Turkish authorities refused permission for it to pass. This resulted in a bit of a stand-off and the carrier being hauled around the Black Sea in circles for 16 months. Eventually, in November 2001 after the Turkish authorities finally relented, the Varyag made its way into the Mediterranean in order to take the long route to China. As it was classified a 'dead ship', it was not allowed through the Suez Canal and had to go through the straits of Gibraltar and round the Cape of Good Hope to reach the Indian Ocean. It finally arrived in Chinese waters in March 2002.

By 2012, the rusting relic of the Cold War had been transformed into China's first aircraft carrier. When I did some of the research for this book, I found a before and after picture - the Varyag as it was when it was sold and the Liaoning as it had been renamed - and the two vessels, their shape and structure aside, bore almost no resemblance to each other. One was a giant lump of rusted metal whilst the other was a fantastic piece of 21st century technology and a symbol of China's ascendance to global prominence.

When I was in China, the Liaoning was still under renovation. However, the first of the Soviet carriers, the Kiev, had also made the journey east, albeit in far less dramatic circumstances. It was sold in 1996 to an entertainment company who wanted to turn it into a theme park and hotel. As the ship's ultimate fate was far more sedate and lacking in military value than the Varyag/Liaoning's, there is far less information about the move east but, by 2004, it had made its way from the Black Sea and was docked in a marshy area somewhere around 50km from Tianjin.

As it seemed a cool attraction, Ossie and I decided to make the trip to see it. I am told that from about 2012 the carrier has been operating as a luxury hotel, but when we got there it was still very much looking like a relic of the Soviet era. It was a fascinating thing to see. The ship had been stripped of a lot of its major workings. For example, the electrics were gone with the power coming from the shore and much of the internal fittings had also disappeared - we didn't know if it was the Chinese or the Russians who had removed them - leaving bare metal. However, there were still some really cool things to see, such as the radar and radio rooms as well as large missile silos that contained what we presumed to be fake versions of the ballistic missiles it once carried. We found it great fun to explore the cavernous hull and marvel at a piece of a period of history that was fast receding from global view.

One of the major benefits of moving to downtown Tianjin from Dawufeng was the almost instant improvement in my health thanks to the huge changes in both hygiene and nutrition that the move brought. However, it would be erroneous of me to paint Tianjin as a bastion of cleanliness and healthy living. In fact, there were plenty of places in the city where health and safety levels were just horrific. For example, I often used to go to an outdoor barbeque joint with friends from Ali Babas for lamb kebabs and cold beers. As it was located in a parking lot behind a cheap chain business hotel, we just called the place 'Car Park' as it had no name or sign. It was Asian street food before it was cool and before it was the subject of hundreds of insipid YouTube channels. Nonetheless, it was a delicious and dangerously cheap place to eat.

On one particularly hot summer evening, we were sitting there with a few frosty Tsingtao beers when we heard an ear-splitting screech from the area in front of where the food was being cooked. We all looked up and were greeted by the sight of three rats, one of which was the size of a small dog, fighting over a discarded chunk of lamb. Interestingly, none of us stopped eating; it was kind of what we expected in Tianjin at the time. In a similar vein, Ossie and I once found ourselves enjoying some beers and noodles at a relatively expensive Japanese restaurant where we would have expected standards to be higher than at a street food vendor's stall, when out of the corner of my eye I noticed a family of rats drop out of the back of a fridge containing beer and soft drinks before scurrying off towards the kitchen.

With such stories in mind, I was always careful in picking places to eat in China. However, as the above anecdotes attest, I wasn't always successful. There was, though, one particular incident in which I was frighteningly off the mark. I was in TEDA to deliver some business writing classes and was hungry. As TEDA was quite spartan in terms of dining options, I plumped for the easy option and headed to KFC. At this point, it is worth taking a second to discuss sanitation and water in China. The situation I had encountered in Dawufeng, where I couldn't even dare cook with water from my tap, was extreme but by no means unusual. There was nowhere in China, not even the big cities like Beijing or Shanghai, where it was safe to drink water from the tap.

Because the water was not at all potable, it was always an issue getting a drink with ice. In most places, I asked for my drink without it as you could never quite be sure whether the ice cubes were made with filtered water or not. The KFC I visited in TEDA, where it slipped my mind to instruct the server, had clearly used tap water to make the ice in my Diet Coke. This proved to be a massive problem for me as, a few hours after eating my chicken burger, I began to feel very ill. What followed was a period of extreme discomfort that highlighted the dangers of poor water quality and also served to give me a taste of China's medical system.

I had been in China for two and a half years when I was struck down with water-borne illness. Up until that point, I had not really been ill at all. I had experienced a couple of headaches and a strain in the knee that I had previously damaged in Korea. Neither wanting nor really needing to see a doctor about these issues, I generally just popped to my local pharmacy - usually with a Chinese friend or colleague to help translate - to get some medication or advice. That was my initial plan when I began to feel a little queasy. However, once the full impact of the tainted water began to kick in, I soon realised that the pharmacy wasn't going to be enough as I was crippled with stomach cramps and was losing the contents of my stomach with great discomfort, regularity and odour.

After a night with very little sleep spent primarily in my bathroom, I realised that I was going to have to avail myself of the Chinese medical system. This realisation left me with a few different options. The first and most appealing in terms of feeling confident in the treatment I would receive was to go private. I had travel insurance that covered serious illness, so the cost would be reimbursed. However, not only did I have a deductible that was pretty steep but also the initial cost of any treatment would be in the hundreds of dollars and it might have been months before I was reimbursed. So, I decided that it would possibly be better to explore the public health system and leave the slick private clinic with western doctors as an expensive backup option. As I was a foreigner, I wouldn't be able to have the same benefits as Chinese citizens for whom half of the cost would be reimbursed. However, my colleagues assured me that it would cost infinitely less than my insurance deductible and would be very safe and clean.

To get to my closest hospital, I jumped into a cab outside my apartment block and collected a colleague, who would translate for me, on the way. I must admit that I was feeling a little bit apprehensive as I had no idea what to expect from a Chinese hospital. Perhaps I was exhibiting a bit of western arrogance, but I presumed it was going to be significantly worse than an NHS hospital in the UK. When I arrived, I discovered that in terms of modernity and shiny equipment, my initial preconceptions were probably correct as the emergency department looked rather like my old school in Dawufeng. The walls were bare concrete, the chairs in the waiting room looked like they were from the 1950s and the whole place smelled strongly of disinfectant - the last bit was no bad thing in a hospital of course.

My initial impression of the hospital may have seemed to confirm a few of my implicit prejudices, but the longer I spent there the more I began to feel impressed with the Chinese medical system. The first element of this was the speed in which I was seen. If I had gone to a hospital in England, I could well have been waiting for hours on end. In Tianjin, I was called through to see a doctor within fifteen minutes. I was also really impressed at the efficiency of the system as things moved quickly and smoothly.

The doctor, who spoke passable English, started things off by asking for a urine and stool sample. I figured that this would be simple enough, but when I encountered a toilet that amounted to little more than a trough in the ground - a tiled and sanitized trough, but a trough nonetheless - I was a little perturbed. Squatting to use the toilet is not uncommon in Asia. It was something I had experienced in both Korea and Mongolia and of which I was no great fan. In Dawufeng, all the toilets in the school at which I worked were all of the squatting variety. In truth, I never used them for anything other than a quick pee as not only were they squatties, but they were also communal with no doors on the stalls. Instead, for anything more serious I just held it and went at home in my cockroach filled bathroom.

As I was no great expert at using the squatty, I found it hugely difficult to balance on the balls of my feet and simultaneously keep my underwear clear of the 'drop zone'. On the few previous occasions where I had no other choice than to use a squattie, I generally went all in and removed my trousers and underwear to avoid potential disaster. As my bowel movements for the preceding hours had been far from solid, I decided it was best to go for that tried and tested technique and hang my trousers behind the door. Thus, I found myself squatting there naked from the waste down - save for a pair of flip flops - trying to defecate into a small plastic cup.

Providing my sample was one of the most chastening and least elegant things I have ever done and it certainly made me regret - for a short period at least - choosing the public hospital. However, my negativity was short lived as barely an hour later the doctor had diagnosed me with bacillary dysentery and set about trying to get me better. She prescribed some antibiotics, some medication to steady my stomach and a solution to help with the dehydration the incessant diarrhoea had caused. The whole experience took less than three hours and, to my surprise and delight, cost me less than $10.

I was genuinely delighted at the experience - the treatment, not the dysentery. Even though the hospital looked and felt a little dated, I couldn't fault the treatment I had received and couldn't help but compare it favourably to the UK. I guess one caveat to all of that would be that to me $10 was not a lot of money, but to some Chinese people it would have been a big sum. So, my pleasure at the economy of the treatment perhaps needs to be placed in a little economic context.

OUT ON THE ROAD

I loved living in Tianjin. It really became a second hometown for me. Even a decade after I left, I still look back on my time there with a huge degree of affection. However, this did not stop me wanting to continue exploring the rest of China. I was lucky enough to get the opportunity to travel around the country for work quite often. I flew pretty regularly to Shanghai, occasionally to Guangzhou and once to Suzhou. The majority of these trips, unfortunately, only really involved going to the CBD of each city. Shanghai - with the fabulous contrast of Liujazhui's huge skyscrapers on one side of the Huangpu River and the fabulous old buildings of the Bund on the other - aside, this was not always so exciting. So, whenever I got the opportunity, I tried to get out and explore further afield. .

Shenyang

My first major trip, which came after about a year in China, was to the frozen north and the city of Shenyang. Even though it turned out to be an amazing trip, it was not my original choice of destination. As I was taking advantage of the Spring Festival golden week, air tickets were predictably expensive and scarce. Just as I had one year before when I was with Ossie, I wanted to go west. Sadly, it was a case of deja vu all over again and I simply couldn't find a way to get to any of the cities on the old Silk Road. Thankfully, Shenyang has a lot of history in its own right, some of which was new to me and absolutely fascinating.

The major reason I originally picked Shenyang was to see some very traditional Chinese history as the city is home to the only imperial palace outside Beijing, the Mukden Palace. Interestingly, though, this proved to be the least captivating of the things to see in town. It was without doubt a beautiful sight and dated back to the Ming dynasty in the 17th century. However, once you have seen the Forbidden City and the Summer Palace, a smaller and less ornate version doesn't really capture the attention too much.

Whilst the older history in Shenyang was not hugely exciting, the more recent history was genuinely gripping. The first element of this was the September 18th Memorial, which provided a haunting prequel to what Ossie and I saw at the Nanjing Memorial. The Shenyang memorial, just as in Nanjing, was truly harrowing but it also taught me a lot about the

Japanese occupation of China that I did not know. The most famous example of Japanese aggression is in Nanjing, but things actually began in Shenyang - known at the time as Mukden - in September 1931 when the Japanese army blew up the railway line and, rather spuriously, blamed the action on the Chinese. They used this as a pretext to launch a full-scale invasion in the northeast, the area often known in the west as Manchuria.

The memorial focused on the 'Mukden Incident' itself but also on the occupation of the region and the atrocities that went along with it. Just as with Nanjing, there wasn't an iota of subtlety in the way things were presented. And, also just as with Nanjing, it hit very hard. The whole exhibit was darker than Nanjing. Part of this might have come from the rather gloomy winter weather, but it also came from the dark granite in which the memorial was built. It gave the place a hugely - and not inappropriate - feel of morbidity.

Just as in Nanjing, there were also plenty of horrific details about murder and torture conducted by the Japanaese forces. There was one particularly gruesome exhibit that detailed methods of torture used by the Japanese on Chinese soldiers and civilians. However, just as with Nanjing, it was the basic reality that had the greatest impact. In Shenyang, this came in the form of a pit that was filled with skeletons of victims. In the dim light it looked almost like a horror movie with the white of skulls shining out of the darkness.

The September 18th Memorial was a hugely sobering place to visit, but I also found it genuinely informative as, I must admit, I knew precious little of what had happened in Manchuria. This was also the case when I visited the city's military cemetery, known quite dramatically as the Korean War Martyrs Cemetery. As Shenyang is one of the biggest cities in China's northeast and close to the Korean border, it was a major staging point for the Chinese intervention in the Korean War. Therefore, it is home to the biggest cemetery and memorial marking the People's Volunteer Army's involvement in Korea.

Just as with most things in China, the PVA in Korea was on a dramatic human scale. It is estimated that somewhere between 2.2 and 2.9 million Chinese fought in the war - although there were never more than 1.4million in theatre at one time - and that casualties numbered between 600,00 and 900,000. The US, on the other hand, suffered casualties numbering under 40,000. Historians in China dispute the casualty numbers and claim that the US military inflated its kill statistics. They argue that casualties were significantly lower and offer somewhere around 300,000 as a more realistic number. Either way, it was still a very large number - one which certainly merited a very large memorial.

The main area of the memorial looked pretty much as you might expect in any such place of a military ilk. It was dominated by a huge pillar topped by a sculpture of a PVA soldier wearing the fur-lined heavy winter gear needed for the bitingly cold conditions on the Korean peninsula. There was also a giant wall engraved with the names of many of those who perished in the conflict. There were also a few pieces of preserved military hardware such as jet fighters and a tank. It was very similar to the memorials I had seen in Normandy and Picardy when I visited those regions with my family as a child. This, of course, did not lessen its impact but it didn't really raise too much in the way of curiosity. Behind the memorial, though, the cemetery seemed far less typical.

Whereas war graves in Europe tend to either be rows of plain white stone or rows of white crosses, in Shenyang the graves were a series of small concrete domes. Each of these came with an inscription written in red Chinese characters on a stone slab in front. At this point, I must confess my ignorance in regards to some of the exact details about the cemetery. I am not 100% sure why the grave sites looked quite like they did. I was confused because they were big and oddly shaped for a single grave. I thought perhaps the domes contained more than one body or they might house unidentified remains of multiple bodies in an unknown soldier type scenario. Regardless of the exact details, the graves were a strange and slightly spooky sight. This may sound trite, but they reminded me of the pods in *Invasion of the Body Snatchers*. It was a very odd sight to see.

In the years since I visited Shenyang, I have done plenty of research - with very little success - to try and find out more practical information about the pods. Even though I was not lucky enough to get the details I was searching for, I did manage to find out about another issue that was very interesting. Whenever I googled the Martyrs' Cemetery, the majority of related articles seemed to focus on an interesting hangover from the Korean War. As the war ended with merely a ceasefire rather than an actual peace treaty - a situation that persists to this day - there were no diplomatic relations between many of the combatants for many years. For example, the US and China had almost no contact whatsoever between the end of the war and Nixon's historic visit to Beijing in 1972. Similarly, China and South Korea only established diplomatic relations in the early 1990s.

A consequence of the frosty relations between the two countries was that the bodies of thousands of Chinese soldiers remained in Korea. Unlike in northern France or other areas in Europe, where bodies from all combatants can be found resting in similar areas, the Chinese wanted the bodies of their soldiers repatriated to the motherland. For half a century, this was impossible. However, the process finally began in 2013 - six years after I had visited Shenyang - as a selection of unidentified remains left Korea to be reburied in the Martyrs' Cemetery.

The Korean War element of the memorial was captivating. I had only ever thought about the conflict from a western perspective. As I described in the previous section of this book, I visited the demilitarised zone and stared at North Korea from a safe vantage point in the South. I also had a great great uncle, who often spent Christmas with us when I was a child, who fought as a gunner in Korea. He often used to joke, "I made 10,000 Chinanem (His words there, not mine) run … but they didn't catch me". However, I had never looked at things from the other side. Therefore, I genuinely felt that even though I was still missing some important details about the cemetery, I had learned a lot. However, there was a quiet and seemingly forgotten corner of the cemetery that I found even more fascinating.

Rather than inscriptions with Chinese characters, the script in one particular area of the cemetery was different. It was cyrillic. When I first chanced upon these, I was a tad confused as, aside from a few military advisers and fighter pilots, the Soviet Union was not directly involved on the Korean peninsula. Upon closer inspection, though, I saw that the dates on the graves and the small memorial were from 1945 - too early for the Korean War. As it transpired, the graves were for soldiers killed during the three-week period at the end of WWII when the Soviet Union declared war on Japan and defeated the Imperial Army in Manchuria. It is a piece of history that is often overshadowed by the fall of the Third Reich and the atomic destruction of Nagasaki and Hiroshima, so I found it interesting. I also found it rather sad. The men involved were hidden away in a tiny nook of the cemetery and thousands of miles from their homes. They had been relegated to the tiniest footnote of history

After the rather morbid couple of hours I spent in the Martyr's Cemetery, I needed a change of pace. So, I pondered a trip to the Winter Zoo. At first, I was rather dubious about this as some of my previous experiences with animal rights in China had not been very positive. In fact, they had been downright horrific. On my first visit to China after leaving Korea, based on the recommendation of the staff at my hostel, I visited Beijing Zoo on a hot summer afternoon. It had been a shock to the system. The animals were kept in frighteningly small enclosures and cages. It was genuinely gut-wrenching. Particularly traumatic was the sight of a polar bear in a concrete enclosure that offered only the barest hint of shade from the 35 degree heat and which contained only a small puddle of brown water. The poor creature looked in terrible health.

As bad as that sounds, the zoo in Tianjin was even worse. Its management seemed to have a policy of not paying for animal food. Instead, they relied on visitors throwing food to the animals. With the monkeys, interestingly, this actually worked to a degree. The keepers stood outside the enclosure hawking bowls of old fruit for a few RMB. Visitors would purchase these and the monkeys would walk right up to you and take a piece of watermelon directly from your hand. Health and safety concerns aside, this method at least ensured the monkeys got enough to eat and the food they ate fit with their diet. For some of the more dangerous animals though, the majority of their nutrition came from visitors throwing food into their cages or enclosures. This meant that you would often see bears eating Pringles or Skittles. It also meant that the animals had learned how to get attention and how to get food. To do this they perform tricks. For example, the bears would stand on their hind legs and reach up towards the viewing platform or - and this one brought a tear to my eye - put their paws together as though praying..

With such precedents in mind, I was wary about what I might encounter in Shenyang. Thankfully, things were much better than I expected and there was a fabulous array of animals on show. When most people think of cold climates, they tend to focus more on Russia, Canada and Scandinavia. China often gets ignored as a winter locale, but it can get very cold in northern China. In Tianjin, the average temperature in

January was more than five degrees below zero. In Shenyang, things were even colder as winter temperatures dropped to more than minus 15 degrees - it was ten below when I was there. Therefore, it was a fantastic location for animals from cold weather climes.

There was lots to see in the winter zoo. The most striking and poignant for me was the polar bear area. Unlike in Beijing, the Shenyang bears looked fit and healthy. Whereas those in the capital looked straggly and dirty, those in the northeast were a pristine white. They had a large pool of very cold water in which to take a dip. Thankfully, they seemed to be just loving it. It was great to watch as one dragged itself out of the water and plonked itself down on a rock and relaxed with a look of supreme satisfaction.

Hohhot

The following year, I had the third and final installment of my ultimately futile battle to find my way further onto the Silk Road. The dance was the same as the previous two years. Tickets to cities like Urumqi or Turpan were either sold out or off the charts expensive. Ossie and I were desperate for somewhere interesting to visit. We toyed with the idea of visiting Dandong on the North Korean border where you can take a speedboat along the river between China and the hermit state. However, aside from the boat ride and the bridge towards Pyongyang, Dandong didn't have too much to see. So, we decided to take a punt on visiting the capital of Inner Mongolia, Hohhot.

Tickets and hotel rooms were super cheap, which in one way was a big plus. However, there was a reason that prices in February were only 30% of what we would expect to pay in the summer months. Inner Mongolia, just like the Republic of Mongolia to the north, is famous for its open grasslands and outdoor pursuits. And, just like its independent neighbour to the north, it is bitterly cold and enveloped in snow in the winter. Therefore, our visit was not hugely well timed as we wouldn't be doing any horse wrangling or camel riding out on the grasslands. But, we were betting/hoping that there would still be some other fun stuff to see and do.

We arrived on a mid-afternoon flight from Beijing - no direct flights from Tianjin - and took a cab to our hotel. We had booked it through the Chinese web-portal Elong, which was sort of an Expedia for the

Middle Kingdom. However, in massive contrast to western equivalents, the Chinese version often loved playing fast and loose with the truth when it came to the details of hotels. The "four-star' venue we booked looked genuinely fabulous on its listing. It was a fifteen storey skyscraper with a fountain in the lobby, a gym, a spa and even a pool. We figured that even if the weather would limit our activities, we would at least be able to enjoy the opulent looking facilities.

Sadly, we were due a very clear lesson in Chinese false advertising - a pretty common phenomenon. Our first indicator that everything was not going to be what we were expecting came when we reached the main doors and found them bolted closed with a rusty old bike lock. This left us a little nonplussed. We peered through the glass doors at the reception desk but saw nobody there. We then banged on the doors to try and get someone's attention as we were both pretty worried that the hotel may have been deserted. After a couple of minutes pounding on the glass, a young woman and an old man dressed in ancient padded Chairman Mao jackets appeared in the lobby and shuffled towards us. The young woman undid the bike lock, half-opened the door and asked, "Pao li Bei Ku?". Close enough!

It very quickly became clear that the hotel - which really looked like it had only just opened and wasn't perhaps fully finished - hadn't received too many guests and certainly not any foreign ones. After a clumsy check-in process in the frigidly cold reception, which was 'heated' by a single bar on an ageing electric fire, we were given a key and shown past the non-functioning fountain to the elevator. It took us to the seventh floor, which was similarly Baltic in its climate. Thankfully, when we reached the room, the heating was on - we presumed it was the only room in the hotel in which the heat was actually being used - and we were able to thaw out our frozen extremities.

After we unpacked our cases, we decided it would be a good idea to go and explore the hotel and its facilities. It would be a disappointing trip. We headed to the second floor where we expected to find the pool and spa. There was neither a pool nor a spa. Instead, there was a 'massage' centre which was - in an echo of our experiences in Nanjing two years before - a poorly disguised brothel. Interestingly, whilst the majority of the hotel was deserted, the knocking shop seemed well-populated with young ladies. Not wanting to partake in the wares on offer, we decided that it was probably best for us to get out so that we could explore the city.

Since it was already mid-afternoon and we felt that we didn't really have time to explore beyond the centre of the city, we decided to visit one of Hohhot's most famous historical attractions: Dazhou Temple. As it was built in the 1500s, we were expecting something with a bit of ancient wonder. Sadly, we were to be disappointed as despite Dazhou being half a millennia old, precious little has actually ever happened there. The Dalai Lama visited in 1586, but after that it was 400 rather sedate years.

Dazhou's slightly anaemic past was slightly underwhelming. However, what the temple lacked in history it more than made up for in aesthetics. Until that point in my stay in China, most of the attractions I had visited were in absolutely pristine condition. This was down to a couple of reasons. Firstly, on a more recent level, everything was being touched up ahead of the Olympics in Beijing and the tourists that would arrive in conjunction with them. A clear example of this was the Temple of Heaven, which was closed for refurbishment and renovation for the first 18 months that I lived in the country.

Secondly, on a slightly older level, many of the historic buildings around China were damaged or destroyed during the Cultural Revolution in 1967 and 1968 when the Red Guards - a student mass movement guided by Mao - waged a campaign of chaos and destruction against what Mao defined as the "Four Olds": old customs, old habits, old culture and old ideas in order to sever China from its traditional past. To do this, they set about destroying and vandalising historical sites across the country. It is estimated that in Beijing alone 4,922 were seriously damaged. Consequently, a lot of them needed to be rebuilt or restored.

For those two reasons, many of the ancient buildings in China that survived the chaos of the late 1960s have a somewhat modern air of perfection about them. For example, when I was finally able to visit the aforementioned Temple of Heaven I was astounded by the beauty and intricacy of the buildings and decorations while simultaneously disappointed by the sanitised feel it conveyed. For a building constructed in the fifteenth century, it seemed odd that there was scarcely a tile out of place or a single crack in the masonry. It almost felt like a theme park version of Chinese history.

After Dazhao, and grabbing a cup of coffee to warm ourselves up, we decided to take a short walk to the city mosque. As we had seen in Xi'an, the further west you travel in China the greater the muslim influence. In truth, aside from the far western province of Xinjiang - where, as I have already discussed, there is a huge amount of repression aimed at the Muslim Uighur population - the Islamic influence is not so strong in China. However, despite the relatively small population, there are plenty of mosques that look amazing and are worth the visit. There are some, such as one that we passed in Yinchuan, that look similar to the architecture you might see in Pakistan or the Gulf. Others, such as the one in Xi'an, have a very Chinese feel and almost look like pagodas.

The mosque in Hohhot was totally different. It really did not seem to fit into any specific architectural category and genuinely surprised us. It was a beautiful but very strange building. The best adjective I could use to describe it would be 'wizardly'. The buildings were built of small black bricks and were covered with ornate Arabic script in emerald green and gold. This, coupled with eaves that seemed to twist and turn towards the heavens, gave it an almost mystical feel. As amazing as the mosque looked though, just as with Dazhou, there was no great historical significance to it. It was originally built in 1693 and, a couple of renovations aside, nothing ever really happened there… apart from me and Ossie visiting, of course!

In such bitterly cold conditions, Dazhou and the mosque were enough for the day. So, we headed back to the hotel - where the fountain remained dry and there was no still no sign of any other guests - to take a shower before heading out for dinner and a few beers. Little did we know that Hohhot would provide us with one of the weirdest and most exciting evenings out we would enjoy in China.

It began with a lamb hotpot. The economy of Inner Mongolia is based heavily on the grasslands that surround Hohhot, so there is a huge focus on dairy products and lamb or mutton. Consequently, there are a plethora of restaurants that serve lamb kebabs and hotpot. We washed our dinner down with a couple of cold beers and then began to think about where the evening would take us. However, as we scanned the area surrounding the restaurant, there seemed to be a paucity of nightlife options.

This situation was not uncommon in China because: i) people tend to go out to restaurants in large family or work-based groups rather than going to bars, and ii) many places tend to close much earlier than they do in the west. In Tianjin, in such a situation, we would decamp to the welcoming confines of Ali Babas. However, in Hohhot, we didn't know whether there was a bar that would be open beyond 10pm. After stepping out of the restaurant and into the cold, we began our search. Initially, we had no luck. We wandered the streets close to our hotel looking for neon lights that might signify a bit of nightlife but found ourselves going around in circles and feeling increasingly cold.

As I began to lose feeling in the end of my nose and we started to think that our search would be in vain, we heard a low rhythmic beating sound. We stopped and tilted our ears to get a better gauge on the sound. It certainly sounded like a bar or a club. Thus began a process of trying to identify where the noise was emanating from. This was no easy task as there didn't seem to be any lights or signs to help us hone in on it. However, eventually, we managed to locate an old derelict looking warehouse that seemed to be the source of the music. To get in, we had to walk down an alley at the side and climb a rickety metal staircase. At the top of the stairs we were greeted by a surprisingly elderly Chinese man in a giant fur-lined Mao jacket. As we might have expected in a smaller and relatively remote Chinese city, he was clearly shocked to see us. Unlike Tianjin or Beijing, we had seen very few *laowai* in Hohhot so we were clearly something of a novelty. He asked us for 5rmb admission - less than £1 - and opened a giant padded door.

Once inside, we were astounded by what we found. Bars in China generally fell into one of two uninspiring categories. Most Chinese bars tended to be very expensive and were aimed at business people drinking expensive - although not necessarily good - scotch. They would usually be dark with shiny tables and would play genuinely woeful Chinese pop music. The majority of bars aimed at the *laowai* tended to be themed affairs such as British, Irish or American. Whilst these usually played much better music and often served some good western food, they were also frighteningly expensive as they catered to expats who would pay western prices for a Chinese beer. Aside from my beloved Ali Babas and The Den in Beijing, there were not too many bars in China that I really liked. Generally, like most Chinese people, me and my friends would enjoy beers with dinner at restaurants … unless we were in Babas. The old warehouse in Hohhot, though, broke the mold.

The first thing that struck us was the music. Even though we were in a very remote corner of China, it was actually good. There was a really cool mix of rock and dance music. The second thing was the decor. It was really cool and massively ahead of its time. The roof girders were exposed and rusted - I guess this was just a reflection of the state of the building rather than an architectural statement - whilst the walls inside were covered in graffiti. It had the look of a British hipster bar, before that was even a thing. The whole place looked like it had been very effectively repurposed, before that was even a word. The only downside was that while they were installing the bar and doing the graffiti, nobody seemed to have thought about installing any heating, so we had to stay wrapped up very warm in our padded jackets and hats.

The Hohhot locals really seemed to love a good night on the tiles. The whole place was packed with hundreds of young people dancing, even whilst wearing their padded jackets and woolly hats, and creating a fantastic atmosphere. It was unlike anything we had experienced in China. Compared to the slick and sanitised Chinese bars or clubs and the overpriced and generally ridiculously inauthentic western bars, it was amazing and very real. We were hooked!!!

We had a fabulous night in the frigid warehouse. We piled back a bunch of 3RMB beers (Barely 25p) and joined the Inner Mongolians on the dance-floor for a raucous evening of fun. Because of this, the next morning we were in no state to go exploring any historical sights. So, we shuffled a few hundred metres down the street to the Holiday Inn to get a good cup of coffee and to fight off our hangovers at the lunch buffet. That was no easy process as cheap Chinese beer rarely sits well in the system and has a habit of hitting quite hard the following day. So, by the time we were done, it was mid-afternoon and we were in need of something to do. A quick scan of our Lonely Planet brought the idea of taking a stroll in Qingcheng Park.

All the pictures we had seen of Qingcheng were taken in the summer and showed lush greenery and families boating on a green lake. In the icy depths of February, we would see a very different landscape. When we arrived at the gate to the park it was like stepping onto the Siberian tundra. The ground was frozen solid and covered in a thick layer of snow whilst the trees were all black and skeletal. It all looked very depressing. However, just as with our warehouse experience the previous evening, we would be surprised by the entertainment on offer.

As we walked along a frozen path, we stumbled upon the frozen lake at the centre of the park. Instead of the rowing boats and pedalos we would have seen in the summer, the ice was covered in young Chinese people doing all manner of winter activities. There were younger kids being pushed or dragged around the ice on rubber rings - this looked unbelievably fun but we were not sure they would let two fully grown adults have a go - as well as older kids using specially customised ice-bikes with spokes on the wheels to allow them to grip the surface and a combination of teens and adults skating around the lake.

What better way, we asked ourselves, was there to clear a stinking hangover than skating on a frozen lake? As it transpired, there were probably many better ways. It didn't go well. Ossie couldn't skate at all and I had only the most basic of levels. I was also handicapped by a lack of availability of skates. I am a UK 9, but the Chinese tend to be a tad smaller in the foot department. Therefore, some of the bigger sizes were not so well-stocked, or stocked at all. The skate rental shack had a 7.5 or a 10.5. I couldn't get my feet into the smaller pair, so I was forced to go for the bigger ones.

The loose skates and my hangover combined to ensure that I managed to face-plant the ice on several occasions. My hilarious and decidedly unsuccessful attempts at skating elicited plenty of mirth from the watching locals. However, this was nothing compared to the attention Ossie received. Even though his skates fit nicely - he is a small fella, so he was able to slide into a pair of size 6s - he was terrible on the ice and could barely go two metres without flapping, flailing and then tumbling quite spectacularly to the ice. After this happened six or seven times, the guys in the skate shack wandered over to the edge of the lake and waved him over. Clearly worried about the foreigner's health, they proffered a strange contraption seemingly designed to help him maintain his balance. It was a rickety old chair, the type my kids sat on in Dawufeng, with a skate blade fastened to the front legs.

The chair, which at no point looked either safe or sturdy, proved to be wildly successful in providing some rather humorous entertainment as Ossie managed to use it as a rudimentary zimmer frame. The sight of a short foreigner nervously pushing a kiddies' school chair around the ice certainly brightened up the afternoon for most people in the park. However, it was far less successful as a skating aid as Ossie continued to plummet to the ice with alarming force … albeit at slightly less frequent intervals. Therefore, he decided that the best course of action would be to give up on the skates completely and go for one of the ice-bikes. Despite these being for children, Ossie managed to squeeze onto the seat. This allowed him to glide around the ice with a modicum of dignity..

Chengdu

The trip Ossie and I took to Chengdu for the October holiday of 2009 was probably the first we took together where our eyes had not been on the Silk Road. Unlike previous trips when we were stumped by the weather or the scarcity of tickets, there were a few slightly more complicated reasons this time. Obviously, we did have to face the familiar problem of finding tickets. However, this was not the main hindrance. By this point, some of the areas in the far west were getting increasingly tense as the government stepped up its repression against the Uighur minority in the region amidst a series of riots in Xinjiang during the summer. This meant it really wasn't a safe proposition anymore.

The other reason we were happy to ignore the far west was that Chengdu had so much to offer. Shenyang had been a pleasant surprise because there was so much recent history that I had not been aware of. Hohhot, in itself, was not the most interesting of cities but we had managed to find ways to really enjoy our trip. Chengdu, on the other hand, clearly had so much to offer: there was history, there was amazing food ... and, there were pandas!

The first thing to strike us about Chengdu was the heat and humidity. Tianjin in October was starting to get cold and was, as it is most of the year, extremely dry. In winter months, it would often be so dry and cold that my skin would feel parched and irritated, even to the point of cracking. Chengdu was the polar opposite. After getting out of the taxi from the airport, we were struck by a wave of moisture from the air. Before we had even managed to get from the curb to the hotel doors, we were drenched.

Unlike our trip to Hohhot, where we had chosen a hotel that was perhaps a little too modern, we were staying in Chengdu's old town. Our hotel was in a two storey building that seemed to date back to the turn of the previous century and was built in traditional Chinese style around an open central courtyard. With the inner workings of the house open to the elements and the ancient frame lacking a little bit of modern insulation, it felt moist everywhere. Our room was beautiful and looked out onto a jade fountain in the courtyard, but the walls were wet and the bedding felt claggy. Rather than unpacking and risking our clothes also getting wet, we left them in our suitcases and decided to head out for dinner.

As we were already in the old town, we didn't need to go far to find something fabulous to eat. A few hundred metres from the hotel we found a row of buildings that, despite being seemingly in the middle of either a renovation or demolition, were serving some fabulous local food. We plonked ourselves down at a rickety table in front of one of these 'restaurants' and waited for the waiter. The 'menu' was simply a choice between chicken, pork and shrimp.. Not really knowing what to expect, we ordered one chicken and one shrimp dish to share and a couple of icy cold beers.

Sichuan, the province in which Chengdu is located, is famous for having the spiciest food in China. I am a massive fan of a bit of heat and love super spicy Indian curry. However, I had absolutely no idea what I was getting myself into. Our food arrived on a giant plate cum shallow bowl and was served in layers. The bottom of the plate was filled with water and was crammed with small dried chillies. Each of these had been sliced so that the spice within would ooze out and create the spiciest sauce I have ever eaten and ever will eat. Above these was a layer of vegetables and then a layer of chicken and then another layer of vegetables and finally some more chicken with a sprinkling of nuts. It looked resplendent and had us salivating.

Eating the plate was a transitional and transformative experience. It began easily and comfortably as we picked the chicken and nuts from the top. It was good but, in all honesty, felt a little bland. However, as we ate our way through the layers of chicken and vegetables and the meat began to settle into the spicy sauce in the bottom, things became far more intense and decidedly less comfortable. By the time we got to the last pieces of chicken, the meat was soaked in crazily hot sauce. Even a single mouthful made us sweat and, I hate to admit, had me close to tears. The only way to take the heat was to power down the frosty beers in quick succession. It was a truly enchanting combination and one of the most memorable meals I have ever eaten.

The spicy food and the super cold beer was a rather schizophrenic experience. In one way, it was addictive as the contrasting temperatures fought a gripping battle on our taste buds. However, conversely, the combination proved to be a gateway into pain. The cooling effect of the beer temporarily eased the heat of the food allowing us to continue when that course of action might not have been so wise. It was all great at the time, but at around three a.m. I woke in the hottest of sweats. Admittedly, the room was relatively humid to begin with, but I was drenched and surrounded by a pool of salty liquid. Not only this, but I found myself feeling as though my skin was wanting to peel off my body. I lay there scratching manically for a few moments before deciding to down the bottle of water I had by the bed and then go to the bathroom. Taking a pee proved to be a necessary but horrific process. The spice had managed to infiltrate every part of my body and it burned like hell. Had I not just eaten the spiciest meal known to man, I would have worried I had a urinary tract infection.

The next morning I awoke on sodden and cold sheets. At first, I thought that I had embarrassed myself by wetting the bed. Thankfully, my shame was short-lived and needless as it quickly became clear that it was sweat rather than urine in which I was lying. As I came round and peeled myself off the sheets, my head was absolutely pounding. However, I managed to rouse myself and jump in the shower to wash off the layer of salt and residual spice that was still clinging obdurately to my skin. Ordinarily, feeling as rough as I did, I would have preferred to lounge in bed for the majority of the morning and perhaps even some of the afternoon. This was not on the agenda, though, because we were going to see the pandas and I was as excited as a four-year old on his first trip to the zoo!

Chengdu is often referred to as the Panda Capital of China as it is at the heart of the mountainous region in the southwest of the country - in Sichuan and the southern parts of Gansu - that provides pandas with their bamboo rich habitat. Therefore, there is lots to see in the city and surrounding areas in relation to one of the world's cutest animals. There were some opportunities for us to get out into the countryside to see the pandas in a more natural habitat, but these were both expensive and complex to arrange. So, instead, we decided to visit the Panda Research Base just outside Chengdu.

As I discussed in the chapter on Shenyang, animal rights in China can often be something of an oxymoron. Therefore, we were a little concerned about what we would find. Thankfully, the Research Base was amazing. However, on the way there, we got a reminder of how bad things can be. To get to the pandas, we had taken a taxi from our hotel but had a bit of a miscommunication when we gave directions and our driver took us to the City Zoo because it also had pandas. Whereas the research base was a fantastic place and treated the animals very well, the city zoo was horrid. Just as with its counterparts in Beijing and Tianjin, the animals there were kept in small concrete-lined cages. It was such a sad sight. The three pandas all looked motheaten and dejected. It was heart-wrenching.

The Panda Research Base was, to our great relief, a very different matter. It was created in 1987 in order to take care of six pandas that were in ill-health. Since then, it has expanded and developed in order to i) research pandas and their breeding habits, or lack thereof, ii) to breed pandas in a safe but natural environment, and iii) to provide education about giant pandas. It was a fabulous afternoon in which we learned a lot and during which our faith in China's attitude towards the animal kingdom was restored a little.

Our visit began with an exhibition about panda breeding, which as we soon learned is not always the easiest and smoothest of processes. The first issue, we discovered, was that the pandas only have a short window to get the job done. Not only are the females only in season from March until May but also couples often only meet for 2 or 3 days at a time during this period. Because of this, the panda population was dwindling for many years and by 2003 there were barely 1,200 living in the wild. In recent years, their number has bounced back a little but there are still less than 2,000.

The exhibition showed lots of case studies of pandas living in the research base and how they had succeeded in breeding. However, the most interesting thing we learned was a more extreme approach to conception. There was a visual display that described two pandas that had been paired together but failed to produce any offspring. To ensure that the pair could procreate, doctors took a radical approach and went for a type of panda IVF. They sedated the male panda and then, eye-wateringly, took a scalpel to his testicles. They removed an amount of 'matter' that was then used to inseminate the female. It sounded rather brutal and painful to me, but it had brought success.

From the exhibition, we moved into the wider area of the base, which includes a large expanse of bamboo forest in which the pandas live. We were able to wander on special paths that wind through these areas and see adult pandas living in a close approximation to their natural habitat. This was utterly fabulous. It was by no means high octane entertainment as the pandas don't really do too much in the way of moving, but it was almost hypnotic. The animals were so calm, peaceful and gentle. All they did was sit in the shade stripping and eating pieces of bamboo. In objective terms, it was quite mundane. However, I simply couldn't bring myself to look away. Despite being so slow and lumbering, the giant pandas were so beautiful.

Dragging ourselves away from the adult pandas was extremely difficult. I had never seen anything quite like it and they were just so cute. However, there was still so much to see in the base. This started about half a kilometre away with the adolescent pandas. Whereas the mature pandas seemed to have grown sedate with their older age, the younger pandas were full of the exuberance of youth. They were housed in a small enclosure - with enough room to wander around and plenty of bamboo to eat - with a climbing frame at the centre. The young pandas seemed to love it. They clambered all over the wooden beams and jumped around. They even indulged in a little play-fighting, which just looked tremendous fun.

The first two panda enclosures with the adults and the adolescents were just awesome. Both Ossie and I were absolutely blown away. However, in terms of pure cuteness, we had seen nothing up to that point! We went around the park in descending order of age. So, having gone from the adults to adolescents, we then made our way to the babies. Even for two cynical ESL teachers, it was too cute to believe. All of the babies made our hearts skip a beat. They genuinely looked like cuddly toys and you just wanted to give them a big hug. However, the greatest thing we saw was a baby panda in an incubator. It was tiny and oddly pink and simply laid there sleeping. You simply cannot imagine how adorable it was.

One of the other things we discovered whilst in the research base was the impact that the Sichuan earthquake had had on the panda population. In May 2008, Sichuan province was rocked by a tremor measuring eight on the Richter scale. At the time, I was sitting in my office in Tianjin - thousands of miles away from the epicentre - and noticed the blinds on my window gently swaying from side to side. At first, I thought it was just the air-conditioning, but soon reports of the tragedy started to flood in. People reported similar patterns in cities as far north as Shenyang. It was a truly devastating natural disaster.

The vast majority of the media coverage associated with the earthquake focused on the human impact as almost 90,000 people lost their lives and tens of millions lost their homes and possessions. There was also a lot of attention paid to the quality of buildings in the region as several schools collapsed frighteningly easily when the ground shook beneath them and, in so doing, took the lives of hundreds and thousands of schoolchildren. This horror came about because local party bosses had been cutting corners with materials in order to pocket the money they saved. However, along with the tragic human cost, there was also a significant environmental impact.

The earthquake struck in the heart of the pandas' natural habitat. It completely destroyed 23% of it and had a direct impact on 60% of the panda population. The quake damaged an area of over 320 square kilometers of land that was rich in vegetation and left it bare. This deprived pandas of food and places to live. It also served to fragment the population with several panda couples separated and left stranded. It left the government and organisations like WWF with a huge job to get the pandas reunited and back into the best environments. Apparently, this took almost 18 months to fully complete.

Seeing the pandas was always going to be the highlight of our trip to Chengdu. Let's be clear, it would be the highlight of almost any trip to any city anywhere in the world. In my life, the only two other experiences with nature that have even come close were seeing sea turtles laying their eggs in Oman and watching elephants take a bath in a river close to Kandy in Sri Lanka. However, we would be doubly fortunate on our trip as close to Chengdu was one of the great sights of Chinese history. The LeShan Giant Buddha might not be as well known as the Great Wall, the Forbidden City or the Terracotta Warriors but it is certainly as stunning. Built in the 8th century, at over 70m in height LeShan is the biggest statue of Buddha in the world and is the biggest statue of any kind from the pre-modern age. We had seen plenty of pictures of the statue before our visit, but they really didn't do it justice!

We booked a driver in Chengdu to drive us out to the Buddha - it was just over two hours - on a wet and misty day. When we arrived, we had to take a long walk up a series of shallow steps that led up towards the Buddha's head. It was quite the sight. It is the size of a three or four storey house - just the head, not the Buddha in its entirety. As we looked across at the face, he had a rather passive expression. The lips were closed, but looked as though they were just about to break into a wry smile. The eyes seemed to be rather blank and almost sleepy. It made us wonder what he was thinking about and what he had been pondering for over a millennium. More eye-catching than the facial expression though, were his ears. He had superbly long lobes - they were probably about four feet long in themselves - that drooped down towards his shoulders.

The Buddha is carved out of a cliff face in a seated position overlooking the murky waters of the Min River. His giant feet are barely 5m away from the waters' edge. To get a better perspective on the Buddha, it was best to walk down to the viewing area at the base in front of his feet. To get there, we took a precarious path that ran down the side of a cliff that overlooks the statue. It being China, even though the path was both narrow and precarious, it was crammed with people. Because of this, we didn't get as much time as we would have liked to enjoy the detail of the Buddha. However, walking next to the figure helped to really put the scale into context: it took us a good long while to get to the bottom!

Once we had reached the bottom, we were greeted by a truly fantastic sight. The Buddha towered above us like a giant skyscraper. In a country like China, scale is always a hugely relative concept. For example, the skyline in Pudong in Shanghai with Shanghai World Financial Centre and Jinmao Tower is an epic view. Those two behemoths dwarf some buildings that would have dominated the panorama of almost any other city. The Buddha wasn't on this kind of scale in pure physical terms, but it managed to create a feeling of being truly gigantic as it dwarfed the people standing at the bottom and the cruise ships that bobbed about on the river. His feet were almost the height of most of the Chinese people and his body towered away from us. It astounded us that something so large was done so many years ago with so little technology.

As fabulous as LeShan was, there was something that struck us as tragic. In Hohhot, it had been interesting to see the signs of wear and age on the eaves and tiles of Dazhou Temple as it provided a refreshing contrast to sanitised and over renovated attractions such as the Temple of Heaven in Beijing. The LeShan Buddha was also not particularly sanitised. However, the situation was nothing like the one in Inner Mongolia. Rather than merely being a bit faded, the Buddha was showing the signs of some pretty serious environmental damage.

When we had stared across at the Buddha's face, his expression was absolutely enchanting. However, it was also alarmingly grimey. He looked like he was in desperate need of a wash - like a small child that had been out playing in the dirt. From the bottom too, the situation was similar. The feet were darkened and the legs also looked off-colour. All of this was caused not by the Buddha's slack personal hygiene, but by the impact of local coal-fired power stations. I didn't know it at the time, but apparently many locals had nicknamed it the 'Crying Buddha' because the grime would run down its face when it rained and made it look like a lady with mascara that was running.

CHANGING CHINA

During the four years I spent in China, it is safe to say that both my life and career changed exponentially and that I saw some unbelievable places and met many interesting people - both Chinese and *laowai*. On a professional level, my job progressed beyond anything I could have ever imagined. When I arrived, I just wanted to experience China and to see a bit of a country that looked really interesting. I had only ever taught children and I spent my first few months teaching kids on a blackboard in a hugely dated classroom. By the time I had been there three years, thanks to the unprecedented development and changes the country was undergoing and the opportunities these afforded, I was wearing a tailored suit whilst teaching employees at major multinational companies in Tianjin and also in other big cities like Beijing Shanghai and Guangzhou. Despite the regular delays and horrific service on Chinese airlines, I absolutely loved being flown around the country for work. It really felt like I had arrived and was getting the true modern China experience. Even today, a decade after the fact, I distinctly remember boarding a flight from Shanghai to Tianjin one cold November evening and pinching myself at the transformation in my life. I clearly recall thinking to myself that it could only have happened in China.

As cool as all that was, no matter how much I changed and evolved during my time in China, I could not have kept up with the speed of change in the country as a whole. The place I encountered when I arrived in 2006 was, in many ways, vastly different to the one I left in 2010. It is not an exaggeration to say that the changes covered almost every facet of life from architecture, to food and even people's attitudes to the world. When I think back on the Tianjin of 2006 and compare it to the one I was living in when I left, the difference is stark.

One of the biggest changes I saw was with transport. As I explained in previous pages, travel in China in my early days was often a slow, dirty and difficult process. I have already detailed the horrors of travelling in rural China, but even travelling between Beijing and Tianjin - two of the biggest cities in northern China - was not very pleasant when I first arrived in the country. The first issue here was that the train was frightfully slow. The two cities are separated by barely 100km but the journey often took over two and a half hours. The second issue was the crowds. Getting on the train was often a complete nightmare. The stations were hugely crowded and horribly managed. For example, buying a ticket from Beijing to Tianjin often involved joining a melee of 50 or 60 people trying to force their way to a single window. Then, once on the train it was often impossible to sit down, even if you had purchased a ticket with an assigned seat because as soon as you boarded the train you would be struck by an impenetrable wall of humanity all crammed into the aisles and any available spaces.

There was a similar situation for transport on a more local level. When I arrived in Tianjin, I tried the local bus service. In truth, it wasn't terrible. The buses were relatively clean and generally punctual. However, in a similar vein to the trains, they were monumentally crowded. In the summer, it was horrifically claustrophobic and sweaty. So, to avoid the crush, I generally travelled around the city by taxi. These were readily available and crazy cheap. In 2006, this was a pretty idiosyncratic experience. Almost all of the cabs were old Chinese made models - by the state-run Xia Li company - that rattled along the streets with bone juddering ferocity. They were made with the cheapest possible materials and had absolutely no suspension whatsoever. As a consequence, a trip across the city would cost me next to nothing but usually left me worried about the integrity of my lowest two vertebrae.

Not only were the Xia Li hugely uncomfortable, but they were also usually rancidly unhygienic. The first issue was the drivers and their love of smoking in the car and then flicking their ash wherever they pleased. The second issue was spitting. The drivers generally loved to clear their noses and either fire it out of the window or shoot it into a cup they kept on the dashboard. Also, in the backseat you would find an empty tin can fastened to the back of the driver's seat for passengers to spit into. The third issue was the bizarre attire they would often sport. Winter was generally fine but in the summer it was not uncommon for me to get into a cab and find the driver sitting in a pair of baggy boxer shorts with his t.shirt rolled up to expose his belly. It may have kept them cool, but it really did not make for a pleasant ride.

By the time I was ready to leave China, things had changed a lot. The train had gone from being a crowded, chaotic and dirty experience to being fast, smooth and uncharacteristically clean. Many of the clanking old diesel trains disappeared and were replaced by sleek white bullet trains linking major cities. The major catalyst for this change was the 2008 Olympic Games. Prior to the games, the government set about creating a high speed rail link between Beijing and Tianjin as part of the development of a larger national system. To facilitate this, they built a new station in the south of Beijing and revamped the station in Tianjin, which involved closing the main station for about a year and using a truly horrific temporary station made from corrugated iron. However, by the time Li Ning - China's first ever Olympic gold medallist and now the owner of a huge sportswear brand - lit the flame in the Bird's Nest stadium, rail travel in China bore very little resemblance to what I had experienced before.

The construction of the new rail infrastructure proved to be interesting to see and was indicative of the growth seen around the country. I spent a lot of time travelling between Tianjin and Beijing for both my job and for football, so I had a ringside seat for all the changes. It was a very odd process. Things seemed to be static for a hugely long time and then so much happened at the very last minute.

Things started pretty well when, in early 2008, new bullet trains replaced the old 1970s diesels. When this happened, we all thought that the new system would be up and running quickly and well ahead of the games. Yet, bizarrely, the rail system operated using the new trains with the old infrastructure for more than six months with strict speed limits. This meant the journey became more comfortable but still took over an hour. Equally oddly, even though the trains had changed, the stations hadn't. So, we had the strange scenario of multi million dollar pieces of rail technology arriving at a station that looked like a series of large portacabins. It all seemed very odd and slightly lacking in logic.

Amazingly, that situation was still in place just days before the games began. With Tianjin hosting some of the Olympic boxing and football, it made you wonder what on earth was going to happen if they didn't get a move on. I took a train on August 2nd - only six days before it all began - and it remained totally chaotic. The journey from the temporary station to Beijing passed through Tianjin's main station, which was slated to open around the 5th. Whilst it was starting to look like a modern station, there was still so much to do. None of the escalators leading to the platform were there, none of the shops had signs or windows and none of the electronic signs had been installed. It looked weeks away from being ready.

As only a country with a cheap labor force of hundreds of millions and a pretty lackadaisical outlook on health and safety can, China really got a move on! I am not sure how they did it - I presume it involved a huge influx of migrant labour coming in from the inland provinces - but, within a matter of days, Tianjin station was transformed from a disjointed building site to a gleaming wonder of modern design. It was simply astounding. The concrete Stalinist style facade remained on the outside but the interior looked like something from a sci-fi movie and was unrecognisable from what was there before. On a more practical level, an increase in ticket desks and the introduction of sleak automated barriers meant that it was so much easier to get tickets and to get on the train without having to wrestle your way to your seat.

Changes in more localised transport were also dramatic. The biggest move was the opening of a new metro in Tianjin, which was superb. However, unfortunately, it didn't go particularly close to either my apartment or my office, so I didn't get to use it too often and was forced to continue using taxis. Thankfully, these also underwent dramatic change. As 2008 progressed, the horrid rickety Xia Li began to disappear and be replaced by shiny new Toyotas produced, as part of a joint venture, at the Xia Li plant in Tianjin. At the same time, the drivers also changed as rules came in to ban spitting and smoking, and to make them wear pants. My journeys became far less colourful, but a great deal more comfortable.

The Olympics were a watershed moment in Chinese history. It was a huge global event that showed the new image of China to the outside world. As I have already noted, this brought huge changes to the faces of both Tianjin and Beijing. This was fantastic for me in terms of the practicalities of my daily life. However, the games also brought some changes that were far less positive and highlighted that even though we were witnessing a period of epic change, China was still a dictatorship and old habits die hard for authoritarian regimes. We saw this in a couple of ways, i) the way the government dealt with historic parts of Beijing, and ii) in the way they dealt with a large number of the foreigners who had been living in the country prior to the Olympics.

Back in early 2006, when Ossie and I were enjoying Spring Festival, we stayed at a hotel in the old hutong area of Beijing, which we used as a base to enjoy the festivities. It was amazing. We enjoyed meeting the people who lived in the area as well as eating in a couple of amazing restaurants there. As the Olympics neared, the area began to disappear and the bulldozers rolled in as a process of 'modernization' began. What had been an area that sprawled over several city blocks and was home to real people and real businesses, was reduced to a couple of streets that were home to souvenir shops and fast food restaurants. Apparently, the government saw street vendors and hole in the wall eateries as a poor reflection on the city, so they were closed and forced away from the centre where they might encounter foreign tourists.

It was soul destroying - both for the city and anyone who had loved its more authentic areas. I returned there in the weeks before the games in the hope of eating at Tian Hai Can Ting once more, but was greeted with large walls blocking off the whole area in which I had previously stayed as a huge amount of construction work was underway. Thankfully, before I left China, I was able to eat there again as Tian Hai had a big enough reputation - it was heralded in Lonely Planet - that the government allowed it to remain but its surroundings were not what they had been.

The destruction of historic parts of China's capital was a crying shame and upset me a little as Ossie and I had a fantastic time whilst we were staying in those areas. However, the impact the Olympics had on China's expat community was far more pressing and had a far greater impact for me personally. To explain what happened and how things worked out, I probably need to start by giving a bit of an overview of the immigration situation in the country at the time. In doing so, I will also need to talk a little bit about institutionalised corruption.

When I arrived in 2006, the recruiter who had set me up in Dawufeng organised a 'Z' visa for me. This was the standard immigration protocol for teachers and allowed us to live and work in China. These were generally issued for a year but, as I was only at the school for a shorter period, mine lasted for six months. To be eligible for one, teachers needed to have a degree and be from an English speaking country. Having a teaching certificate or experience was not usually an issue, which was good news for me. In truth, as China was not always an epicentre of ethics, people from non-English speaking countries and those without a degree were also able to get one as long as their employer passed a little cash to the local visa office. This was all very smooth when I was in Dawufeng, but things changed for me when I moved to the training company.

The Z visa required quite a bit of paperwork, was pretty expensive and the amount issued per organisation was limited - the bigger the company or school, the more visas it could offer. Therefore, the training company I started to work for, which was not huge and consequently not in a position to get a lot of Z visas easily, decided to exploit a well-known and commonly-used loophole. They got me a business visa. This worked quite well as we were operating in the corporate world and branded ourselves as business trainers rather than pure teachers. However, ordinarily, one of those should have lasted six months, at which point the law stated that I should have left the country. To get beyond this, our HR department alternated between visa offices in Beijing and a small town in Shandong province, each of which looked the other way - I presume in exchange for a small envelope of cash - when it came to me and my colleagues leaving the country. This little practice was the same for everyone in the company and was, although technically illegal, commonplace for foreigners across the country.

As the Olympics came into view, the Chinese government suddenly decided that it was no great fan of institutionalised corruption and wanted to stamp out shady practices, particularly in regards to immigration. On the face of it, this seemed like a good move. After all, nobody likes endemic government corruption - aside from those benefiting from it of course - and making the country fairer and more ethical was certainly a great thing. Unfortunately, corruption was so all-encompassing that removing it caused a butterfly effect around the country that would provide me and many other laowai a lot of problems!

Not only would the government's move be hugely inconvenient for me and many friends, but it was also drowning in irony as corruption in most areas of life in China was just so prevalent and so blatant! I am not exaggerating when I say you could see it almost everywhere you looked. In 2008, China came in at number 72 in the International Corruption Perception Index with a score of 3.6, which was a lot closer to countries like Myanmar and Iraq (both 1.3) than Denmark and New Zealand (both 9.3).

During my time in China, there were several high profile examples of overt corruption on massive scales, some of which had genuinely tragic consequences. In the chapter on Chengdu, I cited the example of local Communist party bosses who used low grade materials to build schools and then pocketed the money saved. This ended in tragedy when several school buildings collapsed like a house of cards. Over 5,000 schoolchildren died during the quake with most parents blaming the shoddy construction for the atrocious body count.

Another example came just over a year before the Olympics as Beijing was rocked by scandal when the city's vice-mayor was sacked for allegedly accepting bribes and sexual favours from developers keen to get in on the Olympic building boom. Just after the Olympics, the country was hit by yet another scandal. It was another example of officials cutting corners in order to keep the money saved. It took place at a dairy that produced baby formula where, rather than ensuring the correct nutrients were put into the formula, the mixture was watered down and laced with a chemical that would reduce the production cost whilst allowing it to pass safety tests. The upshot of this was the death of six children from chronic kidney failure.

The move to remove corruption in relation to immigration was all well and good, but as the above examples might suggest it still went on completely unfettered in almost every other domain and I still encountered it on a relatively regular basis. To illustrate this, let me give an example that took place in my office when we tried to get our broadband service improved by China Telecom - coincidentally the same state-run company that had denied me internet access in Dawufeng. This story took place a few weeks after the supposed 'crackdown' on corruption kicked off and when I was worried about my own immigration status.

As we had an office in a relatively modern building, I presumed it would be a simple process to get things updated and a new super-fast connection installed. I was wrong. It was not. Having moved into the new building and having called the telecom office, the engineer arrived carrying his bag of tools and equipment. This gave the impression that he was ready to work and hook us up. However, despite being fully tooled up, he seemed reluctant to actually do anything. After a lot of umming and ahhing, he informed us that he would be unable to do any work for at least one month, maybe six weeks. This seemed ridiculous and, through the translation of one of my Chinese colleagues, I told him so. He really didn't seem unduly concerned by my typically British bluster and declared that he was stepping outside for a cigarette. After he did so, my colleague turned to me and, with a tone of genuine surprise, asked me:

"Paul, what are you doing?"

"What do you mean? I am trying to get him to change our internet".

"Why don't you just give him some cash?"

It was a very blunt question and I was taken aback that she would suggest that I resort to a bit of direct bribery.

"Is that what this is about? Is he trying to shake us down for some cash?"

"Yes, of course he is! You won't get anything if you don't pay him. This is China, that is how it works!"

When the guy returned, I offered him 20RMB in cash - less than a couple of English pounds - which he accepted gladly. He then reached into his bag and pulled out a modem and router box, which he plugged into the wall. In less than three minutes, we were done!

The crackdown on corruption was ironic, but it is difficult to downplay the chaos it would cause for the expat community. For a decent period of time, I was genuinely worried that I would be deported from the country. The problems started about four or five months before the Olympics when our HR department reported that the business visa loophole appeared to have been rather suddenly and unexpectedly closed and that they were unable to renew any more such visas. This meant that the company needed to start getting Z visas, otherwise its employees would be very politely invited to leave China. At first, this wasn't a huge issue as a visa office in Shanghai was happy to complete the process and several of my colleagues were fortunate enough to benefit from this. However, as the Olympics drew closer, things got much more complicated as the government insisted that anyone wanting a Z visa could not apply in mainland China and had to leave the country. At the time, this didn't seem too much of a bad deal as a trip to either Hong Kong or Japan - both of which had open consular offices that were issuing Z visas - sounded fun.

Unfortunately for me, by the time my business visa was due to expire, things had tightened up even more and the government was insisting that foreigners return to their country of origin if they wanted a new visa and that companies would only have a limited number of visas. For a rather nerve-wracking three weeks, it looked like I would lose my job and with it the right to live in China. Thankfully, at the last minute, my company was eventually able to secure enough Z visas to allow me - although not all my colleagues - to stay in the country. To do so though, I had to fly back to the UK ... at my own expense.

Finding out I would be able to get a visa and stay in China was a massive relief. However, that moment proved to be just the start of a very laborious process that involved filling in a mountain of paperwork and travelling thousands of miles. The first step was to take a trip to Shanghai where I had to undergo a blood test at an official immigration clinic - to check I didn't have HIV - and to get my application form stamped. I then had to take that application to the Chinese consulate in Manchester where it was processed and where they stuck the visa into my passport.

I had hoped that flying across the world, and in so doing paying hundreds of dollars, would be the end of the drama and I would be able to rest easy. Sadly, I was sorely mistaken. When I got back to China, our HR manager told me that there was one final step and that I needed to get my visa stamped at my local police station. That process would provide another fantastic example of Chinese corruption irony.

Clearly the guys at the Hua Long Dao station, which was the closest one to my apartment, had not got the memo about stamping out corruption. I went to get the stamp on a Monday morning before going to work. I got there, showed them my passport and then waited for the officer responsible for dealing with visas to come and see me. I waited for over an hour, but nobody came. So, I went back to the desk and asked when he would come. The officer there shrugged his shoulders and walked away. With little other choice, as I needed to get to work, I also shrugged and jumped in a cab to go to the office.

The following day, I returned with one of our HR team in tow. When we arrived, we got the same treatment as I had the day before from the desk officer. We were told to wait. This time, we gave it half an hour before the girl from HR got up and went over to the desk. Just as the day before, the officer really didn't seem inclined to help. However, with the appearance of a packet of a well-known brand of US cigarettes, his demeanour changed almost instantly and he shouted forcefully over his shoulder through a door behind him. About thirty seconds later, a different officer emerged through the door and approached the desk. At no point did he, i) take the cigarette he was smoking out of his mouth, ii) stop talking on his cellphone, or iii) bother to actually check the photo on my passport. He just whacked the stamp on my visa page and walked away.

I was furious and wanted to say something and maybe call them out on their spurious lack of morals, but the girl from HR quietly told me to be quiet and just be thankful that I had the stamp. She reminded me that plenty of other people hadn't been fortunate enough to get one. So, we left as I muttered under my breath about the injustice of everything. I was angry about it all but, in reality, I was very lucky in comparison to many other laowai in China. Within my company, several of our teachers either had to leave the country or jumped ship to bigger companies who were able to offer visa security. I also had friends from Ali Baba's who simply had to leave China. It didn't matter if they had built businesses or lives there, if they were unable to find a new visa, they were gone.

The changes in China's infrastructure and immigration policies - if not its attitude to corruption - were pretty big, but so too was the cosmetic transformation that the face of Tianjin underwent. As a city, it developed immensely and became unimaginably more modern and cosmopolitan. When I moved there in 2006, my life was transformed as I was able to do so many of the things that I couldn't in Dawufeng: live in a vermin free apartment; eat fresh food; buy a decent cup of coffee; have a beer with other *laowai*. However, that change in my life needs to be viewed in a clear context. Tianjin was amazing ... in comparison to Dawufeng.

Even though it was a city of over 15million people, Tianjin was still a long way behind the times in many respects. For example, while there was a huge upturn in my standard of living, there were still a few big holes. For instance, a lot of international products such as good cheese or cooked meats - the Chinese version of ham was purely abhorrent - were difficult to find and, when they could be tracked down, were very expensive. When it came to eating out, apart from local cuisine, it was a similar situation. There were one or two western restaurants that served burgers or steaks at similar prices to those you would find in the UK or

US but, aside from those, the only real options were KFC or McDonalds.

On a more aesthetic level, the city also looked a little outdated in places. In the central business district, there were several new and impressive looking skyscrapers dotting the skyline - these were not quite like the Oriental Pearl but were quite striking nevertheless. However, there were still plenty of gaps between them and there was also a huge amount of old grey concrete buildings that didn't look hugely different to the one in which I had lived in Dawufeng. For example, my apartment complex was very nice and very modern, but barely 300m away the buildings got older and grimmer very quickly. Similarly, Binjiang Dao in the city centre looked like the type of modern shopping street that you would find anywhere in the world. However, if you took one of the side streets that adjoined it, the buildings were suddenly made of corrugated iron and wood.

Three and a half years later and things had changed dramatically. It would be an exaggeration to say that in those years the city became a culinary or architectural capital, but things were very different. Not only was there an explosion in casual food options with several American options such as Subway, Dairy Queen and Cold Stone Creamery opening up, but there was a sea-change in higher quality dining options. In fact, a fully-fledged restaurant district had sprung up in the southern half of the city with Indian restaurants, a French bistro and a series of Japanese places serving top quality seafood and Kobe beef. It would have been simply unthinkable in 2006. The old Italian Concession area had also transformed from a series of beautiful but derelict buildings to a lovely little locale with cafes and some very passable restaurants. We also saw a huge change in shopping options. On a more local level, the Wal-Mart close to my house began to stock a lot more international products. Also, in the city centre a giant Japanese department store opened up with a fabulous selection of gourmet cheeses, German sausages and Hong Kong style dim sum.

The culinary changes to the city were clearly reflected in my physical appearance. When I had moved to Tianjin from Dawufeng, I looked genuinely ill and was almost 10kg lighter than when I had left the UK. By late 2009, I was 5kg heavier and looking very well-fed - there are a couple of pictures from that period that leave me wincing at the rather generous belly I was cultivating.

As time wore on, the city itself also began to look very different. Just in my little niche, there was a huge amount of building work. Within 500m of my front door, there were four or five giant new apartment blocks, a small shopping centre and two new main roads constructed. The centre of the city went in the same direction as two or three of the older buildings on Binjiang Dao disappeared to be replaced by shiny modern buildings with several floors of shops and restaurants.

As I have heaped on about incessantly in this section of the book, China was a country that was changing at a pace like almost no other in history. The growth, development and migration we were seeing made the industrial revolutions in Europe two hundred years before or the migration into the US from Europe a century before look like small potatoes. Therefore, it is unsurprising that Beijing and Tianjin looked and felt very different places in 2010 compared to 2006. However, if you were to ask me what I felt was the biggest change I witnessed whilst there, I might actually swerve away from talking about buildings, trains and business in order to discuss the people and how their lives and perspectives on the world were vastly different

One point that I am sure this book has hammered home is that in 2006 China, in regards not to its politicians or business leaders but to its ordinary people, was a very insular country. It had been closed to the west for the best part of 50 years in the latter half of the 20th century and was scarcely a decade into being a global power. As a consequence, most ordinary Chinese people knew very little of the outside world and saw foreigners as genuine novelties. My experiences on trains to Hangzhou and Datong and with Mrs. Li in Dawufeng were testament to this. People had no idea about life in other countries and were genuinely curious, annoyingly so at times.

I also used to experience a fantastic example of how local people viewed foreigners every time - I am not exaggerating, I really do mean every time - I left my apartment. Even if I simply popped out to the local convenience store for a bottle of milk or nipped to the bank across the street to get cash, the following situation would always play out. As I walked down the street, a Chinese person I did not know would shout "hello" at me. They just loved to do it. They would never say anything else. There was no "How are you?" or "Nice weather today". I just got "hello". To some extent, it was annoying as hell as I was forever turning round to see who had shouted to me. Often, it would be difficult to ascertain who had actually said it as I would turn around and see three or four people staring embarrassingly at their feet or I would only see their back as they zipped past on a bicycle.

It was a common topic of conversation for expats to discuss how many "hellos" we got in a day. For me, even if I was just ambling around my local neighborhood, it would be 20 or 30. If I ventured closer to the centre of the city, it could be in the hundreds. It was never something that genuinely irritated me, but when it happened for the fiftieth or sixtieth time in the same day, I would get a bit tired of it.

A second example of Chinese people's fascination with foreigners came in the form of staring. My goodness, I was stared at a lot. I already touched on this a little when I discussed the parents and grandparents who would freeze and gawp open-mouthed at me whenever I left the school building in Dawufeng. At the time, I assumed that this phenomenon was simply a reflection of living in a small - and to be frank, rather backward - town. In contrast to this, when Ossie and I were visiting Beijing and Shanghai it wasn't such a big issue as we spent a lot of time around major attractions where foreign tourists were a common sight. Tianjin didn't really have too many historic attractions, so despite being a huge city, it was a lot closer to Dawufeng in terms of attitude.

A clear example of this was when I went to the supermarket. Whenever I was purchasing food, I would quickly become the centre of attention. People were clearly interested in what the foreigner was buying. This interest manifested itself in three major ways: i) People would just stand and stare whilst I perused the shelves, ii) More adventurous types would follow me around the aisles checking each individual selection that I made, and iii) The most adventurous would sidle up to my trolley and actually start to pick up and examine the items I was planning to purchase.

I got plenty of attention when I was close to home in Hedong district, but when I walked down Binjiang Dao in the city centre, I stood out like the proverbial sore thumb as I was significantly taller than most of the people around me and my bald head was very different to the sea of black hair that surrounded me. The striking contrast was such that as I made my way along the street people would step out of my way to get a better look at the large hairless foreigner in their midst. It could, rather bizarrely, be compared to Moses parting the Red Sea.

I also loved the outrageous unpredictability of the city in my early days there. For the majority of my time in China, I would wake up in the morning and wonder to myself what crazy sights I would see that day. There were so many! These could be simple things such as people carrying crazy objects on the back of their bicycles. Until I lived in China, I had no real concept of the things you can transport on a bike! Probably the most striking of these was the small washing machine I saw being transported by an old man, which as you might expect looked dangerously unbalanced. However, there were plenty of other odd examples. For instance, I saw several kitchen sinks, a whole host of small items of furniture and even a few animals - why wouldn't you carry a couple of live chickens in a box on the back of your bike? There were also plenty of examples of families travelling together by bike with dad riding, mum sitting above the back wheel and a kid - almost always just one - holding mum's neck. All those examples grabbed my attention as they seemed unusual to me, but they were also evocative of a place with a unique character.

Along with the slightly unusual transport, there were some goings on that were just plain crazy. A particular favourite of mine came one Sunday evening when I took a walk to Wal-Mart to do a bit of shopping. As I walked into the car park, I almost fell into a very large hole that I hadn't noticed as there was nothing to warn me about its location or even its existence. It was almost 2m in diameter and over a meter deep. I have no idea why it was there but it really didn't seem safe. Feeling a little disconcerted from having almost had a nasty accident, I tried to communicate to the car park attendant, who appeared to be supervising the situation, that it really wasn't safe to have a giant open pit in the middle of a car park. As my Chinese was only rudimentary, I wasn't sure if I had got my message across. Apparently, I did as when I popped back the following day after work, the hole was covered up … to a fashion. There was no safety tape, no fencing and no barriers. Instead, there was a giant white 1970s style formica wardrobe complete with a brass-colored rail upon which clothes had once hung. It was a bizarre sight but, in fairness, it did cover the hole!

By 2010, things were just no longer the same. As I have already detailed, the economic, the architectural and the cultural face of the city had changed pretty dramatically. And, so too had many of the people and the general atmosphere around the city. There were still lots of people who would stare at me in the street - it takes more than three or four years to roll back five decades of isolation and secrecy - but, as my time in Tianjin drew on, the city and its residents began to change. The younger end of the population was fast becoming far more cosmopolitan and far better off economically as 10% annual growth created new jobs with higher salaries. In 2006, it felt odd when I discussed frappuccinos and wine bars with some of my corporate students, but by 2009 this was much closer to the norm and more and more of them were increasingly westernized.

Not only did plenty of them drink their green tea frappuccino from Starbucks and chattinto their iPhones but many of them also now bought clothes from global brands like Zara and Uniqlo and drove expensive foreign cars. This new and rapidly growing generation was far more cosmopolitan than their older relatives. They had come of age in the new China, the one that was already open to the rest of the world. They never knew secrecy and isolation. They weren't hugely shocked to see a bald foreigner walking down the street and they certainly weren't so interested in the cost of rice in the UK or the average salary of a worker in London..

I had moved to China for the challenge and to experience something different. In 2006, that was exactly what I got. However, in 2010 as I took an air-conditioned Toyota taxi after leaving my office on the 23rd floor to go to a Japanese teppanyaki restaurant where well-off locals and expats were paying $30 a head for all you can eat and drink menus featuring shrimp, lobster and filet mignon, I began to feel that I was no longer really enjoying such a challenging experience.

When I taught a class with an openly gay man in his early 20s who wanted to talk about Lady Gaga and ask about the gay scene in the UK and a young woman who wanted to ask about fashion in the UK and whether Ugg boots were as popular in London as they were in China - I couldn't really give either of them much insight in all honesty - I began to feel I really was in a different world to the one I had been looking for when I first arrived. I began to miss the rattly old Xia Lis, the flood of bicycles around the city and everyone saying hello to the random *laowai*.

A Sweet Sorrow

The faster Tianjin grew and the glitzier it became, the more I began to ask myself what I was still doing there. The change was an awe-inspiring sight to see and it was fabulous that the standard of living had risen for so many people, but it felt like my time there was drawing to a close. However, it was most definitely not an easy decision to leave. China was a highly addictive drug. I really hope that this book has conveyed just how much I loved my time there and just how fascinating a country it was. Even today, I still consider my four years there as one of the defining periods of my life. Whenever friends, family or new acquaintances ask me about the 13 years I spent living overseas, it is China not Korea or France or UAE that people focus on. Because of this, I faced a huge degree of separation anxiety - far more than when I left Korea. I knew it was time to leave, but it was very difficult to actually tear myself away.

I would also argue that much of my reticence to leave came from something I would describe as Middle Kingdom Syndrome. As I have mentioned already, the Chinese call their country *Zhong Hua*, which translates to Middle Kingdom - a term I have used regularly throughout this book - which reflects the belief from imperial China that their country represented the centre of global civilisation. It was a balls-out arrogant moniker to apply!

The ancient Chinese certainly had a rather arrogant take on things, but they were not alone in their perspective. It was also shared by many foreigners living in China. The common idea amongst many British, American and European businessmen - and it generally did tend to be men as there were far fewer female expats - was that because China was growing so fast, it was the only place in the world to be working. They believed that China had usurped the US and Europe to become the centre of the modern business world. This gave rise to the common notion that living and working anywhere else was simply foolish.

I have to be 100% honest here and admit that my Middle Kingdom Syndrome was pretty damn strong and my arrogance about life in China was impressively obnoxious. Whenever I was back in the UK for a holiday and people asked me about working in Tianjin they got a lengthy lecture on why it really was the best thing in the world. However, in the middle of my fourth year in China, I began to start having doubts. Initially, I didn't really give them much attention. Why would I? I was living in the centre of the world! But, a visit from my mother began to change my mentality.

When she stepped off the plane from Manchester, I had a few nagging worries about the continued relevance of life in China, but I had no immediate plans to leave. I still firmly believed that I was working in the most exciting place on earth. However, seeing my mummy changed my perspective. As I touched on earlier, the only holidays many Chinese people got each year were during the Golden Weeks. Annual leave that could be taken as and when they wished - like we have in the UK and Europe - was an unheard of luxury.

For many expats, the situation was better, but not by much. Rather than the 25 or 30 days I could expect in the UK, I had just ten, almost all of which I had to use in order to go home at Christmas. With the cost and problems of travelling during the Golden Weeks, this meant that I found it difficult to get home more than once a year. In four years in China, I managed to travel home just six times - one of which was my enforced visa run. Each of these trips was for one week or less.

Not seeing my family was always a difficult downside to living in China. For the majority of my time there, the experience felt like a reasonable trade off. However, as I began to realise that the country wasn't quite gripping me in the way that it had in 2006 and 2007, that balance began to shift and my mother's arrival was the final tipping point. Seeing her made me question whether it was worth being so far away from home if I was no longer finding China the marvel that I once did. The short answer was that it wasn't and that I was ready for a change. So, I decided that it was time to look for something that would allow me to travel home a lot more.

EPILOGUE

Even though I took an early morning flight from Beijing airport and, as a consequence, stayed in an airport hotel on my final night in China, I consider the ending of this story to have come on my penultimate day in the Far East. I stood outside the Kiessling bakery in Tianjin and hugged Ossie good-bye. We had done similar in Korea in the knowledge that we would meet again soon. However, four and a half years later, things were different. Careers needed to be pursued - it is a lot easier and more fun to backpack around at 25 or 26 without a care in the world than it is at 30 with the shadow of middle-age and sensible life decisions looming - and families would be acquired. It had been a wild ride. Eleven years hence, I am not sure what I miss most, the adventures in China - Korea to a lesser extent - or my buddy with whom I shared plenty of beers and some amazing times.

Printed in Great Britain
by Amazon